THE POLITICS OF BAD GOVERNANCE IN
CONTEMPORARY RUSSIA

The Politics of Bad Governance
in Contemporary Russia

Vladimir Gel'man

UNIVERSITY OF MICHIGAN PRESS

Ann Arbor

For questions or permissions, please contact um.press.perms@umich.edu
Published in the United States of America by the University of Michigan Press
Printed and bound by CPI Group (UK) Ltd, Croydon, CR0 4YY
Open access e-book first published August 2022;
Additional formats first published November 2022

A CIP catalog record for this book is available from the British Library.
Library of Congress Cataloging-in-Publication data has been applied for.
ISBN 978-0-472-07562-1 (hardcover : alk. paper)
ISBN 978-0-472-05562-3 (paper : alk. paper)
ISBN 978-0-472-90298-9 (open access ebook)

DOI: https://doi.org/10.3998/mpub.11621795

The University of Michigan Press's open access publishing program is made possible thanks to additional funding from the University of Michigan Office of the Provost and the generous support of contributing libraries.

S | H   **The Sustainable History Monograph Pilot**
M | P   Opening Up the Past, Publishing for the Future

We are eager to learn more about how you discovered this title and how you are using it. We hope you will spend a few minutes answering a couple of questions at this URL: **https://www.longleafservices.org/shmp-survey/**

More information about the Sustainable History Monograph Pilot can be found at https://www.longleafservices.org.

CONTENTS

Digital materials related to this title can be found on the Fulcrum platform via the following citable URL: https://doi.org/10.3998/mpub.11621795

LIST OF FIGURES AND TABLES

PREFACE and ACKNOWLEDGMENTS

Since the classic statement by Samuel P. Huntington, who observed that "the most important political distinction among countries concerns not their form of government but their degree of government,"[1] scholars of comparative politics have focused to a great degree on the politics of governance across the globe. While major historically oriented analyses trace the evolutionary logic of governance from ancient times to the present day,[2] and numerous experts develop highly sophisticated datasets with long batteries of indicators addressed to governance-related issues,[3] we still know little about the factors behind various patterns of governance and their dynamics in different states and nations. Answering the questions of why governments govern better in some countries than in others is essential for political scientists and policy analysts, politicians, and policymakers, as well as for civil activists and citizens in various countries. Certainly, accomplishing such a daunting task would require long-standing collective multidisciplinary efforts by the international scholarly community, something that lies beyond the scope of a single academic book. However, I believe that there is a need to address these questions based on analyzing the politics of governance in one country, namely post-Communist Russia. According to many accounts and assessments, present-day Russia is governed much worse than it should be and explaining its patterns of governance by putting this country-level analysis into a broader theoretical and comparative perspective may shed some light on the phenomenon of governing states beyond a single case study of a certain outlier. Therefore, I wrote this book with some hope that it might be of interest both for scholars of Russia and for experts in comparative politics of governance.

In this book, I would like to challenge a conventional wisdom that dominates the research of governance and development, namely the assumption that all countries, at least in theory, aim to improve their performance in order to achieve prosperity, and exceptions from this rule can be considered deviations. Such a view is typical for academics who teach their students with the mission of promoting scholarly excellence—we all want to be proud of our A-students with excellent grades, great knowledge, and outstanding skills. However, I grew up in communities of C-students within the late-Soviet educational establishments, where almost nobody cared about gaining knowledge, where the scholarly cheating was nearly ubiquitous, and where the skills of making good informal connections[4] paved the way for high grades and better jobs. Those A-students who behaved otherwise (myself included) were regarded as outsiders in these communities, to say the least. Over time, I realized that communities of C-students—in Russia and elsewhere—are the norm, and A-students are almost an exception, rather than the reverse. C-students may convert themselves into A-students (similarly to the conversion from Saul to Paul the apostle) only under serious pressure that may provide strong incentives for improving their performance. Without these incentives, C-students will not pursue academic excellence (even though many of them could perform much better) but rather will prefer some manner of muddling through to minimize their scholarly efforts, showing little care about their future. In the worst-case scenario, they may demonstrate educational decay and deterioration in various political and institutional contexts and even irreversibly turn into F-students. Even though we all prefer A-students to their C-counterparts, understanding the rationale behind poor performance requires additional in-depth analysis of the causes and mechanisms of mediocrity, carelessness, and dishonesty to a larger degree than those of excellence, high motivation, and integrity.

In a way, states and nations are similar to students' communities. Without strong domestic and/or international incentives, they may not strive toward better performance and may not be interested in improving the quality of their governance. Similar to C-students, the rulers of these states and nations govern their countries much worse than they should, and at the same time may receive certain short-term benefits from their mediocre performance at the expense of their fellow citizens and of generations of their successors. I would argue that the persistence of patterns of bad governance is primarily driven by politics because of the combinations of ideas, interests, and incentives of rulers and elites. In other words, I consider bad governance to be an agency-driven phenomenon, and therefore a scholarly focus on the causes and mechanisms of the politics of governance is necessary for addressing the questions of good and bad governance. This focus may help not only to explain the peculiarities of Russia's underperformance but also to explore how and why practices of bad governance emerged, persisted, and evolved over time in various political and institutional contexts. My book is aimed at such an exploration.

This book resulted from several academic endeavors. First and foremost, I was extraordinarily lucky to work in two universities, two cities, and two countries—at the European University at Saint Petersburg (EUSP) in Russia, and at the University of Helsinki (UH) in Finland. Being part of two different scholarly communities enormously benefited this book project and other research ventures. I would like to thank my colleagues from both EUSP and UH for the great intellectual atmosphere and for our fruitful exchange of ideas. Kaarina Aitamurto, Sari Autio-Sarasmo, Daria Gritsenko, Boris Firsov, Anna-Liisa Heusala, Marina Khmelnitskaya, Ivan Kurilla, Katalin Miklossy, Ella Paneyakh, Katri Pynnöniemi, Mikhail Sokolov, Anna Temkina, Veli-Pekka Tynkkynen, Pavel Usanov, and Veljko Vujacic provided me with great food for thought in various ways over the years. Special thanks go to my superiors at the EUSP and the UH, who made it possible for me to be a servant of two masters and move back and forth between Russian and Finnish environments, similarly to a dolphin who jumps back and forth between the fresh waters of the sea and the open air. I am greatly indebted for this unique opportunity to Grigorii Golosov, Markku Kangaspuro, Oleg Kharkhordin, Markku Kivinen, and Vadim Volkov—all of them supported me both in intellectual and in administrative terms. My coauthors of various scholarly pieces, Hilary Appel, Andrey Starodubtsev, Dmitry Travin, and Andrey Zaostrovtsev, greatly contributed to some chapters and paragraphs of this book and offered me invaluable experience of successful academic collaboration. In addition, former students, who later became scholars themselves, helped me to formulate and crystallize some of the elements of my writings—many thanks to Aleksey Gilev, Kirill Kalinin, Anton Shirikov, Andrey Shcherbak, Anna Tarasenko, and Tatiana Tkacheva. Two other former students, Egor Lazarev and Margarita Zavadskaya, were the first readers of the book manuscript, and their friendly yet critical suggestions and recommendations provided many valuable insights. The financial support received from the Academy of Finland and the Department of Political Science at the EUSP enables me to cover many costs related to this book project.

Drafts of various chapters were discussed in academic seminars and workshops held at the EUSP, the UH, Columbia University, the Higher School of Economics at Saint Petersburg, Perm State University, Princeton University, Sciences Po Paris, the University of Dundee, the University of Michigan, Uppsala University, and Yale University. Major conferences of the Program on New Approaches to Research and Security (PONARS Eurasia) and ASEEES annual conventions served as key milestones in crafting the building blocks of this book. There is no way to thank all the participants and discussants, whose questions and comments were important. I owe special debts to Mark Beissinger, Irina Busygina, Anna Dekalchuk, Gilles Favarel-Garrigues, Timothy Frye, Sam Greene, Sergei Guriev, Henry Hale, Alexander Libman, Leonid Polishchuk,

Kirill Rogov, Cameron Ross, Andrey Semenov, Gulnaz Sharafutdinova, Maria Snegovaya, Konstantin Sonin, Regina Smyth, Lucan Way, and Susanne Wengle. The efficient administrative support from Anna Gasanova, Tatiana Khruleva, Eeva Korteniemi, Anna Korhonen, and Ira Österberg made this project feasible. Aleksei Pobedonostsev and Sergei Kim provided significant technical assistance with some data and visualization. The friendly, detailed, and nuanced linguistic assistance by Alexei Stephenson was essential for making the manuscript readable. I truly appreciate the great interest and excellent encouragement of Elizabeth Demers from the University of Michigan Press, who endorsed this book project and made it possible—without her it would probably not have happened—and the whole publishing team deserve many warm words for their help. Three anonymous reviewers of the book manuscript made several useful comments and critical points. Last but not least, my wife Oxana supported me over all these journeys, constantly demonstrating many instances of good governance in our family: my outstanding debts to her will probably never be fully paid. Needless to say, none of the above persons and organizations are responsible for any errors and flawed interpretations. All arguments in this book solely reflect my own viewpoints, which may not coincide with their opinions.

The early versions of some parts of this book previously appeared in the form of articles. Elements of chapter 1 are based upon "Political Foundations of Bad Governance in Post-Soviet Eurasia: Towards a Research Agenda" (*East European Politics* 33, no. 4 [2017], © Taylor & Francis), and elements of chapter 2 use parts of "The Vicious Circle of Post-Soviet Neopatrimonialism in Russia" (*Post-Soviet Affairs* 32, no. 5 [2016], © Taylor & Francis). Chapter 4 is based on "Opportunities and Constraints of Authoritarian Modernisation: Russian Policy Reforms of the 2000s" (*Europe-Asia Studies* 68, no. 1 [2016], © University of Glasgow, reprinted by permission of Taylor & Francis Ltd. on behalf of the University of Glasgow), coauthored with Andrey Starodubtsev. Chapter 5 is based on "Politics versus Policy: Technocratic Traps of Russian Policy Reforms" (*Russian Politics* 3, no. 2 [2018], © Brill). Chapter 6 is based on "Exceptions and Rules: Success Stories and Bad Governance in Russia" (*Europe-Asia Studies* 73, no. 6 [2021], © University of Glasgow, reprinted by permission of Taylor & Francis Ltd. on behalf of the University of Glasgow).

This book deals with many difficult issues of bad governance, analyzing rent-seeking and corruption as cornerstones of a certain politico-economic order, and the reader might become depressed because of the gloomy pictures of these practices and their effects. However, one should not fall into the deadly sin of sloth—the most useless, fruitless, and hopeless of all deadly sins. This is why I wrote this book with something of a "bias for hope"[5] that it will make a small contribution to overcoming pathologies of bad governance in Russia and elsewhere. I dedicate this book to the many activists, journalists, scholars, civil servants, and ordinary citizens who resist the politics of bad governance in one way or another and who struggle for good governance in their respective countries and all over the world.

Saint Petersburg—Helsinki
September 2021

THE POLITICS OF BAD GOVERNANCE IN CONTEMPORARY RUSSIA

CHAPTER 1

The Politics of Bad Governance

A Framework for Analysis

I T IS A GIVEN that the quality of governance makes a difference. It determines the developmental trajectories of states and nations, as well as the everyday lives of its citizens. Why are some countries governed worse than others? In particular, why is contemporary Russia governed so much worse than one would expect, judging by its degree of socioeconomic development? In the comparative perspective, contemporary Russia represents an example of a high-capacity authoritarian state that exhibits the main features of bad governance, such as a lack and/or perversion of the rule of law, near-universal rent-seeking, ubiquitous corruption, poor quality of state regulation, widespread abuse of public funds, and overall ineffectiveness of government. These features have been demonstrated in numerous recent assessments of Russia vis-à-vis many other countries, conducted by various reputable international agencies.[1] The evidence presented there is endorsed by investigative journalists,[2] policy analysts,[3] political activists,[4] and filmmakers,[5] and the combination of different sources portray a rather gloomy picture of patterns of governance in Russia—this country performs worse than some of its post-Soviet neighbors[6] and the other countries that belongs to BRICS (Brazil, Russia, India, China, South Africa) group.[7] However, one should go beyond these critical assessments and address more fundamental questions about the sources and mechanisms of bad governance in Russia and beyond. Why did bad governance emerge and persist in certain countries, and to what extent can the quality of governance be improved over time by certain policies?

Scholars and observers have addressed these issues since ancient times but have not provided comprehensive answers as of yet. Perhaps the first full-fledged vivid exploration of issues of quality of governance appeared in visual arts. In 1338, the city council of Siena, then a medieval oligarchic republic, commissioned two sets of frescoes to decorate the council hall (*Sala dei Nove*) in its residence, Palazzo Pubblico, from the local artist Ambrogio Lorenzetti. The following year, Lorenzetti produced the series of frescoes, known as *The Allegory of Good and Bad Government*, which are still located in Palazzo Pubblico today. These artworks, justly considered masterpieces of early Renaissance secular painting, presented six scenes of contemporary Siena and its neighboring areas, and through images, reflected normative ideas of good and bad governance that are still important almost seven centuries later. Art historians,[8] and political theorists such as Quentin Skinner,[9] have mostly focused on the set of three frescoes that represent the Allegory of Good Government (*Allegoria del Buon Governo*). Such a focus is driven not only by the fact that this set has been portrayed extensively and preserved in better shape as a piece of art, but mostly because it represents the major civic virtues, such as Peace, Fortitude, Prudence, Magnanimity, Temperance, and Justice, guided by symbols of Faith, Hope, and Charity. All of these symbols and features were essential for an understanding of good governance in the fourteenth century and have not lost their relevance in the present day. In a sense, they are not much different from a twenty-first century approach to good governance, where, for example, the highly reputable Quality of Government Institute (the QoG Institute) at the University of Gothenburg has placed a major emphasis in its research on "trustworthy, reliable, impartial, un-corrupt and competent government institutions."[10]

However, what about the Allegory of Bad Government (*Allegoria del Cattivo Governo*), which was so vividly presented in the paired set of Lorenzetti's frescoes and is presented on the cover of this book? One should pay attention to its central character, a devious-looking figure adorned with horns and fangs, and apparently cross-eyed. This figure is identified as Tyranny, who sits enthroned, resting his feet upon a goat (a symbol of luxury) while holding a dagger. Below the tyrant, the captive figure of Justice lies bound and swaddled, while the figures of Cruelty, Deceit, Fraud, Fury, Division, and War flank him, and above the tyrant float the figures of Avarice, Pride, and Vainglory. These symbols and features, according to an advice book for the city magistrate of that time, were considered the "leading enemies of human life."[11] Since the frescoes came as a pair, the whole scene demonstrated a mirror opposite of that of the Allegory of Good Government, creating a powerful reminder to the members of the city council of what they should and should not do in governing the city.

A viewer, or a reader of this book, who is familiar with politics in contemporary Russia may find a striking similarity between the image of the tyrant in Lorenzetti's fresco and the appearance of Russia's long-standing ruler,

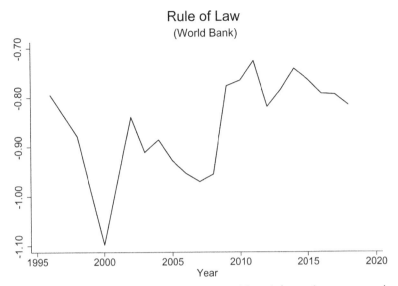

FIGURE 1. Rule of Law in Russia, 1996–2018, World Bank (range from-2.5 to +2.5)

Vladimir Putin. Besides the apparent visual resemblance, there are important substantive parallels between the interpretation of the nature of bad governance in fourteenth-century Siena and an understanding of this phenomenon in twenty-first-century political science. The common point is that unconstrained autocratic rule is considered the main source of bad governance both then and now, and numerous vices that result from it—be they related to deceit, fraud, avarice, cruelty, or war—cause harsh and often insuperable obstacles to justice and contribute to numerous pathologies for the development of states and societies. The question of the causes and effects of bad governance has not lost its relevance since the medieval period, and in the twenty-first century, the time is ripe to reconsider these issues from a scholarly perspective.

This is a book about how and why Russia, a highly developed, urbanized, well-educated, and relatively wealthy country, which demonstrated a promising potential for further advancement after the collapse of Communism and a series of complex post-Communist transformations,[12] became a country with a trajectory of durable bad governance over the recent decades. Even though calls to improve the quality of governance in Russia have been made many times by political leaders and top officials, during the period of the 2000s and the 2010s there was little (if any) progress in many important dimensions of governance, regarding the rule of law control of corruption and especially, regulatory quality, as figures 1 through 4 demonstrated.[13]

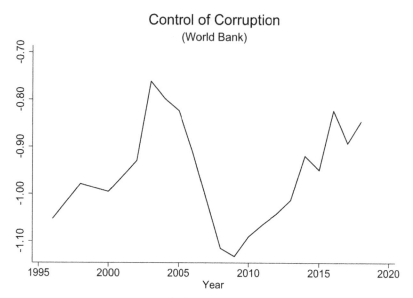

FIGURE 2. Control of Corruption in Russia, 1996–
2018, World Bank (range from-2.5 to +2.5)

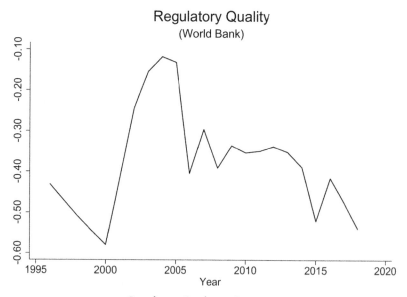

FIGURE 3. Regulatory Quality in Russia, 1996–2018,
World Bank (range from-2.5 to +2.5)

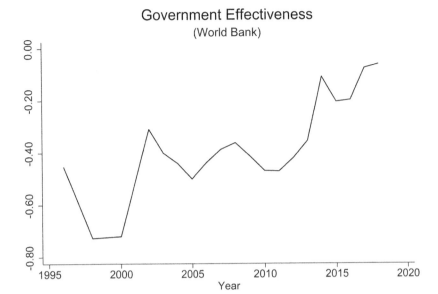

FIGURE 4. Government Effectiveness in Russia, 1996–
2018, World Bank (range from-2.5 to +2.5)

What are the sources and mechanisms of governance in Russia? Should bad governance be expected to persist endlessly under authoritarian rule, or can the quality of governance be improved over time by certain policies? The recent discussions attempting to explain good and bad governance in various countries, regions, and policy areas have been quite extensive.[14] The question is: How can we place present-day Russia on this global governance map? Should we consider Russia to be an outlier or, rather, a laggard vis-à-vis many other developed and developing states?

Indeed, in 1984, a *Financial Times* journalist noted that Russia's predecessor, the Soviet Union, should not be regarded as "Upper Volta with missiles."[15] However, such a statement soon lost its initial meaning of juxtaposition and instead became a sort of label for the country during the period of Soviet collapse. At that time, it sounded deliberately offensive, and most probably unjust, given the fact that Upper Volta (renamed in 1984 to Burkina Faso) was one of the poorest African nations. Almost four decades later, however, this statement has, in a sense, proved to be correct. Judging by the data from the *Rule of Law Index* by the World Justice Project, the *Corruption Perception Index* by Transparency International, and the World Bank's *Governance Matters*, Russia has exhibited worse performance than Burkina Faso (still one of the poorest African nations) in five out of six key parameters of quality of governance (see table 1).

TABLE 1. Why Russia is Not Burkina Faso

Indexes	Russia	Burkina Faso
Rule of Law Index (World Justice Project), 2020	0.47 (rank 94 out of 128)	0.51 (rank 70 out of 128)
Corruption Perception Index (Transparency International), 2018	28 (rank 137 out of 180)	40 (rank 85 out of 180)
Rule of Law Index (World Bank), 2018	-0.82	-0.45
Regulatory Quality Index (World Bank), 2018	-0.54	-0.39
Government Effectiveness (World Bank), 2018	-0.06	-0.58
Control of Corruption (World Bank), 2018	-0.85	-0.11

SOURCES: *World Justice Project Rule of Law Index 2020* (Washington, DC: World Justice Project, 2020) https://worldjusticeproject.org/sites/default/files/documents/WJP-ROLI-2020-Online_0.pdf range from 0 (min) to 1 (max)
Corruption Perception Index (Berlin: Transparency International, 2020) https://www.transparency.org/cpi2019 range from 0 (min) to 100 (max)
Worldwide Governance Indicators (Washington, DC: World Bank, 2020) http://info.worldbank.org/governance/wgi/ range from -2.5 (min) to + 2.5 (max)

Although the validity of these and other cross-national rankings of states is the subject of numerous heated discussions,[16] they may be used at least as a proxy for positioning certain countries on the global map of governance. While there is a high degree of correlation between the level of socioeconomic development (measured as GDP per capita) and the quality of governance in many countries, Russia seems to be an important, if not the only, major outlier from this tendency, especially regarding the rule of law and control of corruption, as figures 5 through 8 demonstrated.

This is why an in-depth focus on analysis of Russia's "deviant case"[17] may not only be useful for an understanding of the causes and effects of bad governance in this particular country, but also may shed some light on this phenomenon in a broader comparative perspective—which is essentially the goal of this book.

This introductory chapter is focused on setting the scene for the further exploration of issues of bad governance in Russia and beyond. After a short excursion to cover key concepts and definitions, it will explain the framework for analysis used in this book, present my main arguments, and outline the trajectory of bad governance in post-Communist Russia and its dynamics. The structure and contents of the following chapters will be briefly outlined in its concluding paragraphs.

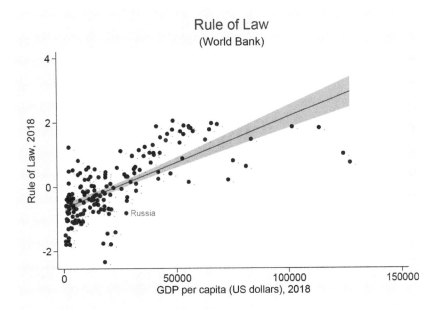

FIGURE 5. GDP Per Capita and Rule of Law, 2018, World Bank (range from -2.5 to +2.5)

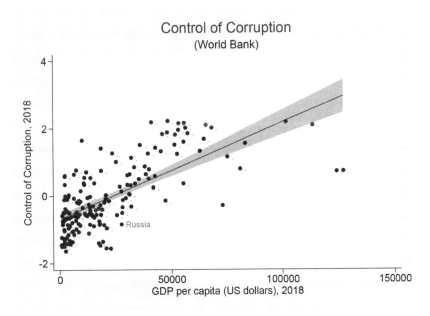

FIGURE 6. GDP Per Capita and Control of Corruption, 2018, World Bank (range from -2.5 to +2.5)

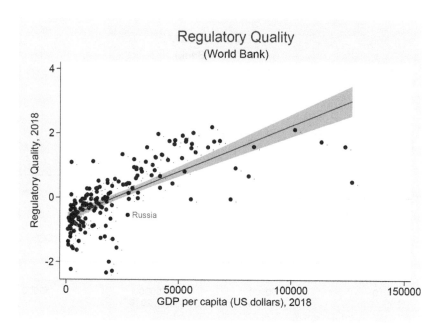

FIGURE 7. GDP Per Capita and Regulatory Quality,
2018, World Bank (range from -2.5 to +2.5)

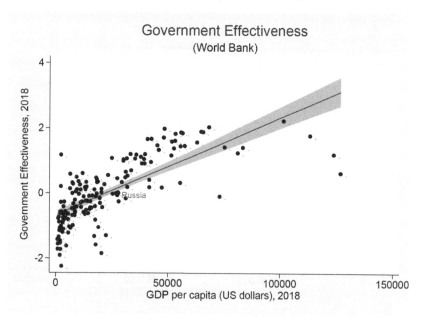

FIGURE 8. GDP Per Capita and Government Effectiveness,
2018, World Bank (range from -2.5 to +2.5)

What Is Bad Governance?

One influential political scientist has defined "governance" as the "government's ability to make and enforce rules, and to deliver services, regardless as to whether that government is democratic or not."[18] From this viewpoint, governance as a category of analysis is different both from state capacity, which is related to the state's coercive and infrastructural potential to implement certain policies, and from state autonomy, which is related to the ability of the state apparatus to adopt and implement policies irrespective of political influence. Explicitly or implicitly, such an approach lies behind numerous studies on the subject, both theoretically and comparatively oriented ones and those focused on particular countries, regions, and policy areas.[19] Although the causes and mechanisms of bad governance have been analyzed by political scientists since the times of Machiavelli, modern discussions of this phenomenon are fueled not only by a major rise of scholarly interest in various aspects of governance[20] but also by the emergence of new research tools and databases assembled by various institutions and teams of analysts.[21] However, the very notion of "bad governance" has to a certain degree remained an elusive term, one constructed as an antonym to "good governance"; the latter, in turn, is also based on multidimensional criteria and lacks a universally accepted definition.[22]

The most widely used approach in the field is related to the World Bank's Worldwide Governance Indicators program,[23] where the understanding of good governance is based on six major pillars, or dimensions: (1) Voice and Accountability; (2) Political Stability and Absence of Violence; (3) Government Effectiveness; (4) Regulation Quality; (5) Rule of Law; and (6) Control of Corruption. While categories 1 and 2 relate to the quality of political regimes rather than to the quality of governance as such, the other four parameters, categories 3–6, establish the features of various dimensions of good governance. Scholars of the QoG Institute greatly expanded the understanding of good governance, adding to this list some other important dimensions of governance, such as accountability, efficiency, impartiality, and legitimacy, and employed this framework for analysis in several important scholarly contributions.[24] However, such a comprehensive approach may contradict the good old Occam's razor principle, or the law of parsimony, and go beyond necessity. This is why in this book I will mostly rely upon the minimalist definition of good governance offered by the World Bank because it better fits the purposes of my analysis. Thus, the four constituent elements of good governance are: effective government performance, decent regulatory quality of the state, adherence to the basic principles of the rule of law[25] and political and institutional constraints on corruption.

If one perceives bad governance as an alternative juxtaposed to good governance in the manner of antinomy (such an analytic approach was, for example, employed in a recent study of Russian modernization[26]), then the key features of bad governance can be constructed as opposites of the principles of good governance in all of these four dimensions. Thus, bad governance can be understood as a combination of these attributes: (1) a lack of the rule of law and/or perversion of its basic principles; (2) a high degree of corruption, which penetrates all layers of governance; (3) a combination of high density, poor quality and selective implementation of state regulations (labeled here as the phenomenon of the "overregulated state");[27] and (4) general government ineffectiveness, except for certain crucial policy areas and/or priority projects and programs (often conducted under special conditions).

These attributes are related to governing the state in a narrow sense. Meanwhile, although lack of democracy and weakness of political rights, as well as political instability and violence, could be considered elements of bad governance in certain political and institutional contexts, these qualifications merely describe the qualities of political regimes, and cannot be attributed as features of bad governance by default. While some studies have demonstrated a conditional impact of democracy and authoritarianism on the quality of governance,[28] their impact is often indirect and not always straightforward. The antinomy of features of good and bad governance is summarized in table 2.

Although in substantive terms such a negative definition of bad governance based on antinomies may be far from satisfactory, this approach is a logical consequence of the normative bias inherent in the perceptions of many social and political scientists. This normative bias in analyses of bad governance has also contributed to the extension of its attributes far beyond the aforementioned list, not only with regard to governing the state, but also in various aspects of social policies and state-society relations, such that the term has become a byword for a set of diverse negative tendencies.[29] This broad interpretation is highly questionable, because it combines in the same category various phenomena that do not always relate to the quality of state governance and/or may stem from different causes; such an approach is dubious, being a form of "conceptual stretching."[30] At the same time, however, equating bad governance solely with widespread corruption, as some scholars argue, would be a wild oversimplification.[31] Although corruption is an unquestionable element of bad governance, it should be regarded as a symptom (rather than a cause), and not the only symptom. Moreover, such an

TABLE 2. Antinomies of Features of Good and Bad Governance

Pillar of Governance	Good Governance	Bad Governance
Government Effectiveness	Generally effective and efficient government	Government may be effective mostly in certain crucial policy areas and priority projects and programs, conducted under special conditions
Regulation Quality	A decent regulatory framework, maintained by strong institutions and unbiased state bureaucracy	"Over-regulated state," which combines high density and poor quality of state regulations with their selective implementation
Rule of Law	Adherence to basic principles of the rule of law	Lack of the rule of law and/or perversion of its basic principles
Control of Corruption	Low level of corruption, which is limited by political and institutional constraints	High level of corruption, which penetrates all layers of governance

equation may result in an imperfect diagnostic of bad governance as a phenomenon being attributed to many very different yet highly corrupt governments in a similar way. If one were to compare political diagnostics with medical ones, it is as if a doctor equated a banal flu with pneumonia judging solely by patient symptoms like high temperature, fever, and cough, without relying on a lung X-ray or other tests. This is why I rely upon a different definition of the syndrome of bad governance that is based on the four major characteristics of governing the state presented above: lack and/or perversion of the rule of law, unconstrained corruption, poor quality of state regulations, and general ineffectiveness of government (some exceptions to this rule will be discussed in detail in chapter 6).

These characteristics need to be clarified for a better understanding of their role in governing the state: To what extent do they serve as symptoms of certain pathologies or, rather, to what extent may they be considered norms of bad governance? In other words, the mode of study of bad governance should be switched from normative assessment to a positive analysis. This also means that one needs to shift from the above-stated description of symptoms of bad governance as a specific syndrome to a causal explanation of why it emerges and develops and how it can be overcome (and indeed, whether it can at all). From this perspective, one must admit that bad governance is not only the opposite of good governance, but also a distinctive politico-economic order that is based on a set of formal and informal rules, norms, and practices, quite different from the norms of governance. In turn, this politico-economic order, although it may be perceived as one of the many instances of a "limited access order"[32] and of the prevalence of "extractive" political and economic institutions,[33] demonstrates several political foundations that make it a peculiar subtype of such orders. To put it bluntly, among the many countries belonging to these categories in the past and in the present, there are some countries that are governed intentionally badly because the political leaders of these countries establish and maintain rules, norms, and practices that serve their own self-interests. These political foundations are identified hereafter as a "constitution" of bad governance, or its informal institutional core.[34] In other words, they are treated as de-facto "rules-in-use"[35] serving as key institutional arrangements of the politico-economic order that sets up the framework and mechanisms for governing the state:

1. Rent extraction is the main goal and substantive purpose of governing the state at all levels of authority.
2. The mechanism of governing the state tends toward a hierarchy (the "power vertical") with only one major center of decision-making, which claims a monopoly on political power (the "single power pyramid").[36]
3. The autonomy of domestic political and economic actors vis-à-vis this center is conditional; it can be reduced and/or abolished at any given moment.
4. The formal institutions that define the framework of power and governance are arranged as by-products of the distribution of resources within the power vertical: they matter as rules of the game only to the degree to which they contribute to rent-seeking (or at least do not prevent it).
5. The power apparatus within the power vertical is divided into several organized groups and/or informal cliques, which compete with one another for access to rents.

These political foundations are important for understanding the main features of bad governance as the basis of a respective politico-economic order and principal tools for its maintenance in governing the state. Indeed, if the state is governed in order to extract rents, then various forms and manifestations of corruption[37] serve not as deviations from the norms of good governance but rather as means to achieve this goal. Similarly, poor quality of state regulations and perversion of the principles of the rule of law (hereafter "unrule of law")[38] not only contribute to extraction of rents but also reduce the risk of breakdown of hierarchical power pyramids, and manage the conditional nature of the political and economic actors' autonomy. The creation and frequent changing of both "fuzzy"[39] and overly rigid formal institutions against a background of purposively selective law enforcement also serve these goals. In other words, I consider bad governance to be a social mechanism that emerges as an effect of the above stated politico-economic order based on a drive for rent extraction by major political and economic actors. The logic of formation of this mechanism may be illustrated in a graphic form (see figure 9).

In many ways, the emergence and maintenance of bad governance is similar to the rise of the political monopoly of autocratic rulers and their cronies, which is a by-product of the drive for power maximization of would-be dominant political actors given existing constraints or lack thereof.[40] The pattern of creation of bad governance is similar to that of authoritarian regime-building:[41] the drive for maximization of rents contributes to consistent building of those bad institutions (corruption, poor regulations, and the unrule of law), which may be considered effects of bad governance similar to the figures in Lorenzetti's fresco. They maintain a socially inefficient equilibrium in order to serve the vested interests of actors with strong bargaining power.[42] As a result, the ineffectiveness of government under these conditions becomes an unavoidable consequence of bad governance, although its scope and effects may vary in different sectors of economy and policy areas and during different periods of time. However, ineffectiveness of government is tolerated by rent-seeking actors and by societies at large as long as it does not produce major immediate challenges to the politico-economic order itself. Thus, bad governance is a functional, purpose-built, and even acceptable mechanism for many (if not most) political and economic actors, at least as a short-term solution

The implications of such a framing of bad governance for further analysis are straightforward: it is perceived as a primarily agency-driven rather than structure-induced phenomenon. Although certain structural conditions such as material, institutional, and organizational legacies of the past, the capacity and autonomy of the state, and international linkages of certain countries affect quality of governance across the globe, and there is no reason to consider bad governance in given countries (including Russia) to be inevitable. Indeed, bad governance is created by people who have strong temptations to exploit their power for private purposes: if they do not face major constraints, they may impose this mechanism on society. The issue, however, is that some of these self-interested, rent-seeking actors who aim to build bad governance can achieve their goals (often for a long period of time), while others fail to do so due to a variety of reasons.

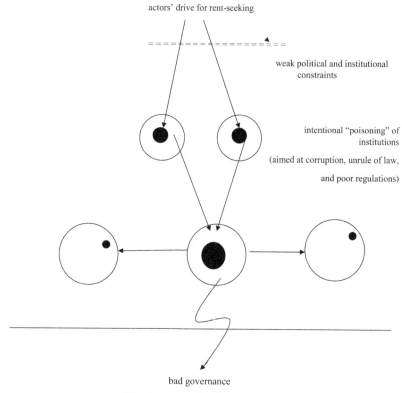

actors' drive for rent-seeking

weak political and institutional
constraints

intentional "poisoning" of
institutions

(aimed at corruption, unrule of law,

and poor regulations)

bad governance

FIGURE 9. The Genesis and Effects of Bad Governance

In essence, bad governance is a stable yet inefficient equilibrium: it can rarely be shaken, and re-equilibration is possible even after major exogenous shocks. As will be explored later in this book, post-Communist Russia, with its uneven political and economic dynamics, may serve as a prime example of this kind of low-level equilibrium. The stability of bad governance becomes self-reinforcing over time, while the apparatus of the state can only improve the quality of governance to a limited degree: its ability to pursue structural reforms aimed at improving effectiveness of government is severely constrained. The durable nature of bad governance in Russia and beyond demands reassessment and more in-depth analysis.

Bad Governance: Why?

The existing scholarship on good and bad governance is rather diverse and pays attention to different causal mechanisms, which in turn, are based upon the impact of political, economic, societal, and cultural factors. The influential institutionalist approach, which predominates in political economy literature, focuses on the decisive influence of overarching institutional settings, such as the prevalence of "extractive" versus "inclusive" institutions[43] or of "limited access" versus "open access" orders[44] in patterns of governance. These orders and/ or institutions, which emerged historically in various contexts, may persist for decades or even centuries, determine patterns of political competition and accountability (or lack thereof), and provide major conditions for good and bad governance in the long run. Another influential macrolevel societal approach tends to emphasize the major impact of social capital,[45] social embeddedness and personal networks,[46] which in turn, affects the position of interpersonal and institutional trust[47] as essential components of the quality of governance. At the same time, the dark side of social capital (such as clientelism, patronalism, "amoral familism," and the like)[48] provides fertile grounds for long-term persistence of bad governance, therefore making it increasingly difficult to combat over time. Several influential studies, both contemporary and historical,[49] discuss the validity of these arguments, thus encouraging scholars of Russian governance to follow these frameworks as major guidelines.

Overall, there is a dismal consensus among specialists: the common assertion of durable bad governance has become the default vantage point for almost all writings about Russia and other post-Soviet countries.[50] However, the popular explanations of such a persistence in the literature vary considerably. Some authors tend to be excessively shallow in their approach. They emphasize the pernicious role of Putin and his entourage, portray the entire process of politico-economic changes as a Manichean struggle between reformers ("good guys," the crusaders of good governance) and rent-seekers ("bad guys," the defenders of bad governance)[51] and blame the latter group of actors for building a "kleptocracy" and "crony capitalism"[52] if not "mafia states."[53] While the factual grounds for such a criticism are often correct, explanations of this kind are often insufficient, as in the political realm most "guys" are neither good nor bad by default. The same political actors may endorse policy reforms aimed at improvement of quality of governance or adopt measures that may have devastating effects on governance. In fact, Vladimir Putin contributed to advancements of some policy reforms in the early 2000s (discussed in the chapter 4), but he also paved the way for many practices of bad governance.

The alternative is focusing on excessively deep explanations, as many experts attribute roots of bad governance in Russia to secondary effects of negative legacies of bad informality,[54] which tend to reproduce "single power pyramids"[55] in Russia and post-Soviet Eurasia over centuries. Some critically minded observers of Russia have deterministically argued that there is an inescapable path-dependency[56] and deeply embedded patrimonial rule in Russia[57] that cannot be overcome at all, or at least not in the foreseeable future. Such a perception cannot be used to explain why Russia, both historically and in the present, has been able to build and maintain decent quality of governance at least in some policy fields prioritized by political leaders, sometimes pursue successful policy reforms, and demonstrate certain "success stories" of state-driven projects and programs (discussed in the chapter 6). If any given country is doomed to be governed badly forever, then how can we explain these advancements: Why do good apples still grow on such a bad tree?

In this book, I address the issue of causes and mechanisms of bad governance in Russia and beyond from a different scholarly optics, which is not especially country-specific and context-bounded, but based on a more general rationale of state-building, political regime dynamics, and policy-making. I argue that although these days, bad governance is almost universally perceived as an anomaly, at least in developed countries, in fact human history is largely a history of ineffective and corrupt governments, while the rule of law and decent state regulatory quality are relatively recent matters of modern history when they emerged as side effects of state-building.[58] Indeed, the picture is quite the opposite: bad governance is the norm, while good governance is an exception. This paradox is not only a side effect of the worst features of human nature (although the personal qualities of many rulers, both contemporary and historical, are imperfect, to put it mildly). The problem is that most rulers, especially if their time horizons are short and the external constraints on their behavior are not especially binding, tend to govern their domains in a predatory way because of the prevalence of short-term over long-term incentives.[59] While the examples of careless rulers who governed their respective states quite badly are numerous,[60] we may wonder why some countries have established and developed good governance despite these incentives.

In the past, good governance did not emerge by default because of the good will of benevolent and prudent leaders and/or experts,[61] but as a forced response by rulers to two interrelated challenges. First, fierce international rivalry led to numerous wars and bloody military conflicts, and those states that demonstrated ineffectiveness in both economic and military terms bore heavy losses and were even conquered by their more effective adversaries. This is why, according to Charles Tilly, rulers had to invest tremendous efforts in maintenance of control over their territories and in building effective state machinery, enabling them to exercise a monopoly on legitimate violence,[62] collect necessary taxes,[63] and use both the coercive and the infrastructural power of their states[64] for survival in a highly competitive international environment. Over generations, these rulers faced the need to make governance more suitable for international competition not only in military but also in economic terms, thus paving the way to modern good governance.

Second, the ineffectiveness and corruption of governments prompted the rise of domestic political conflicts because of pressure from various political and economic actors and citizens at large. These conflicts often went beyond the rulers' control and contributed to the spread of uncontrolled violence and civil wars, which developed into major threats to the very existence of the states and ruined their social orders. The classical analysis of economic history, which focuses on the emergence of the rule of law and transition toward good governance after the Glorious Revolution in late seventeenth-century England, serves as an illustration of the impact of these challenges.[65] As Douglass North and his collaborators have demonstrated, the monarchy's inefficient policy contributed to the fiscal crisis of the state and the subsequent chain of violent political crises (revolution—dictatorship—restoration). This lasted for some decades until competing actors reached the solution of building a new order via empowering the parliament and establishing a limited government that was constrained in terms of borrowing money. It was only later that good governance played an important role in the long-term and sustainable economic growth that helped Britain to enhance its positions in foreign policy arenas and protect itself from international challenges.

However, in the contemporary world the nature of international and domestic challenges to bad governance is qualitatively different to that in the past. Against the background of the rise of new authoritarian regimes after the end of the Cold War[66] amid the global antidemocratic tide in the twenty-first century,[67] the new nondemocratic leaders faced relatively short time horizons (especially true for personalist electoral autocracies)[68] and were therefore tempted to govern their countries badly, to the point of notoriety. Still, not all modern autocracies have necessarily resulted in comprehensive bad governance, as some of them (most notably, China) were able to provide certain political and institutional constraints to rent-seeking and corruption, especially at subnational level.[69] Nevertheless, examples of authoritarian good governance are relatively rare. Dani Rodrik summarized these tendencies in a brief statement: "for every President Lee Kwan Yew of Singapore there are many like President Mobutu Sese Seko of Zaire (now called the Democratic Republic of the Congo)."[70]

Meanwhile, the nature of constraints on bad governance has dramatically changed in the present day. Since large-scale wars are more or less matters of the past, corrupt and ineffective governments are no longer at risk of conquest by foreign nations or loss of power through defeat in war. International challenges to autocratic rulers are indirect and take effect in the medium term. Though the risk of losses in international economic competition because of bad governance may be a rather frustrating nuisance for corrupt and ineffective governments, such challenges are far from critical for the survival of political leaders. Sluggish economic growth, a decline in foreign investments, and capital flight bring negative consequences for the countries involved but they do not always put the ruling groups at risk of losing power and wealth, at least in the short term. In terms of control over domestic conflicts and violence, one might argue that bad governance is a functional mechanism that maintains a delicate balance among elites, thus preserving the political status quo[71] if domestic pressure from political and economic actors and society at large is sporadic and can generally be kept under control by the ruling groups. Under conditions of bad governance, ruling groups, in turn, can co-opt some rent-seeking actors as their loyal followers or use selective coercion and repressions toward other actors. Thus, domestic pressures that may disequilibrate bad governance can also be diminished. And if and when both international and domestic pressures are weak enough, then bad governance, once established and entrenched, may reproduce itself over and over again despite (or even thanks to) regime and leadership changes.

Why Bad Governance in Russia?

Perhaps the best description of the emergence of bad governance in the existing literature was provided not by scholars, but by a novelist, William Golding.[72] His *Lord of the Flies* is worth reading as a classic example of the making of bad governance, in this case on an uninhabited island by a community of teenagers.[73] According to Golding's plot, the trajectory of governance on this island went from a failed attempt to build an electoral democracy, through a short-lived informal oligarchy, to a seizure of power by the most brazen teenager who excluded his rivals from the community, reshuffled a coalition of his followers, and established a harsh repressive tyranny, which resulted in a catastrophe. In the novel, the encroachment of external actors (namely, navy officers) put an end to this trajectory, but in real life, the catastrophe of bad governance could have continued virtually forever. One should admit, however, that Golding's characters were not doomed to bad governance because of unfavorable initial conditions: they were just ordinary teenagers left to their own devices. The main lesson of *Lord of the Flies* for political scientists is that bad governance is a natural logical outcome of the power maximization drive of successful brazen politicians who face insufficient constraints to their aspirations. Later, this argument was reformulated by leading scholars of authoritarianism who asserted that bad governance is typically the best politics for dictators:[74] to a certain extent, the experience of post-Communist Russia and some of its neighbors in Eurasia fits these suppositions.

In this respect, the rise of bad governance in post-Communist Russia conformed to the logic of *Lord of the Flies*: indeed, it is practically the main outcome of the transformation of the Russian state after the collapse of the Soviet Union.[75] This is what happens if and when ruling groups lack immediate domestic and international challenges and meet little resistance to making their dreams come true. They can rationally and purposively maintain a politico-economic order that is unavailable to ruling groups in other political conditions: post-Communist leaders have often faced almost no constraints on their aspirations of rent-seeking and building single power pyramids. In brief, the syndrome of bad governance in post-Soviet Eurasia arose as a side effect of several major transformations, including the decay and collapse of the Soviet state and post-Communist state capture[76] first from the outside (by oligarchs) and then from the inside (by top bureaucrats). Major rent-seeking ruling actors aimed to privatize gains and socialize losses during the process of political and economic changes, and many of them encountered few, if any, constraints on achieving these goals in the turbulent post-Communist political environment.[77] Thus, they consciously, consistently, and deliberately continue to build and maintain socially inefficient institutions, or "rules of the game."[78] But given the short-term horizon of their planning, which is often constrained by the performance legitimacy of the ruling groups,[79] and because of the dubious prospects of successful hereditary succession,[80] these actors most often act as "roving" rather than "stationary" bandits.[81] They steal state resources to the point where the label "kleptocracy" is not merely opinion journalism but rather an adequate description of various leaders' governance of Russia and post-Soviet states.[82] It is no wonder that the winners of post-Communist regime changes and economic reforms, who were able to secure their positions vis-à-vis domestic competitors and international influences, have used various political and institutional devices to preserve bad governance, although their degree of success has varied across states, sectors, and policy areas. At the same time, the numerous losers among Russian citizens have rarely raised their voices about bad governance—bottom-up protests dealt with certain governance-related issues or (to a much lesser degree) with the autocratic tendencies of the regime as a whole,[83] but not with the politico-economic order as such. Also, Russia, unlike its post-Communist counterparts in Eastern Europe,[84] has encountered little influence from international actors in terms of pressure toward improving the quality of governance: Western leverages were weak,[85] and more recently a drive for "sovereignty" of the Russian state at any cost has been serving as a shield aimed at the preservation of bad governance.

Despite these tendencies, Russia does not fully fit into the model outlined by Bruce Bueno de Mesquita and Alastair Smith.[86] They argue that the survival interests of political leaders contribute to an intentional decay of quality of governance more or less universally. However, the Russian state was and is still able to conduct prudent policies and successfully pursue major developmental goals if and when they are strategically important for political leaders. Apart from rent-seekers, Russia's "winning coalitions" have also involved numerous technocrats who have effectively provided quality expertise and put forth effort to prevent major governance failures and have often designed and implemented policy advancements, even though their results are sometimes far from desired. Certain state-driven development programs have brought positive effects. The problem is that such a coexistence of various patterns of governance (in the jargon used by some international agencies, it is referred to as "bad enough governance")[87] is rather imperfect and results in numerous contradictions. At best, these winning coalitions enabled certain fool-proofing in governing Russia[88] during the twenty-first century, but they were a poor fit for further development of the country.[89] Following Rodrik's parallel stated above, one must admit that governance in Russia resembles neither Singapore under Lee Kwan Yew nor Congo under Mobutu Sese Seko, but rather combines elements of various models. However, this combination also contributes to the reinforcement of bad governance in the manner of a vicious circle. This vicious circle may be reproduced over time under different rulers, and attempts to overcome bad governance, if and when they occur, face strong resistance and often have only a limited impact on the quality of governance. I argue that the mechanism of bad governance in Russia and beyond cannot be broken without major regime changes, and even these changes will not necessarily bring about its defeat and the improvement of quality of governance, at least in the short term.

As I consider bad governance to be a primarily agency-driven phenomenon, its construction in post-Communist Russia and beyond may be regarded as an equivalent to the deliberate poisoning of the societal organism.[90] Unlike other causes of major diseases—such as inheritance or trauma—it has been an outcome of the purposeful actions of numerous actors, driven mostly by their self-interest but also by certain ideas that guided the processes of post-Communist transformation. In one way or another, this poisoning achieved its goals because of the fertile grounds and the lack of antidote amid the cultivation of bad governance via the efforts of Russia's rulers and their cronies. Before turning to a detailed analysis of the mechanisms of bad governance in Russia, I will briefly outline the trajectory of its rise and further evolution, with an emphasis on the major critical junctures and drivers of continuity and changes.

The quality of governance in the Soviet Union was exceedingly poor. However, it was very different from what is understood as bad governance in terms of this book: rent-seeking and corruption as goals of governing the state. The political regime in the Soviet Union was highly institutionalized: it placed major formal and informal constraints on the behavior of elites, at least after Stalin's death.[91] Even though major violations of these rules occurred from time to time, they were largely considered deviations rather than norms.[92] Nevertheless, attempts to rearrange the Soviet model of governance during Gorbachev's perestroika were poorly prepared and changed the quality of governance from bad to worse amid a major crisis of the Soviet economy and the state.[93] In the end, the Soviet Union collapsed under the avalanche of simultaneous economic troubles, political tensions, and ethnic conflicts.[94] To some extent, the Soviet collapse, which contributed to a dramatic decline of state capacity in Russia and in the entire post-Soviet region,[95] had the unintended consequence of serving as a trigger event for the rise of bad governance during the following decades because of the grave weakening of political and institutional constraints to rent-seeking.

No wonder that the "roaring" 1990s in Russia demonstrated plenty of examples of bad governance against the background of major political conflicts, a deep and protracted economic transformation recession, and the fragmentation of the Russian state in both vertical and horizontal dimensions. These include various developments such as "state capture" by economic interest groups,[96] spontaneous state devolution from the federal center to regional fiefdoms,[97] the criminal business of private protection[98] and the like. After this turbulence, the period of complex "triple transition" (regime change, market transformation, and nation-state building)[99] ended by the early 2000s. Then the Russian economy attained an unprecedented growth rate, and the Russian state partially restored its capacity. Soon after, agents of state capture became peripheral or were integrated into the new institutional environment. "Oligarchs" lost their control over the political agenda and were placed into subordinate positions within the state-led corporatism;[100] regional bosses lost their leverages of power and became dependent upon the federal center and large nationwide companies;[101] criminal "violent entrepreneurs" were either legalized or marginalized,[102] and so forth. To paraphrase the title once coined by Theda Skocpol, the Russian state was being brought back.[103] One might expect that the conservative post-revolutionary stabilization of the 2000s[104] would not only extend the time horizon of major actors, but also open up room for a new gradual drift of Russia toward eradication of bad governance, similarly to overcoming growing pains. Over time, however, these tendencies in Russia became even stronger.

In the early 2000s, the Russian leaders launched several programs of state-driven policy reforms aimed at improving the quality of governance, and some of them brought major positive effects, even though they were only partial.[105] Still, the drive for policy reforms was short-lived, and gradually these reforms lost priority status in the agenda of Putin and his entourage.[106] At the same time, political changes aimed at democratization were intentionally and systematically pushed out of the menu of options for political leaders and policy reformers alike for the sake of an "authoritarian modernization" strategy (analyzed in detail in chapter 3).[107] Over the course of the next decade, this strategy was implemented in a controversial way—an electoral authoritarian regime was successfully built and consolidated in Russia,[108] yet the "narrow" economic modernization faced numerous problems, including those related to the quality of governance. In fact, Russia's ruling groups effectively used the strengthening of the state and economic growth to pursue their opportunistic interests. Speaking more broadly, one might argue that the restoration of state capacity and economic growth does not by default lead to the overcoming of bad governance. Quite the opposite, the Russian experience of the 2000s has demonstrated that the "medicine" of authoritarianism can be even worse than the illness of bad governance itself; the post-traumatic stress resulting from this method of healing can easily turn into a pernicious chronic disease. In many ways, Russia in the 2000s fits the bitter statement of Adam Przeworski: "as any order is better than any disorder, any order is established."[109] This maxim is also true for the politico-economic order of bad governance that was established in Russia at that time.

The period of the 2010s brought new controversies to the politics of bad governance in Russia. On the one hand, the rapid economic growth that had served as a driver of Russia's development before the 2008–2009 global crisis was exhausted, and over the last decade growth has been sluggish. On the other hand, the Russian annexation of Crimea in 2014 and the subsequent rise of international tensions amid domestic isolationist trends have contributed to further aggravation of bad governance. The political leaders who invested a lot of effort into the preservation of the political status quo easily sacrificed the quality of governance for the sake of keeping political "stability" at any cost, and have tended to prioritize political loyalty over efficiency in all layers of government.[110] At best, improvements of quality of governance have affected various issues of secondary importance, and their effects have been rather modest. More important, overall, the goals of economic growth and development have been consigned to the periphery of the Russian leadership's agenda, being overshadowed by geopolitical ambitions.[111] In effect, the consolidated authoritarian regime in Russia[112] has become the main (although not the only) pernicious factor in the further deterioration of the quality of governance in the country. However, unlike in the case of Soviet collapse, this deterioration looks not like a sudden breakdown but rather like a gradual yet steady decay.

The present-day low-level equilibrium of bad governance in Russia is also maintained by the high costs of overcoming it, which may increase over time. These costs are related not only to the complexities of possible political regime changes (if and when they occur) but also to the need for major elite turnover. In fact, the short-term beneficiaries of bad governance in Russia are numerous: they are not only limited to top state officials and oligarchs, but also include the staff of law enforcement agencies and many public sector employees, so it is difficult to expect that their resistance to revision of the politico-economic order will be eradicated easily. Meanwhile, even small steps toward democratization are not on the agenda of Russia's political leaders, as they tend to find other recipes to maintain "bad enough" governance. These recipes may be summarized as "3D"—deregulation, digitalization, and decentralization—but they can affect only technical rather than substantive issues of the quality of governance in the absence of a "4D" solution, which should include democratization as the number one item on the political agenda. However, the recent experience of democratization in some other post-Soviet countries (most notably, Ukraine) as well as the recent resurgence of bad governance in some East European countries (Hungary may serve as a prime example in this respect) tells us that democratization, though necessary, is not a sufficient factor for improving the quality of governance. This is why bad governance in Russia should be considered to be not just a short-term side effect of the one-off "poisoning" efforts of Putin and his entourage. By the 2020s, the consequences of this "poisoning" (which has continued over time in a systematic manner) have turned into a major long-term chronic disease that may be curable only with serious systematic treatment and outstanding efforts by the Russian political class and Russian society at large. The detailed analysis of causes, mechanisms, and possible evolution of bad governance in Russia, as well as lessons from the Russian experience for other states and nations, will be discussed further.

Plan of the Book

This book begins by setting the stage for exploring the politics of bad governance in Russia and beyond in terms of definitions, theoretical claims, and applications of these arguments to analysis of the trajectory of bad governance in Russia after the Soviet collapse. Chapter 2 focuses on mechanisms of bad governance in Russia and major factors in its maintenance. Apart from emphasis on the self-interest of major political and economic actors and on the instrumental use of bad governance by Russia's elites, it also focuses on the use of various "legacies of the past" as tools for legitimation of bad governance and as ideational role models for Russia's rulers and many citizens. It also discusses attempts at building efficient institutions aimed to improve the quality of governance in Russia in parallel to the existing mechanisms of bad governance and the limits of possible changes.

The following two chapters examine the origins of bad governance in post-Soviet Russia and attempts to constrain it via mechanisms of policy changes under conditions of authoritarian politics. Chapter 3 discusses the project of "authoritarian modernization" consciously and consistently pursued by the Russian elites after the Soviet collapse in the 1990s and especially in the 2000s. It focuses on the controversies of this project in terms of ideas, institutions, and policies, and the major flaws of authoritarian modernization that greatly contributed to the rise of bad governance. Chapter 4 examines one of the key elements of authoritarian modernization in Russia, namely the politics of policy reforms of the 2000s aimed at facilitating Russia's economic development and improving the quality of governance. It provides an explanation for why these reforms resulted in only partial and temporary improvements and how this experience played a role in the subsequent building and consolidation of bad governance in Russia.

The next two chapters concentrate on other elements of the mechanism of governance in Russia, which aims to prevent major failures and bring certain advancements despite the overall gloomy picture of the quality of governance. Chapter 5 focuses on the role of technocrats in governing Russia—those policymakers who conduct certain policies reasonably well and perform functions of fool-proofing against the most dangerous vices of bad governance. Still, the influence of technocrats on policy-making in Russia is limited, and its effects should not be overstated. Chapter 6 examines "success stories," or outstanding examples of state-directed programs and projects aimed at major achievements in certain policy fields during both the Soviet and the post-Soviet periods of Russian history. Although a rare combination of top-level political patronage and effective policy entrepreneurship sometimes results in major breakthroughs, these success stories often prove short-lived, and rarely contribute to major diffusions of advancements beyond "pockets of efficiency" cultivated under special conditions. This is why hopes for spreading elements of good governance beyond certain limits appear illusory.

Chapter 7 aims to place the phenomenon of bad governance in Russia into a broader comparative perspective and consider the implications of the analysis of the Russian case beyond the region. I argue that the drive to make bad governance work is not particularly a country-specific and context-bounded process. Rather, Russia's experience may be perceived as a negative role model for many rulers across the globe who would like to minimize the political and institutional constraints of bad governance. In the conclusion, the book discusses prospects for improving the quality of governance in Russia, as well as related opportunities, challenges, and risks the country may face on this thorny path.

CHAPTER 2

___

Post-Soviet Bad Governance: A Vicious Circle?

Introduction: Russia's Greatest Rent Machine

On New Year's Eve 2015, the residents of more than two dozen Russian regions received an unexpected and unpleasant holiday gift from the authorities. They were notified that the commuter trains (*elektrichki*) that link many cities and towns with regional capitals were being cut *en masse*; in some regions they were completely abolished. Although the frequency of commuter trains had already been reduced, together with a steady rise in rail ticket prices, the elimination of many trains at once caused major public discontent, especially in those areas where no other public transportation had been provided. Soon after, one of the leaders of the Russian opposition, Alexei Navalny, accused both the state authorities and the top managers of the company Russian Railways (RZhD) of "genocide of the Russian people,"[1] while in some Siberian regions, attempted collective action by local residents contributed to threats of rail traffic blockages. The rise in social tensions became so striking and visible that in February 2015 Russian President Vladimir Putin, speaking before TV cameras, asked state officials and the RZhD leadership to fully restore commuter trains. Shortly afterward, the return of passenger traffic was announced in the media (although it was only a partial return), so the previous status quo was restored, at least for a while.

Although at first glance this episode illustrates an accident of mismanagement of public transportation, the fact is that the abolition of commuter trains was a logical outcome of the changes to Russian railroads that had been implemented during the previous decade.[2] In 2003, in accordance with a decision by the Russian government, the long-existing state agency, the Ministry of Railways (MPS), was transformed into the state-owned company RZhD, which received the key assets of the railroad sector; later on it became a joint stock company. Subsequently, the Russian railroads underwent a series of structural reforms intended to liberalize the sector. Many reform projects, oriented to follow best international practices, proposed that RZhD should separate profitable cargo transportation from unprofitable passenger traffic, while state policies should pave the way toward a competition between private companies in the market of cargo transportation. But in reality RZhD not only preserved but even strengthened its monopolist position as a provider of passenger transportation; it de-facto unilaterally dictated extraordinarily high tariffs and requested that the state cover the increasing losses of its subsidiary companies, which were in charge of operating commuter trains. These companies, in turn, leased trains and equipment from RZhD and paid it extraordinarily high fees for the use and service of trains (owned by RZhD), while their losses were fully compensated from the Russian state budget. In 2011, the responsibility for covering these losses was transferred from the federal government to the regional authorities, which do not have the funds to feed RZhD's appetites (and in fact have to cover many other expenditures due to previous requests from the federal authorities)[3] and lack the capacity to resist RZhD. Moreover, in January 2015, in accordance with a request by RZhD, the Russian federal government drastically increased fees for the use of rail infrastructure, thus aggravating the heavy financial burden on regional authorities to subsidize commuter trains.[4] Putin's subsequent call for action did not change the economic model of commuter trains; at best, responsibility to cover losses was to some extent transferred from regional budgets to federal coffers (with the annual amount estimated at twenty-two billion rubles at that time), but the taxpayers still had to pay any bills presented by RZhD.[5]

Although experts rightly observe that the problem of subsidizing unprofitable, yet socially important, commuter trains is hardly unique to Russia and is relevant for railroad reforms elsewhere,[6] so the case of RZhD was atypical not only due to the scope of these problems but also due to its solution. In essence, reforms resulted in the transformation of a state agency, MPS (a legacy of a centralized planned Soviet economy), into a gigantic monopoly, RZhD, which was formally owned by the state and operated on the market, but was in practice outside state control and operated for the benefit of its top managers. Vladimir Yakunin, appointed as CEO of this holding in 2005, was one of the key members of Putin's "inner circle" as one of his *dacha* friends since the 1990s.[7]

Yakunin became famous not only because of his conspicuous consumption of luxury material goods (his big estate near Moscow has been nicknamed *shubokhranilishche*, or "fur storage") but also because of his spike in international status as a public intellectual. Being a doctor of political sciences who chaired the Department of Public Administration in the Faculty of Political Science at Moscow State University,[8] Yakunin is also a patron of the Russian Society of Political Scientists and president of the World Public Forum "Dialogue of Civilizations" (DOC). DOC, in turn, has held numerous international events with participation from global celebrities, and among other things, sponsored publication of a book, *Conversations with the World's Foremost Thinkers*, produced by a highly reputable US university press and edited by leading international scholars—an interview with Yakunin was included there alongside Nobel Prize winners.[9] Despite widespread criticism of Yakunin in the media and some attempts to cancel his job contract as CEO, long-term close connections with Putin made him nearly invincible and gave Yakunin *carte blanche*; RZhD became a fiefdom of this crony of Putin, while its business operations remained in the shadow of numerous offshore companies connected with Yakunin (some of them were linked with his son, who resides in London).[10] However, the incident with the attempted cancellation of commuter trains did not go unnoticed. In essence, Yakunin's appetites were considered too voracious, while his threats to cancel train services came across as blackmailing the Russian state by an oligarch, which was unacceptable for Russia's leadership in political terms.[11] In August 2015, Yakunin was forced to leave his post at RZhD; later he became a full-time chair of the DOC Research Institute with headquarters in Berlin (positioned as a global think tank), gained a German residence permit,[12] and more or less disappeared from Russia's public scene. The new CEO of RZhD, Oleg Belozerov, rearranged some of the corporate governance practices that had emerged under Yakunin's rule, but by and large, according to analysts, the principles of bad governance in this state-owned company did not change much under new leadership.[13]

In other words, after major reforms, a formally state-owned monopoly, the biggest employer in the country, was taken over by a private individual who turned RZhD into a tool for rent maximization and placed the burden of costs (arbitrarily set by himself) on taxpayers' shoulders. To paraphrase the *Boney M* hit of the 1970s, this model of governing the railroads can be best described as "Russia's Greatest Rent Machine." Its social costs became much higher than those of the MPS model, which emerged in the 1930s under the leadership of Stalin's close subordinate Lazar Kaganovich.[14] MPS served as one of the pillars of the Soviet planned economy, had priority access to state resources including labor and investments, and had relatively high status in state distribution of welfare and other goods. Later, its role decreased because of technological changes and the decline of the Soviet economic model, and by the time of the Soviet collapse its impact on rent-seeking was relatively modest. While the crisis of the MPS model in the 1990s has been widely recognized,[15] the consequences of the 2000s reforms may be considered a turn from bad to worse.

The case of RZhD is not the only example of bad governance in Russia's public sector: quite the opposite, this example is a rather typical episode of

exploitation of a state-owned company for the private benefit of its top management. Over the last decades, investigative journalists and anticorruption activists have uncovered many examples of abuses of public resources by top managers
of state-owned companies, as well as by top Russian state officials.[16] Yet despite
the great public attention, in most instances official reaction to these revelations
has been conspicuously absent, and Yakunin remains one of the few visible persons in Russia who lost his post because of a scandal related to bad governance.

In a broader perspective, the transformation of RZhD into "Russia's greatest
rent machine" exemplified the failure of one of the sectoral reforms that formed
a large-scale program of socioeconomic changes in Russia under Putin.[17] But
why did the good intentions of policy reforms aimed at accelerating economic
growth and improving the quality of governance pave a road to the hell of crony
capitalism and bad governance in post-Soviet Russia? I argue that the causes of
these mutations of post-Soviet modernization are related to the emergence and
maintenance of intentionally built political and economic institutions of bad
governance. These institutions should not be perceived merely as inherited from
the Soviet (or pre-Soviet) past; rather, they were purposefully developed after
the Soviet collapse to serve the interests of ruling groups in Russia and other
post-Soviet states and consolidate their political and economic dominance.[18]
Thus, policy reforms brought partial results at best, and very often contributed
to a vicious circle of socially inefficient changes that served privileged private
interests. I also argue that this vicious circle cannot be broken by attempting to
"borrow" socially efficient institutions or "cultivate" them step-by-step within
the given political constraints. Further embedding of post-Soviet bad governance may increase the risk of its reinforcement and self-reproduction regardless
of possible political regime changes. I believe that the incentives for rejection of
bad governance in Russia and some other countries may (though not necessarily
should) be strengthened by a combination of domestic pressure and external
influence, with certain restrictions of those countries' sovereignty and possible
compulsion from major international actors.

The structure of this chapter is as follows. First, after an overview of discussions on the sources and mechanisms of post-Soviet bad governance, I present
my own approach to analysis of its effects on post-Soviet policy-making, and its
political foundations and constraints. I then explore mechanisms of governance
within the framework of post-Soviet political institutions (the "power vertical")
and focus on policy reforms that have brought few returns and/or have resulted
in unexpected and undesired consequences (the models of "borrowing" and
"cultivating" institutions). In the conclusion, I discuss some implications and

considerations regarding the possible role of international influence in breaking
the vicious circle of post-Soviet bad governance.

The Sources of Post-Soviet Bad Governance:
The Long Arm of the Past?

As stated in chapter 1, the following are the foundational principles of post-Soviet
bad governance as a politico-economic order: (1) rent extraction is the main goal
and substantive purpose of governing the state at all levels of authority; (2) the
mechanism of governing the state gravitates toward a hierarchy (the "power vertical") with only one major center of decision-making, which claims a monopoly
on political power (the "single power pyramid"); (3) the autonomy of domestic
political and economic actors vis-à-vis this center is conditional; it can be reduced and/or abolished at any given moment; (4) the formal institutions that
define the framework of power and governance are arranged as by-products of
the distribution of resources within the power vertical: they matter as rules of
the game only to the degree to which they contribute to rent-seeking (or at least
do not prevent it); and (5) the power apparatus within the power vertical is divided into several organized groups and/or informal cliques that compete with
one another for access to rents.

These principles are the essence of an informal institutional core, or de facto
constitution, of the politico-economic order of bad governance. The ruling
groups build the shell of formal institutions (such as official constitutions, laws,
and regulations) around this "core." However, this shell is not just a camou-
flage aiming to hide the ugly face of bad governance; it also serves as a functional mechanism for authoritarian power-sharing and rent-sharing that aims
to maintain a balance of power among the insiders of the regime's "winning
coalition."[19] Although authoritarianism in both its "electoral"[20] and "classical"
("hegemonic")[21] formats to some extent is a mechanism of maintenance of bad
governance in the political arena, it may be vulnerable because of the risks of
intraelite conflicts and regime subversion. These risks emerge when the political monopolies of ruling groups are undermined and autonomy of political and
economic actors becomes limited in certain ways, so regime changes or threats
thereof are not so rare. But if the regime can avert these risks, then bad governance may become invincible (if one puts aside risks stemming from exogenous shocks).

Many explanations of bad governance in post-Soviet Russia are focused on the
negative role of the repressive and ineffective autocratic state machinery, which

is deeply embedded in centuries of Russian history. It is no wonder that its most widespread explanations relate to the effects of various legacies of the past.[22] While in the case of Third World countries (which are largely perceived as hotbeds of various forms of bad governance) the whole frame of reference revolves around colonial legacies,[23] but in post-Soviet countries, scholars look for sources of bad governance in virtually all stages of Russian and Soviet history. They assign responsibility for its embeddedness to the inescapable legacy of pre-Petrine Russia with its lack of private property and arbitrary rule of autocratic leaders,[24] or to the legacy of Communist regime, which in its late developmental stage demonstrated decay and "degeneration" into neo-traditionalism,[25] or to an overlapping of socioeconomic backwardness with imposed Soviet dominance in certain Eastern European countries.[26] Some scholars who use similar arguments in their analyses of post-Soviet politico-economic order refer to terms such as "patronal politics"[27] or "*sistema*,"[28] and also focus on their effects on politics and governance through the lenses of various legacies of the past. In any case, the "legacy" argument is structural in nature: explicitly or implicitly, bad governance is assumed to be like an inherited chronic disease of the sociopolitical organism that cannot be cured at least in the foreseeable future. By its very nature, this eternal and unavoidable "matrix,"[29] or "track" (*koleya*),[30] is put in place once and forever: it cannot be changed because of irreversible path dependency. The reasoning of this analysis, however, is vulnerable to criticism because of its lack of heuristic value and its frequent reliance on the principle of fitting theory and evidence into prearranged answers. The policy relevance of the approach looks even more dubious: if in any given country or region bad governance is the product of a "wrong" history that cannot be altered, one might say that this country is best eliminated (similarly to the fate of the Soviet Union) or conquered by other states that are more capable and efficient in terms of the quality of governance. Nevertheless, in the twentieth century some countries with even more problematic matrixes or tracks of history (ranging from Japan to Turkey) took the route of radical systemic changes necessary for altering their legacies and moving onto the right path; judging from this perspective, a similar path is not precluded for Russia, at least in theory.

In terms of answering empirical questions, one should consider that the rise of post-Soviet bad governance was a consequence of the purposeful actions of political and economic actors who aimed to maximize benefits for themselves during the process of redistribution of power and resources in the turbulent post-Soviet environment. For example, in the case of RZhD, the governance of the biggest state-owned company by Yakunin did not result from the legacies passed down in this sector or in the Russian economy as a whole. Neither Kaganovich nor his MPS successors ever dreamed of a degree of freedom like Yakunin's in arbitrarily governing their respective domains. Of course, political decay during the last decades of the Soviet Union greatly contributed to large-scale exploitation of public resources for the private purposes of top state managers, and instances of bad governance such as the infamous "Cotton Affair" in Uzbekistan in the 1980s were most probably just the tip of the iceberg.[31] Overall, however, in the Soviet Union instances of uncontrolled rent-seeking were limited at that time and never considered a norm of elite behavior. Rather, RZhD was turned into its CEO's fiefdom after the distribution of rent sources among the members of the post-Soviet "winning coalition"[32] led by Putin and his close allies. The maximization of power in politics and the maximization of rents in the economy should be perceived as rational goals of the ruling groups who achieved them in several post-Soviet countries in the wake of political regime changes and market economic reforms. Some analyses of the dynamics of political and economic changes after the Soviet collapse have demonstrated that complex transformations make it easier to achieve these goals, where otherwise they could be more difficult.[33] The new politico-economic order has served as an instrument of the ruling groups, and institutions have maintained its continuity and solidified the existing configurations of political and economic actors. Unlike the legacy argument, a focus on purposeful institution-building treats post-Soviet bad governance as an outcome of conscious "poisoning" of the social and political organism by certain actors belonging to the ruling groups. However, identifying possible cures for this kind of disease is far from straightforward.

That said, there is no reason to deny that "history matters"[34] for an understanding of bad governance. Rather, the question is framed differently: How exactly did this "mattering" of the past become a constituent pattern in the practice of governing the state today and tomorrow? Regarding governance, the legacy of the past is loosely understood as a set of historically established obstacles to good governance that emerged before the Soviet collapse for various reasons and persisted for an indefinite period. But this perception of a legacy fails to explain why it has a different impact on various countries and policy areas and how exactly it affects post-Soviet institutions and practices. In search of alternatives to determinism, Stephen Kotkin and Mark Beissinger redefine "legacy" as "a durable causal relationship between past institutions and policies on subsequent practices or beliefs, long beyond the life of the regimes, institutions, and policies that gave birth to them."[35] They also outline several causal mechanisms for transferring institutions and practices from the past to the present and the future, including: material or "parameter setting"; organizational and institutional or "fragmentation" and "translation"; and ideational or "cultural schemata." Many legacies of parameter setting relate to the limitation of certain institutional and/ or policy choices due to material constraints left over from the past; organizational and institutional fragmentation involves direct inheritance of some parts of previous institutions from the old regime, while translation means using old institutions for new purposes; and cultural schemata refers to perceptions generated by past regime practices that make a certain sort of conduct either normal or unacceptable.[36] Parameter setting results from certain limits set by the physical and technological infrastructure inherited from the Soviet past that posed major barriers to structural reforms.[37] By contrast, cultural schemata, modes of thinking and perceiving reality, were embedded in the past but outlived it and gave birth to the new post-Soviet normative ideal, which could be labeled a "good Soviet Union."[38] This has served as the basis for a "mental model"[39] for post-Soviet elites and societies and affected organizational and institutional legacies to a great degree as a normative ideal.

One might argue that various legacies of the past affect the present and the future mostly because of how they are transferred. This is especially true for ideational legacies: "history matters" if certain actors can use it purposively for achieving their goals in various areas, including governing the state. The time horizon for the impact of these legacies cannot be indefinitely long. In post-Soviet Eurasia, it is relevant for the recent life experience of one or two generations who often interpreted the Soviet collapse and subsequent post-Soviet political and economic changes as a major trauma and framed their perceptions of the late-Soviet experience as a paradise lost. When it comes to the mechanisms for bringing these legacies into the current agenda, material, organizational, and institutional legacies impose high costs on improving the quality of governance and contribute to the preservation of the status quo. But the scale of these costs may decrease over time because of the emergence and spread of new institutions and practices not embedded in the past. Meanwhile, ideational legacies define understanding of the means and possible goals of the process of institution-building and serve as tools of ruling groups in this process.

In essence, the "legacy of the past" is largely a socially constructed phenomenon in post-Soviet Eurasia and beyond and should be regarded not as a structural constraint but as an agency-driven phenomenon. Regarding governing the state, cultural schemata work as instruments for maintaining bad governance in two mutually related ways. First, they establish a retrospective vector of public discussion where the Soviet past is considered the main (if not only) "point of departure." History is not only a subject for historians but penetrates all aspects of public life in the region. The imagined past experience has become a normative marker in projecting the future of post-Soviet Eurasia, including but not limited to state governance. This is why previous institutions and practices have become building blocks for institution-building and policy-making. Fragmentation and translation serve as means to achieve these goals. Second, referring to the past has become the key argument in legitimating political and policy choices, other mechanisms of governance, institutions, and policies not related to the past (irrespective of their adherence to best practices of good governance) are often not perceived as legitimate by society at large. In a sense, the instrumental use of such a legacy in Russia is not so different to the slogan "Make America Great Again," so vigorously and successfully promoted by Donald Trump in his 2016 presidential election campaign. In other words, ideational legacies (in Russia, in the United States, or elsewhere) are phenomena intentionally produced by elites to serve their political goals of power maximization.

The "good Soviet Union," an imagined politico-economic order that somehow resembles that of the Soviet past while lacking its inherent flaws, bears little resemblance to the late-Soviet experience. I believe that these elements of the Soviet legacy are selectively and deliberately chosen for the sake of power maximization of the post-Soviet ruling groups. They include the hierarchy of the power vertical, "cadre stability" on all levels of government (that is, low elite circulation), a closed recruitment pool of elites and their formal and informal privileged status, state control over major media, state repressions toward organized dissent, and so on. Meanwhile, other elements of the late-Soviet politico-economic order, such as relatively low inequality and certain state social guarantees, have been discarded without meaningful resistance. In addition, the "good Soviet Union" includes certain features that did not exist in the real Soviet Union but are very important for ruling groups: not only a full-fledged market economy and no shortages of goods and services, but also a lack of institutional constraints on rent-seeking and the creation of an external interface for legalization of incomes and status abroad. The assertion that the "good Soviet Union" is a deliberate construction by post-Soviet ruling groups and their entourages is no wild exaggeration. In the 2000s, they obtained that which they wanted but which was unavailable to their late-Soviet predecessors in terms of status, power, and material well-being, and their efforts to preserve this normative ideal have borne fruit in many ways.

The use of the Soviet legacy as a set of real and/or imagined building blocks for post-Soviet institution-building and practices of governing the state contributed to the preservation of the status quo of bad governance through fragmentation or translation of this social construct into major choices and solutions. Examples include the transformation of government structure after the Soviet collapse regarding the state apparatus,[40] and practices of control and accountability in law enforcement agencies,[41] both of which extended the lives of outdated institutions and organizations, thus contributing to the ineffectiveness of government. This approach affects policy-making regarding the organization of state bureaucracy and its motivations.[42] As a result, the "good Soviet Union" as a normative ideal has not produced incentives to overcome bad governance and improve government effectiveness, even should these be declared policy goals. Rather, the "good Soviet Union" as a foundation of the post-Soviet "mental model" has become a successful instrument for the legitimation of a politico-economic order of bad governance—at least within the mid-term perspective, until the current generation of post-Soviet rulers and citizens leaves the public scene.

To summarize, the role of the "legacy of the past," which has preserved bad governance in post-Soviet Eurasia and beyond may be primarily considered in ideational terms: these normative ideals and role models affect policy choices and many organizational and institutional solutions. This legacy, which has allegedly doomed some countries to corruption and ineffectiveness, is largely a social construct that is created and maintained by ruling groups for the sake of power maximization. The countries of Eastern Europe and the Baltics have to some extent denied this normative ideal and thus increased their chances to overcome bad governance. However, those countries of post-Soviet Eurasia that see the sources of modern government in their imagined glorious or inglorious past could create a vicious circle of bad governance.

The Power Vertical as a Hierarchy of Bad Governance

The term "power vertical" is usually used to describe the hierarchical model of subnational politics and governance in Russia and other post-Soviet countries.[43] It implies formal and informal subordination of levels of authority and a web of informal exchanges between them (for electoral authoritarian regimes, vote delivery is one of the major resources in these exchanges). But similar mechanisms are employed not only in territorial but also in sectoral governance (including the public sector). One might observe sectoral power verticals within the law enforcement apparatus, educational institutions, and some NGOs. Private business is also involved in numerous informal exchanges within the power vertical, but it enjoys a broader autonomy.[44] These exchanges include not only distribution of rents but also compliance (or noncompliance) with formal rules and norms and changes in formal institutions. The power vertical is widely perceived by many Russian citizens as the legitimate mechanism of governance because of the possibility of hierarchical top-down control over lower-level officialdom. These perceptions are reinforced by the post-Soviet experience of the 1990s with its protracted decline of state capacity and major distortions of law and order after the Soviet collapse;[45] this experience also serves as an additional argument for using the power vertical as the main, if not the only, tool of governance. As long as the lower layers of the power vertical can distribute financial and material resources and perform functions of social patronage, this (imperfect) mechanism of governing territories, enterprises, and organizations persists.

The use of the power vertical as a pillar of politico-economic order in Russia leads to a major increase in agency costs and to the aggravation of principal-agent problems within the hierarchy of governance.[46] For instance, while in China these problems in the system of territorial governance are partially resolved via competition among subnational agents and their mutual policing (provincial Communist bosses can be promoted to the national leadership if and when they demonstrate excellent economic performance),[47] but post-Soviet countries employ other solutions. Eugene Huskey labels them "the politics of redundancy."[48] In other words, parallel hierarchies in charge of control and monitoring emerge at various layers of the power vertical; presidential administrations exert political control over federal and regional governments, presidential representatives in federal districts do the same vis-à-vis governors and city mayors, and so forth. Numerous state agencies in charge of regulation and monitoring in various sectors of the economy, with their own territorial branches, are also used as tools of control. Very often, such a multiplicity of agencies (including those in the law enforcement apparatus) contributes to interagency rivalry: this, in turn, also aggravates principal-agent problems within the power vertical.[49] At first sight, strict adherence to top-down hierarchical relations against the interests of the power vertical's lower echelons should require the full-fledged threat of punishment of subordinated actors by the top leadership for virtually all instances of wrongdoing, misbehavior, and poor performance.[50] But in fact, although the systematic use of state repressions against lower-level officials of the power vertical is rather widespread, it is often driven not by political demands from the Kremlin but rather by private interests of various actors from competing agencies and layers of the state hierarchy.[51] The hierarchy of the power vertical is far from an army-like chain of command, and it operates according to a different logic.

The popular argument that the power vertical serves merely as a tool of subordination and control is rather incomplete and incorrect. The power vertical should be considered as a provider of informal selective incentives. The status of its insiders rewards them with extra benefits as they receive certain exclusive gains unavailable to those actors not included in the power vertical. The major condition for lower-level beneficiaries is that their opportunistic behavior should not prevent the political leadership from achieving its strategic policy goals. In the most general sense, these goals include the preservation of a stable politico-economic order in which the ruling groups run unchallenged and maintain the relative well-being of the population-at-large. Thanks to economic stability, the principal at the top of the power vertical pyramid can reward his agents through access to rents. Thus, corruption is not merely a side effect of bad governance but rather an indispensable part of the mechanism of bad governance within the framework of the power vertical.

In its quest to maintain the loyalty of local actors, the political leadership is forced to use both carrots and sticks. The multiple tools of control include not only the appointment, dismissal, and replacement of officials, but also exclusion from access to rents and "contracted" criminal investigations against officials and businessmen, or threats thereof with the use of *kompromat*.[52] These instruments not only maintain loyalty to the power vertical but are also used as an additional mechanism of control. Almost every actor can easily be accused of criminal acts, and the threat of criminal prosecution is an even more efficient tool for maintaining control than its actual use. Consequently, actors are genuinely interested in the successful implementation of policies that serve both the goals of political leadership and their own self-interests. One should note that punishments take place under two kinds of circumstances: either because actors' rent-seeking activities contradict the policy goals of the political leadership or (more rarely) because their poor performance and/or voracious rent-seeking appetites undermine the legitimacy and stability of the politico-economic order (as the case of Yakunin tells us).

Thus, the power vertical is a relatively cheap (in terms of agency costs) and successful (in terms of incentives) solution to the principal-agent problem: the principal informally offers conditional rent access to loyal and capable agents. This mechanism maintains state capacity in governing multiple political and socioeconomic arenas. The state serves both the collective interests of the power vertical's insiders as a group and the private interests of all its agents, ranging from presidents and prime ministers to local school directors who are allowed to steal public money designated for renovation of the school building if during elections they will deliver votes at the polling station located at their school.[53] As for outsiders to the power vertical, the opportunity to access rents is a major incentive not only for political loyalty but also for personal career choices: for example, many graduates of Russian universities admit that the goal of their pursuit of higher education was a chance to get jobs in the state apparatus or in major state-owned companies such as Gazprom.[54]

Within the post-Soviet context this mechanism of governance demonstrates some specific features. They include, inter alia, the specific divisions among and between the layers and corridors of the state machinery and competition between various agencies and informal cliques for rent access and for positions in the informal hierarchy of decision-making. For example, Russian law enforcement agencies experience stiff competition between the Office of the Prosecutor General and the Investigative Committee, even though the latter agency is formally subordinated to the former.[55] Russian big business demonstrates a rivalry between Gazprom and Rosneft, which emerged almost by chance,[56] and so forth. But these contradictions are mostly structural, because both state agencies and state-owned companies are affected by sectoral power verticals that link lower-level actors to their patrons at higher levels of authority or even in the top leadership. This mechanism plays a powerful role in the informal system of governance because it cannot be bypassed in the process of appointments or dismissals in the lower echelons of the power vertical, and it is important for the survival of all actors in their behind-the-scenes struggles against powerful competitors.

In the media discourse, these phenomena are often regarded as the "new Politburo" or the "struggle between the Kremlin's towers,"[57] but such labels are rather superficial. Parallels between the power vertical under the post-Soviet politico-economic order of bad governance and the Soviet hierarchical model of governance do not touch upon the basic differences in goal-setting, institutions, and incentives. In the Soviet Union, the Communist Party exerted control over the state apparatus, was able to impose sanctions on violators of formal and informal rules of the game, and in a sense, imposed limits on the spread of bad governance. In the post-Soviet environment, the personalist nature of the political regime and the interests of powerful members of winning coalitions establish other constraints: all personnel decisions must include the maintenance of the balance between sectoral power verticals and cliques, and the use of "divide and conquer" tactics for prevention of open intraelite conflicts. The emergence of informal alliances and rivalries between actors who compete for rent access is an unavoidable side effect of the informal distribution of resources among agents. This competition drastically increases agency costs and worsens rather than improves the quality of governance. Although the fruits of economic growth may satisfy the appetites and interests of the most powerful rent-seekers and diminish their rivalries, these contradictions cannot be eliminated.

If the power vertical did not receive demands for policy reforms from the top leadership, and only reproduced the status quo, then even given a minimal inflow of resource rent and very sluggish (if not zero) economic growth, this model of governance could reproduce itself similarly to that of some Third World countries.[58] However, the imperative of "narrow" modernization (outlined in more detail in chapter 3) drives the political leadership to launch numerous policy reforms, which are to be implemented by agents of the power vertical at various layers of authority. These reforms imply not only structural changes (such as the establishment of new agencies) but also changes of goals and criteria for policy evaluation. Bureaucrats and officials must demonstrate "efficiency," which is broadly understood as the achievement of certain formal indicators, ranging from mandatory conducting of auctions and tenders in the state procurement system to a certain quantity of scholars' publications in journals listed in the Web of Science and Scopus databases. Policy reforms often destabilize the power vertical, but their effects on the quality of governance are not so obvious. Sometimes the state of affairs even degrades vis-à-vis the previous status quo, as in the case of the replacement of old Kaganoviches with new Yakunins. Why do the policy reforms sometimes have such dismal results?

The Challenge of Policy Reforms

The symbiosis of the informal core and the formal shell of bad governance, which outwardly seems to share features with advanced states and markets, ranging from formally independent courts to the commercial operations of state-owned companies such as RZhD, maintains a stable yet inefficient equilibrium. This fact explains a contradiction that has been described by scholars of African politics: in theory, under conditions of bad governance, the state of affairs in a given country should inevitably worsen, but in fact disequilibrium is relatively rare.[59] Formal institutions are not the only reason for this. The stable increase of rent in Russia in the 2000s has also helped to maintain the status quo despite short-term economic troubles.[60] Unlike the states and regimes in sub-Saharan Africa which that are widely perceived as "dictatorships of stagnation,"[61] Russia until the 2010s displayed an opposite trend—the drive for economic growth in the 2000s served as the main source of maintenance of this politico-economic order. It was only after 2014 that the priorities of Russia's leadership changed, and economic growth was sacrificed for the sake of "stability" (the preservation of political status quo).[62] Nevertheless, Russia's ruling groups were (and to some extent still are) interested in growth and development not only to increase the amount of rents and to satisfy the appetites of numerous rent-seekers but also because of the need for both domestic legitimation of the political regime[63] and the legitimation of foreign policy in international arenas. In addition, visible and internationally recognized achievements of successful development, such as global mega-events (like the Olympic Games, the G8/G20 summits, or the inclusion of Russian universities in the top 100 of world ratings) serve as a source of conspicuous consumption and of status rent both for Russia's ruling groups and for society at large.

Thus, post-Soviet bad governance implicitly assumes the aspiration of ruling groups to successfully implement policy reforms. They aim to achieve a high degree of socioeconomic development and to accomplish at least some policy reforms oriented toward attaining these goals. This agenda is shared not only by the ruling groups of post-Soviet Russia but also by significant parts of the citizens. However, under the conditions of bad governance this agenda faces numerous obstacles. First, policy reforms must be implemented by the state bureaucracy with all its problems and vices (analyzed in chapter 4). Second, policy reforms that may infringe on the interests of influential rent-seekers will be curtailed, especially if their implementation is not endorsed by a powerful coalition of supporters. The failure of police reform in Russia under the presidency of Dmitry Medvedev may serve as a prime example in this respect.[64] Third, in these circumstances policy reforms often lead to unintended and undesired consequences. These consequences depend not only on specific policies in certain areas but also to a great degree on the hierarchical mechanism of governance within the framework of the power vertical and its institutional constraints on policy reforms.

The role of the power vertical in bad governance is important for an understanding of the pattern followed by socioeconomic policy reforms. The top political leadership is the sole mastermind of reform programs and plans: although alternative policy programs are proposed by independent experts from time to time, they usually remain ignored by political leaders. As demonstrated in chapters 5 and 6, these programs are developed both by ideationally driven experts contracted by the power vertical and by career-driven policy entrepreneurs from among the mid-range officials, and sometimes even by invited foreign consultants.[65] Reform programs are implemented by various layers and hallways of the power vertical, while the political leadership retains a monopoly on policy evaluation, which is not an arbitrary personalist choice by political leaders: it takes into account the interests of the members of the winning coalition as well as public opinion. But under the conditions of authoritarianism, political leadership enjoys more room for maneuver than in most democracies. These conditions favor an "insulation" of reforms and reformers from the pernicious influence of interest groups,[66] yet they also impose almost unavoidable constraints on policy reforms in virtually all areas. The main constraint is related to the fact that the informal institutional core is untouchable by any reform: at best, reforms can affect only formal institutional shells. No wonder that many reform proposals are already planned to be partial, incomplete, and compromise measures even at the preparatory stage (not to mention further decision-making and implementation). Initially good intentions are emasculated and perverted by rent-seekers who are interested in privatization of gains from policy reforms and in socialization of their losses. These problems are acknowledged by reformers themselves, who often already expect these negative outcomes at the beginning of policy planning.

But the main problem of post-Soviet bad governance for policy reforms is related to its informal institutional core, which not only inhibits changes to the formal institutional shell but also exerts a distorting influence on the directions and effects of policy changes. In essence, any policy reforms cause major distributive consequences. In political terms, policy adoption and implementation implie a process of building coalitions of potential beneficiaries of the reforms and the accommodation of their interests with those of the potential losers. These negotiations often damage the quality of policy-making because of the influence of "distributional coalitions," which may block any positive changes.[67] In the wake of democratization, these tendencies often contributed to populist policies (as in Latin America in the 1980s), and these risks were among the main concerns of Russian reformers in the 1990s.[68] However, the politico-economic order of bad governance is also compatible with distributional coalitions, and their influence has increased over time:[69] the major beneficiaries of the politico-economic order of bad governance are small privileged groups of rent-seekers. Thus, the power vertical became a mechanism of rent-sharing among members of winning coalitions who transferred the costs of policy reforms to other actors and/or to society at large. They do not face the constraints imposed by formal institutions; rather the informal institutional core is deliberately tuned for distributive effects of this kind. Thus, the privatization of gains and socialization of losses have become inevitable effects of policy reforms under bad governance. The rapid economic growth of the 2000s in Russia to some extent diminished these effects, but later these contradictions of policy reforms became explicit. The sharp increase in military expenditure and simultaneous cutting of expenditures on public health and education was a logical extension of this approach to policy reforms. Furthermore, these effects may increase until the potential decline in the inflow of rents causes major conflicts between rent-seekers.

The reform of RZhD clearly illustrates these tendencies. Yakunin, being CEO of the holding and one of the key members of the winning coalition, maximized benefits for RZhD and for himself. The company became a monopolist holding, managed by Yakunin on behalf of the Russian state in the manner of a fiefdom, without any external control over its operations. The benefits of the reforms for the company were apparent: RZhD no longer had to subsidize unprofitable commuter trains, was able to unilaterally set tariffs, received outstandingly high fees for the use of its assets by its own subsidiaries, and prevented competition on the market. Costs were transferred not only to passengers (individual consumers of monopolist services) but also to all taxpayers. As long as regional budgets were able to satisfy RZhD's appetites, this situation was considered unacceptable only by opposition activists like Navalny and did not attract major public attention, and further transferring of costs from regional to federal budgets may have diminished the salience of this problem but did not change its causes.

The other problem of policy reforms under bad governance is related to the fact that the hierarchical power vertical is the only instrument for their implementation and an imperfect one. Reformers and their patrons among the top political leaders assume nearly by default that without strict and tight top-down control, the lower layers of the power vertical have no incentives even for their routine performance (let alone policy changes). In other words, they expect that schoolteachers will not teach students and police officers on the ground will not combat street-level crime. Given the lack of other mechanisms of accountability (fair elections, free media, civil society NGOs, influence of public opinion, and so forth), these concerns are quite reasonable. The good intentions of efficient governance are opposed by the weak incentives for policy changes in other political and institutional contexts,[70] and post-Soviet Russia is by no means exceptional in this respect. Yet the politico-economic order of bad governance is the least likely environment for successful implementation of major policy reforms. Since the list of beneficiaries of these changes is limited to a narrow group of rent-seekers, reformers must force other actors to conduct reforms that may not bring them any benefits. At the same time, policy programs and plans of reform are based on the logic of "high modernism":[71] the criteria for successful implementation of changes by the lower layers of the power vertical are reduced to a limited number of formal quantifiable indicators (widely used across the globe within the framework of the "new public management" approach). The formalization of these requirements to some extent aims to reduce excessively high agency costs within the framework of the power vertical. However, this approach contributes to the spiral of overregulation: virtually every new policy change results in a drastic increase of the scope and density of regulations of almost all routines at the lower layers. Hence, the amount of paperwork and related costs skyrockets—police officers, schoolteachers, medical doctors, and all personnel on the ground in many organizations (both state and private) are mired in producing numerous reports to state inspection agencies instead of conducting their primary job functions. As a result, the goals of policy changes are replaced by the attainment of required numbers in reports at any cost: these reports become the main if not the only criterion of evaluation of policy performance.

The system of reporting in the law enforcement agencies, which focuses on the percentage of criminal statistics vis-à-vis respective previous periods, only aggravates numerous pathologies, and replaces the task of combating crime.[72] Similarly, numerous inspection agencies discover those violations of laws and state regulations that require the least effort to detect and prove. The introduction of the Unified State Exam (EGE), the mechanism of assessment of high school graduates in Russia (analyzed in detail in chapter 4), serves as a particularly notorious example of this approach. Soon after its introduction in 2009, the presidential administration included the proportion of school graduates who fail to pass the EGE into the list of criteria for assessment of the performance of the regional chief executives appointed by the Kremlin.[73] This innovation encouraged regional and local officials (ranging from heads of education departments to school teachers) to minimize the number of failures on exams every year, causing numerous prominent scandals (such as the over-performance of school graduates in republics of the North Caucasus). At last, in 2014, the list of criteria changed again, and regional chief executives could no longer be punished for the failures of teenagers in the EGE. But due to these changes, the percentage of failures could greatly increase, resulting in schools' performances worsening. As such, the requirements for passing the EGE were eased to such a degree that achieving minimally acceptable grades was not difficult for even the least capable pupils.[74]

Another case of policy reforms is the attempt to improve the business environment in Russia in accordance with Putin's May 2012 decree. The key indicator chosen for implementing these changes was Russia reaching 20th place in the annual global report *Doing Business*, produced by the World Bank. This report is based on evaluating the conditions of small and medium businesses via analysis of regulatory frameworks and surveys of entrepreneurs. Although most analysts were skeptical about the chances of such progress (in 2012 Russia was in 120th place), in the 2018 annual report Russia reached 31st place out of

189, outperforming countries like France and Japan. This achievement, however, was possible because the World Bank experts (including Russia's representatives) changed the methodology of their report and included more indicators of sub-national regulations: the changing set of criteria alone elevated Russia's rank by thirty places in comparison with the 2014 annual report.[75] As state officials received a top-down signal to reach certain numbers at any cost, achieving better numbers turned into a goal in itself. In a way, such an approach to the quantitative indicators of governance (for improving a country's positions in global rankings or for whatever other purposes) was not much different from the use of the state-sponsored doping program for the sake of Russia's victory in the Sochi Olympics in 2014.[76] In the end, in August 2020 the World Bank announced that it would stop publication of *Doing Business* reports because of the serious flaws and falsifications in the collection and use of the data.[77] Regardless of Russia's positions in rankings by World Bank reports, the problems for doing business as such were more serious: the impressive progress in quantitative indicators was achieved at a moment of stagnation in the Russian economy, record-high capital flight, and so forth.[78] Needless to say, these approaches to policy reforms in various areas brought only partial and incomplete results at best, or even became limited to short campaigns that included the construction of Potemkin villages and contributed to the waste of resources.

Having said that, one should admit that Russia in the 2000s enabled at least partial implementation of policy reforms (analyzed in more detail in chapter 4), and in some policy areas socioeconomic reforms were far from a total failure.[79] But reforming the formal institutional shell without changes in the informal institutional core of post-Soviet bad governance brought major positive effects only under certain circumstances. If and when policy adoption and implementation did not require the involvement of many layers and hallways of the power vertical, and reformers were insulated from numerous rent-seekers because of the priorities and sincere support of the top political leadership, then major advancements could be achieved. But when policy reformers employ alternative strategies for institutional changes, policy reforms in various areas often result in unexpected and undesired consequences.

"Borrowing" and "Cultivating" Institutions: Useless Recipes?

Most of the experts involved in the preparation and development of plans and programs of policy changes in Russia clearly understand the pernicious effects of the informal institutional core of bad governance on policy reforms. However, being hired by the authorities, they refrain from openly criticizing major obstacles to implementing the latter's policy-making. Similarly, to many experts from international organizations who work in Third World countries,[80] they use an Aesopian language full of euphemisms such as "poor quality of institutions" or "unfavorable institutional environment," referring to numerous "legacies" and "institutional traps." Since discussing major revisions of the foundational principles of bad governance (and hence the rejection of the entire politico-economic order) is a kind of taboo, the experts seek ways not to undermine these obstacles but to bypass or circumvent them. The key idea is not to demolish existing informal institutions but rather establish new and parallel formal institutions that are based on other principles than the institutional core of bad governance. It is expected that the new formal institutions will be more efficient, and for this reason they may become embedded over time. According to these ideas, parallel institution-building can gradually supplant the informal institutional core and pave the way for a further strengthening of "inclusive" economic institutions[81] and in the distant future, toward a slow step-by-step adoption of inclusive political institutions. This approach perfectly fits the logic of narrow modernization and leaves reformers wide room for maneuver in institution-building.

In reality, two complementary strategies for institution-building, namely "borrowing" and "cultivating" institutions, have been proposed as possible solutions by a group of leading Russian experts from the Higher School of Economics.[82] "Borrowing" implies transplanting those institutions that have proved their efficiency in various political and institutional contexts (not necessarily Western ones) and could be adopted in Russia for economic growth and development without a major risk to immediately undermining the informal institutional core. "Cultivating," by contrast, assumes that new norms, rules, and mechanisms of governance in certain policy areas can be initially established as experimental innovations under deliberately designed favorable conditions and may later be applied to other policy areas. In theory, both strategies look reasonable and are often suggested by international experts in developing countries.[83] But the practice of bad governance puts them into question because of their essential flaws.

Borrowing institutions, which includes transferring advanced models and practices of governance, is faced with a process dubbed "bastardization."[84] Initially, this term was used to indicate the declining quality of goods produced in Russia using foreign technologies: domestic managers have few incentives to maintain quality control and often intentionally violate technological standards against the background of imperfect quality of corporate governance. Similarly, one might observe bastardization of transferred institutions by those actors who conduct their adoption and implementation in post-Soviet countries. To some extent, this process is inevitable, because the transfer of certain institutions would impose excessively high costs on mid-developed states (including post-Soviet countries). For example, the EGE in Russia is simultaneously used as a final test for school graduates and an entrance exam for universities, while in the United States and several other countries these two forms of tests are conducted separately. The adoption of a cheaper solution caused several problems in implementing the EGE.[85] But more often the cause of bastardization reflects the "interests of those with the bargaining power to devise new rules."[86] The adaptation of borrowed institutions to Russia's conditions is accompanied by their intentional and deliberate distortion by powerful actors interested in the preservation and strengthening of the informal institutional core of bad governance.

A typical example of bastardization of borrowed institutions is the experience of implementing the "open government" initiative in Russia under President Dmitry Medvedev. The idea of a more open and transparent government with active participation of ordinary citizens in policy discussions and the extensive use of modern information technologies was vigorously advocated by Medvedev's team as a part of his political rhetoric of "virtual liberalization."[87] The Russian state designated special funding for these purposes, and a minister responsible for open government affairs was appointed to the cabinet.[88] However, the mechanism was adopted from the Western practice of e-government, which implies the use of the Internet both for provision of state services and for feedback between citizens and the state (including civic legislative initiatives and the like). In the Western political context, e-government works as a complementary mechanism to democratic governance, an addition to free elections, independent media, rule of law, and so forth. In Russia, however, open government was designed as a substitutive mechanism of governance,[89] and intended to work instead for these political institutions, which had been eliminated and/ or weakened in the 2000s. From the viewpoint of governance in the West, e-government served as an additional tool that helped to increase the efficiency of the post-Weberian state apparatus. But in Russia, open government was considered a substitute for the administrative reform that had failed in the 2000s. This failure occurred not least because of the work of Medvedev himself, who had been responsible for overseeing it while he was serving in the presidential administration.[90] It is no wonder that the early promises of open government remained largely unfulfilled; its role was limited to technological issues of the websites of state and municipal agencies and some opportunities for ordinary citizens to submit their letters of complaint via the Web. Open government has not empowered Russian citizens. They remain powerless petitioners, vis-à-vis state officials, who may or may not respond to these complaints at their own discretion. The final episode of bastardization of open government occurred in February 2015, when the Anti-Corruption Foundation (led by Alexei Navalny) proposed a legislative initiative on ratification of Article 20 of the United Nations Convention against Corruption (UNCAC), which implied, inter alia, criminalization of illicit enrichment of state officials (Russian authorities had previously refused to ratify this part of the UNCAC). Navalny and his team gathered one hundred thousand signatures from Russian citizens via the Web, which was a mandatory condition for further inclusion of this citizen legislative initiative into the parliamentary agenda. But since this proposal was against the interests of Russia's ruling group, the open government board (appointed by state officials) declined the legislative initiative using flimsy excuses.[91] The ideas of openness, transparency, and civic activism became irrelevant in this case.

The other approach that aims to constrain the informal institutional core is purposeful cultivation of new norms, rules, and mechanisms of governance and their gradual extension to new areas and policy fields in order to develop new formal institutions. This approach includes not only promotion and advancement of spontaneously emerging good practices but also experimental establishment and embedding of new norms, rules, and mechanisms of governance by reformers who, in turn, are explicitly or implicitly backed by the political leadership. Since large-scale institutional changes are often countered both by the power vertical and by public opinion, the cultivation of institutions sometimes serves to prepare more fertile ground for certain policy innovations. In fact, the experimental nature of policy changes allows their details to be tested, thus averting the risks of full-scale institutional failures. From this viewpoint, cultivating new institutions is an appropriate technological solution that also makes it possible to overcome resistance to major policy reforms. But in most cases, failures to cultivate new institutions are caused by political rather than technological factors. Most large-scale institutional innovations are rather costly, face resistance from various rent-seekers and bureaucratic inertia, and also need public legitimation. The patronage of the top political leadership is necessary but often insufficient to accomplish these goals. This is why cultivating institutions is often accompanied by using special organizational devices, known in the Latin American context as "pockets of efficiency" (analyzed in chapter 6).[92] Their essence is that the political leadership prioritizes a limited number of pet projects, which are implemented not within the framework of the power vertical hierarchy, but via deliberately created organizations and groups that enjoy exceptional official status and may operate beyond standard routines. Thanks to their relative autonomy and effective patronage, these organizations and groups may escape bureaucratic control, bear lower agency costs in comparison with their standard equivalents, and have more room for maneuver thanks to promises of breakthroughs. Sometimes these promises are fulfilled, but this whole venture is rather risky. In the context of Russian military history, the "Toy Army" of Peter the Great may be considered the closest equivalent to pockets of efficiency in the late seventeenth century: it served as a launching pad for a regular military establishment. The Soviet atomic bomb and space programs to a great degree relied upon special design bureaus (also known as *sharashki*), which may be regarded as the Stalinist version of pockets of efficiency.

Pockets of efficiency are short-lived because of the fortunes of the political leadership and its changing priorities and problems with continuity (outlined in a more detailed way in chapter 6). Even if pockets of efficiency perform well and accomplish their initial tasks, they rarely survive the subsequent routinization and the loss of exclusive status. At the same time, their good practices are often poorly diffused and may be rejected by other state agencies unless they are imposed top-down by the political leadership. Finally, the pockets are efficient precisely because of their relatively small size: when they begin to expand their scope and become "too big to fail," they may face degradation because their modes of governance often copy the institutional core they aimed to combat. Often, the informal institutional core of bad governance is able to rebuild pockets of efficiency, rather than vice versa, and the potential incubators of new institutions may contribute to rent-seeking and serve the goals of the power vertical similarly to their predecessors.

To summarize, one might argue that the parallel coexistence of the informal institutional core and new norms, rules, and mechanisms of governance may be instrumental in policy reforms in certain areas but cannot resolve their fundamental contradictions. The politico-economic order of bad governance imposes high barriers to implementing the agenda of policy reforms. Neither the borrowing nor cultivation of institutions as such can increase the chances of their success. Rather, these plans may be sacrificed for the sake of the regime's survival, and at a certain point may be launched again, thus contributing to a vicious circle of elusive chances for successful socioeconomic advancements. The experience of the politico-economic order of bad governance in the Third World[93] demonstrates that such a circle's pernicious influence cannot be easily constrained by new norms, rules, and mechanisms of governance; it can reproduce itself under various conditions.

International Influence: The Limits of Imperialism?

The influence of international factors on domestic changes in post-Soviet Eurasia is often discussed in terms of Western-led democracy promotion, specifically regarding regime cycles and color revolutions (or lack thereof),[94] while in Russia this influence after the Soviet collapse has always been modest, to put it mildly. But to what extent does international influence affect the quality of governance rather than regime dynamics in Russia and beyond? The answer to this question is far from obvious, and not only because post-Soviet rulers perceive foreign influence in any domestic arena as a threat to their dominance and tend to resist it in various ways.

Following Steven Levitsky and Lucan Way, one can distinguish between international linkages and leverages: the former mechanisms connect a country with an increasingly globalized world in terms of communications, technologies, and knowledge, while the latter mechanisms emerge from attempts by international actors to affect domestic developments.[95] As they rightly argue, the combination of relatively high linkages and low leverages (typical for Russia and some countries of post-Soviet Eurasia) provides only weak incentives for democratization. The same is true for governance, especially given the fact that international actors in the region and beyond pursue diverse goals and take different kinds of actions, while their potential for positive influence on the governments of other countries is rather limited.

In the most general sense, international leverages may help overcome bad governance only if and when they work complementarily to domestic efforts on this front rather than being a substitute for them. If ruling groups are unwilling to combat bad governance domestically, then any aid or assistance from the World Bank, the International Monetary Fund (IMF), the European Union (EU), and so forth, will have little impact. Moreover, the governments of the recipient countries often manipulate their donors, thus aggravating principal-agent problems, while the donors have limited opportunities to improve the situation. Without the domestic will to improve the quality of governance, international influence can result in partial changes in certain policy areas at best or even legitimize the preservation of the status quo of bad governance. In this respect, assessments of Russia's cooperation with the IMF in the 1990s are to be treated rather critically, to say the least.[96] The typical practices of postponement of policy decisions, partial and selective implementation of policy recommendations, Potemkin-style showcase advancement of best practices at the expense of donors, and unfulfilled (and often unrealistic) promises result from a lack of genuine interest on the part

of the recipient governments in combating bad governance and from a lack of
enforcement mechanisms on the donor side. From this perspective, Russia in the
1990s looks no better than its African counterparts.[97] Moreover, the efforts of
international donors in the region have often been counterproductive,[98] and if
linkages are curtailed when countries become internationally isolated, or even
isolate themselves (like Russia after 2014), the odds of improvements in quality of governance are severely diminished. Conversely, these developments fuel
the domestic legitimation of bad governance under the slogan of "protection of
national interests," while international legitimation loses any relevance at all;
internationally isolated or self-isolated rulers realize that they have nothing to
lose outside their respective countries.

International linkages may be regarded as a double-edged sword in terms of
bad governance because of the rise of the offshore economy, the outsourcing of
many important functions (such as legal resolution of commercial disputes) to
foreign jurisdictions, and plenty of exit options for post-Soviet elites who aim to
legalize their status and wealth in the West,[99] thus hedging domestic risks. However, one should not underestimate or completely deny the positive effects of
international linkages on the quality of governance. Both the practical needs of
adjustment to international standards and the international diffusion of policy
ideas and best practices may contribute to driving countries toward good governance in certain sectors and policy areas despite the intentions of their rulers.
Juliet Johnson argued in her perceptive analysis of the rise of post-Communist
central banks that the engagement of the emerging community of top banking
officials in international networks played an important role in building the institutional independence of central banks and the prudency of their policies.[100]
Similar effects of internationally driven steps forward can be found in other
areas, ranging from major improvements in national statistics systems[101] to tax
reforms,[102] and attempts to advance Russia's universities to the top of global
rankings (described in chapter 6). These signs of progress are similar to the pockets of efficiency that have been promoted internationally where domestic actors
have not prevented their formation (or sometimes have even supported them).

In terms of overcoming bad governance, the only winning combination involves both the domestic political will to implement structural reforms and institutional and policy changes and strong international linkages and leverages.
These two conditions are complementary rather than substitutive, as international pressure alone (without domestic drivers) may have only temporary and
shallow effects. The EU's employment of conditionality with respect to East
European countries and commitment by East Europeans vis-à-vis their West

European partners may serve as the main positive, if short-lived, example of that kind. The large-scale revision of domestic legislation and law enforcement practices in Eastern Europe was important not only from the viewpoint of regulatory quality in certain policy areas and of the effectiveness of governments. In essence, these conditions implied international constraints on domestic sovereignty and a certain (though limited) possibility of enforcement of EU rules and regulations regarding East European governments. Leverages became reasonably effective mechanisms for constraining bad governance: if following the rules of the game imposed by Brussels did not greatly improve the quality of governance in Romania or Bulgaria, these rules at least created barriers to its major deterioration. Without EU accession, these and some other countries would probably be governed no better than their counterparts in post-Soviet Eurasia.[103]

However, in the case of East European countries, EU-led external constraints on state sovereignty become possible due to a voluntary choice by their elites and citizens. In Russia this issue is far from the agenda, to say the least. The problem here relates not only to the resistance of post-Soviet ruling groups and/ or the attitudes of Russian citizens but also to the incredibly high costs for those nations that would impose constraints on the sovereignty of other states. Even for the EU, attempts to enforce the integration of Eastern European states have been quite costly, and this process is far from complete. Moreover, as soon as EU leverages weakened over time after the accession of East European countries, at least some of these countries—first and foremost, Hungary and to some degree, Poland—experienced major setbacks and reemergence of some institutions and practices of bad governance in the 2010s.[104] For Russia and its neighbors in post-Soviet Eurasia, the possible costs of external imposition and enforcement of new rules and norms aimed at overcoming bad governance would be prohibitively high. This is why the absence of an external intervention in the post-Soviet politico-economic order, which would contribute to preserving the status quo, is the more likely scenario: both fears and hopes of Western-imposed constraints on sovereignty in the region appear to be unjustified. Thus, direct international influence on the quality of governance in Russia is most likely to remain insignificant, with some exceptions.

Meanwhile, insulating bad governance in Russia from outside influence under the guise of state sovereignty serves as a tool for preventing any improvements. State sovereignty serves as a shield for ruling groups; it helps to protect them from any weakening political and economic power and from undesirable institutional changes. The idea of defending sovereignty at any cost (including banning foreign NGOs and limiting the import of Western foods and cultural products) is not paranoia but a rational strategy of the political leadership, who claim sovereignty of their country while preserving and enlarging their personal wealth. In theory, external constraints on state sovereignty imposed by advanced countries may (but not necessarily will) create barriers for the informal institutional core, and in the longer term lead to a revision of the politico-economic order of bad governance. One cannot exclude the possibility that further aggravation of Russia's confrontation with the West, which was launched after the 2014 regime change in Ukraine and annexation of Crimea, may turn into a major challenge of this kind. From this viewpoint, Russia's possible defeat in a major conflict with the West may pave the way to external constraints on its sovereignty and provide certain incentives for a gradual replacement of existing political and economic institutions of bad governance by more inclusive rules and norms. One cannot even imagine the potentially outstandingly high costs for such a complex transformation in Russia. Yet the costs of preserving the vicious circle of post-Soviet bad governance may be even higher for Russia and for the outside world.

To summarize, the emergence and consolidation of bad governance in Russia and beyond has been driven by the weakness of constraints on conscious and consistent construction of a politico-economic order where rent extraction is the major goal and substantive purpose of governing the state. It has also been affected by the combination of the following negative factors: (1) ideational reliance upon a "good Soviet Union" as a normative ideal for the ruling group and society at large; (2) decline of open elite competition and reproduction of the ruling groups; and (3) weak Western influence on Russia and a lack of mechanisms for international enforcement. At the same time, some advancements that were achieved in certain sectors and policy arenas in Russia because of a winning combination of domestic and international efforts had meaningful if limited influence on government effectiveness. However, the question of why constraints on bad governance emerge in some countries, sectors, and policy areas but not in others is worth further exploration. While an answer that places particular emphasis on the process of institution-building and institutional performance sounds plausible, variations in governance can be also explained in terms of the differences in access to rents in various sectors and policy areas and barriers to such access. One might also expect that bad governance in post-Soviet Russia is a long-term feature of its future development. The next chapters will be devoted to an in-depth analysis of its mechanisms.

CHAPTER 3

Authoritarian Modernization

Illusions and Temptations

THE AUTHORITARIAN MODERNIZATION PROJECT sounds tempting in various political and social settings. This project is perceived in the narrow sense as a set of technical policy measures aiming to achieve a high level of socioeconomic development through rapid economic growth, while the broad aspects of political modernization (that is, political freedoms) either remain beyond the current modernization agenda or are postponed to a distant future. The attractiveness of authoritarian modernization, advocated by numerous scholars and experts during the Cold War,[1] greatly increased in the twenty-first century fueled by recent economic advancements in China and once again endorsed by numerous experts, policymakers, and citizens across the globe.[2] There is a strong temptation to implement successful socioeconomic policies with a free hand, without the constraints and defects inherent to democracies, as authoritarianism allows the government to be insulated from the impact of political parties and policy preferences of the mass public.

Post-Communist Russia may be regarded as an instance of this phenomenon: not only are ideas and policies of authoritarian modernization deeply rooted in Russia's Soviet and imperial past, but its current agenda also fits certain interests and expectations of both Russia's elites and society at large.[3] To a certain degree, authoritarian modernization became Russia's response to the numerous challenges of the complex process of post-Communist transformation of Russia, which included simultaneous political regime changes, economic reforms, and state-and nation-building (known in the jargon of the 1990s as the "dilemma of simultaneity" amid the "triple transition").[4] During this process Russia's elites and citizens alike sacrificed democracy for the sake of a market economy and a strong state,[5] and this choice affected various dimensions of Russia's further development including the quality of governance.[6] I argue that the pursuit of authoritarian modernization in post-Communist Russia became one of the main origins of the politico-economic order of bad governance in the country. This is why it is necessary to explain how authoritarian modernization emerged as a mainstream of Russia's political and socioeconomic trajectories and how this project has contributed to bad governance.

The main problem of authoritarian modernization is that "success stories" of its policies are relatively rare, with the major notable exception of China. In the second part of the twentieth century, autocracies demonstrated a much higher diversity of economic growth rates and developmental trajectories than democracies. In fact, this diversity led to Dani Rodrik's comment (cited in chapter 1) about the uniqueness of success stories like Singapore amid many stories of failure like the Congo: a few examples of building effective states and prosperous economies in autocracies coincide with numerous cases where dictators drive their countries into decay and deterioration. From this perspective, the political and economic trajectories of post-Communist Russia resembled pendulum-like swings. In terms of the political regime, after the great liberalization under Gorbachev, during the 1990s and especially in the 2000s, the country quickly deteriorated into a personalist electoral autocracy.[7] In terms of socioeconomic development, after the deep and protracted transformation recession of the 1990s, Russia demonstrated impressive growth in the 2000s, which resulted not only from the steep rise of global oil prices but also from policy changes launched by the government.[8] In terms of state-building, Russia avoided the threat of disintegration in the 1990s and greatly strengthened its coercive and distributive capacity in the 2000s,[9] yet remained an inefficient state with a poor quality of governance.[10] Some authors have argued that these tendencies are natural for a country with the highly problematic legacies of Communism[11] and weak linkages with the West,[12] but have expressed hopes that they may be overcome over time through decades of growth and development with preservation of the political status quo.[13] However, other observers (including the author of this book) have expressed major skepticism of such hopes and prospects.[14]

Since 2014, after Russia annexed Crimea and dragged itself into a major conflict with the West against the background of its geopolitical ambitions, rising economic problems, and questioning if not complete denial of policy goals of growth, development, and international integration, the agenda of authoritarian modernization in Russia has been dramatically challenged. No one believes that the experience of the golden age of rapid economic growth and great expectations from 1999 to 2008 will return, at least in the foreseeable future. Yet now the time is ripe to reconsider the role of the authoritarian modernization project in Russia's political and economic changes at the end of the twentieth and the beginning of the twenty-first century with an emphasis on the central ideas, institutions, and policies that contributed to this project and its implementation. This focus will help to explain the role of authoritarian modernization in the making of bad governance in Russia. Discussing these issues is essential not only for an understanding of the logic and peculiarities of post-Communist changes in Russia but also for mapping Russia's trajectories onto the global map of varieties of modernization, both in contemporary and historical comparative perspective.

Indeed, why have Russia and its neighbors in post-Soviet Eurasia pursued authoritarian modernization after the Soviet collapse (unlike some countries of post-Communist Eastern Europe)? What is the ideational agenda behind this project and why does it dominate Russia's post-Communist political landscape? What are the mechanisms that maintain this project and how have they adopted, absorbed, and affected various institutions and practices of governance in Russia? Why has this project brought diverse results in various policy areas, and why have the consequences of certain policies become rather controversial from the viewpoint of governing the country? And why, despite so many controversies, shortcomings, and flaws, has this project remained attractive in the eyes of a large proportion of Russian elites and Russian citizens? This chapter is intended to address some of these questions and propose several tentative answers, which will be also discussed in the following chapters, aimed at analyzing the impact of the authoritarian modernization project in post-Communist Russia on Russia's politics of bad governance.

The Discreet Charm of Authoritarian Modernization

The concept of modernization (like any major concept in the social sciences) has its own distinct history. Since the boom of modernization theory in the 1950s and 1960s,[15] through nearly universal criticism in the 1970s and 1980s, there has been a large question mark hanging over the term "modernization." However, more recently this conceptual framework has been revived with regard to analyzing the influence of social, economic, political, and cultural changes on the developmental trajectories of states and nations in a comparative and historical perspective.[16] This is why in present-day scholarly jargon, modernization is merely associated with progress and development in various directions (be it human capital, economic prosperity, and/or political freedoms) as well as with certain policies in various areas aimed toward such progress in one way or another. These policies are often labeled "reforms," although some critics tend to portray them in a negative light as instances of "neoliberalism."[17] Scholars of different disciplines and academic schools attempt to discover the causal mechanisms of developmental progress and regress in various countries and understand the logic of why some of them over time tend to move toward the "open access order"[18] and the prevalence of "inclusive" economic and/or political institutions, while others do not.[19]

One of the most contentious issues of modernization, which arises in numerous discussions, is related to the impact of political regime dynamics on modernization—to what extent the success and failure of modernization depends upon democracy and/or authoritarianism. Can socioeconomic development be pursued successfully simultaneously with political democratization ("broad," or democratic modernization) or rather, should economic growth and development precede political opening ("narrow," or authoritarian modernization)? Yet, from a distant historical perspective, major European modernizations were authoritarian nearly by default,[20] and in the second half of the twentieth century this issue came to the forefront in the atmosphere of bipolar rivalry between Communist and capitalist systems during the Cold War. At that time, some proponents of development theories, alongside international organizations such as the World Bank, openly endorsed ideas of authoritarian modernization, mainly for political purposes[21] perceiving them as an instrument for countering Communist expansion and opposition to populist economic policies.[22] This approach is deeply rooted in scholarly literature[23] and is fueled by success stories of various authoritarian reforms, ranging from South Korea in the 1960s–1980s to Chile under Pinochet. The idea of authoritarian policy-making was popular at that time among many international experts in the World Bank and other agencies, as they believed that authoritarianism would be able to implement those unpopular policies that are so often blocked under democratic regimes.

The triumphant perception of global democratization after the end of the Cold War[24] was short-lived, and discussions on the advantages and disadvantages of authoritarian modernization, dating back to the 1960s, reemerged within the context of post-Communist changes.[25] Support for the project of narrow authoritarian modernization came from the proponents of the Chinese developmental trajectory amid numerous problems of democratic development in various parts of the globe.[26] These discussions were also relevant in the Russian domestic context, as sacrificing democratization for the sake of economic reforms became a mainstream of Russian politics and policy-making soon after the Soviet collapse against the background of the "roaring" 1990s.[27] This approach was vigorously advocated in 2009 by then-president Dmitry Medvedev in his manifesto on Russian modernization.[28] Judging from this perspective, contemporary Russia may be regarded as a laboratory for authoritarian modernization, with its dilemmas, challenges, and constraints. Since the failure of Gorbachev's reforms, when political opening and inconsistent economic half-measures contributed to the collapse of the Soviet Union, Russia's rulers have tended to limit or curtail political freedoms and prioritize economic development and state-building in their agenda. While this development has brought mixed and controversial results, the question of the impact of various factors on implementing the authoritarian modernization project remains open, and reexamining the post-Communist Russian experience with an emphasis on its ideas, institutions, and policies might shed some light on these issues. In particular, how did the sources and mechanisms of authoritarian modernization in Russia (and elsewhere) affect the rise of bad governance?

The main arguments for the authoritarian modernization project—in Russia and elsewhere—are both ideational and pragmatic (their lines are complementary rather than antinomies). In terms of ideas, the authoritarian modernization project is based upon normative criticism of the political and social empowerment of citizens in modernizing countries as a source of major instability, conflict, and disorder.[29] A sequence that implies a gradual construction of a strong and efficient state and long-term economic growth and development, as well as possible postponement of democratization for many decades, is considered a desirable alternative; although it is not a combination of the best of both worlds, it is at least an avoidance of their worst combination. In pragmatic terms of conducting policy reforms, authoritarian modernization is preferred over a democratic one because the process of democratization as such presents a risky environment for building efficient states and markets. In essence, democratic regimes are full of inherent defects that make economic reforms problematic. Among these defects, the following are the most important:

1. competitive elections result in "political business cycles," which contribute to short-term populist policy solutions and prevent the implementation of long-term developmental plans;[30]
2. the separation of powers allows powerful veto players to block major policy decisions and/or dilute their substance;[31] moreover, for federal states, the difficult combination of horizontal and vertical separation of powers may contribute to the risks of "joint decision traps";[32]
3. multiparty governments and coalition politics result in adopting compromise policies, which also bring instability because of the fragility of party cooperation;[33] and

4. the representation of interest groups and political parties stimulates the domination of distributional coalitions that are engaged in rent-seeking and aimed at state capture (that is, turning state policies into hostages of private actors) by leveraging their access to governmental posts to reward their allies.[34]

These pitfalls are unavoidable in various political contexts. Many experts have noted the inefficiency of policy reforms under democracies, ranging from Latin America[35] to Eastern Europe,[36] where both the interests of political actors and the institutional settings hindered efficient socioeconomic policies or even contributed to their failure. This criticism is so widespread that it has contributed to hopes for reform-minded leaders, supported by teams of well-qualified experts, who would be capable of modernizing their respective countries without the fear of losing power and/or being trapped by populists and rent-seekers. It is no wonder that some authors have suggested implementing major socioeconomic reforms in Russia under conditions of authoritarianism as a response to the "dilemma of simultaneity."[37] Again, within the framework of this argument, democratization is considered at best a distant side effect of step-by-step creation of efficient institutions that provide stable long-term economic growth. Given the fact that the average economic growth in both democratic and nondemocratic regimes in the second half of the twentieth century was nearly the same,[38] it is unsurprising that the authoritarian modernization project has been perceived as a plausible recipe for several countries, including post-Communist ones, by some experts,[39] despite major criticism from others.[40]

Why is the evidence for the performance of authoritarian modernization so mixed, to say the least? In fact, the experience of the various states and societies involved is different in terms of their initial conditions and international and historical environment. Not many countries combine the advantages of relative underdevelopment and strong potential for catching up with advanced states and societies[41] with an "embedded autonomy" of the state apparatus[42] and a "Weberian" quality of bureaucracy,[43] as well as with a relatively high level of human development. This combination cannot emerge by default and/or be built by design, at least in the short term. On a related note, few of these countries can effectively conduct export-oriented policies against the background of deep international engagement and a favorable global economic and political climate.

Also, one should consider the effects of varieties of authoritarianism given their differences in longevity and performance. While among hegemonic autocracies, monarchies and one-party states are better suited to conducting long-term developmental policies and improving their quality of governance, but personalist regimes are rarely successful in this respect because of their relatively short life expectancy.[44] They suffer from the same defects as democratic polities, that is, political business cycles and distributional coalitions of rent-seekers do not disappear under conditions of electoral authoritarianism. But these regimes also rely heavily on mechanisms such as a politicized state-controlled economy and the patronage and buying of loyalty of the elites and the masses alike.[45] All of these instances provide incentives for politicians and bureaucrats that prevent the implementation of major policy changes. In addition, they also face the risk of leadership change as an outcome of electoral conflicts and elite breakdowns, and this key challenge contributes to a short-term planning horizon in electoral authoritarian regimes vis-à-vis their hegemonic counterparts.[46] Since the regime's survival depends on mass support to a greater degree than either in hegemonic autocracies or in democracies, large-scale modernization (even in a narrow format) is a risky project for electoral authoritarian regimes and their leaders who tend to avoid long-term developmental goals.[47]

Yet another important constraint for authoritarian modernization is the limited set of political tools available to a regime to achieve such a project's goals. In pursuit of policy reforms, authoritarian leaders can rely on bureaucrats, *siloviki,* or the hegemonic (or dominant) party, or a combination of these pillars.[48] However, these mechanisms are rarely useful for implementing reforms. For efficient use of bureaucracy (one tool of authoritarian modernization that was employed in Russia) the reformers need a decent quality to the state apparatus: a high level of professional qualification among officials, strong incentives for them to achieve the goals set by the reformers, and an embedded state autonomy (the bureaucracy's insulation from the influence of interest groups).[49] Leaders cannot develop these conditions from scratch, they can build these mechanisms only over a long period of time. However, the longevity of authoritarian regimes is usually much shorter than what is necessary to build an efficient state bureaucracy.

Finally, the ideational considerations of political leaders and their perceptions of the past, present, and future of their respective countries greatly influence their policy agendas in terms of priorities, directions, and choices. Even those leaders who aim at authoritarian modernization may opt for different role models and pursue different strategies. And even the good intentions of policy reforms do not always lead to success, given the fact that conducting policy changes is not only a technocratic matter of expertise and advice but also a political matter of the balance of interests and incentives among the powerful members of authoritarian winning coalitions, which are built and maintained around rulers. The hidden but stiff competition among various segments of elites often explains why policy reforms may be sacrificed for the sake of the regime's stability in order to prevent possible elite breakdown.[50]

From this perspective, the Russian experience of authoritarian modernization, both historical and contemporary, is rather contradictory. On the one hand, Russia was and still is in the second echelon of countries in terms of socioeconomic and human development, well above the global average level, and numerous attempts at its modernization in the nineteenth, twentieth, and twenty-first centuries were essentially intended to catch up to advanced states and societies. Still, the poor quality of the state, and especially of its bureaucracy, which for a long time has operated within the framework of patrimonial governance, has remained the weakest link of Russian modernization over decades and centuries,[51] although the rapid changes after the Great Reforms of Alexander II greatly reduced the time lag between Russia and its European neighbors.[52] Apart from Russia's imperial past, numerous experts have devoted many pages to discussing the negative effects of Communist legacies on contemporary developments,[53] so the initial conditions of post-Soviet modernization in Russia already do not sound very promising. On the other hand, the semi-peripheral position of Russia in the global economy and the outstandingly high role of natural resource sectors in its development, alongside the difficult consequences of Soviet strategic planning, have contributed to major "bear traps" of post-Soviet modernization.[54] Certainly, the relative isolation of Russia from the outside world in terms of both linkages and leverages[55] and the juxtaposition of Russia to the West in terms of international politics—both during the Cold War and after the annexation of Crimea—were hardly productive for modernization.

Regarding the political regime dimension, two attempts at Russia's democratization—after the monarchy was overthrown in 1917 and after the collapse of Communism in 1991—have failed. The former resulted in civil war, and the latter coincided with the breakdown of the Soviet state. In both cases, these failures paved the way for the emergence of authoritarian regimes on the ruins of unfulfilled democratic promises. However, the Soviet authoritarian modernization under Stalin caused a colossal number of victims and heavy losses of human potential while its economic achievements were questionable.[56] The post-Stalin rejection of repressions as the main tool of governing the country brought mixed consequences to Soviet socioeconomic development, and over time the potential of Soviet modernization was completely exhausted.[57] The post-Soviet authoritarian modernization project, to some extent, also emerged on the ruins of unfulfilled promises of democratization and economic reforms under Gorbachev,[58] while the mixed results of the market changes of the 1990s after the Soviet collapse contributed to the rise of the Russian economy in the 2000s[59] against the background of increasing authoritarian tendencies.

The electoral authoritarian regime that emerged in Russia after the Soviet collapse of the USSR is not unique, but it has several features defined by the pattern of post-Communist transformation. In the 1990s, policy reforms faced the problem of a weak state with a high level of horizontal and vertical fragmentation.[60] As a result, the central government resorted to compromises with oligarchs and regional leaders, which raised the social costs of the reforms.[61] Strengthening state capacity, alongside the rapid economic growth of the 2000s, allowed the central government to implement its policies relatively successfully and reduce the influence of oligarchs and regional leaders alike.[62] But the poor quality of public administration and the bureaucracy's inefficiency were major constraints.[63] By the time of the Soviet collapse, the bureaucratic machine had already been suffering from deep institutional decay, and the post-Soviet period deepened these problems. Electoral authoritarianism provided incentives for the use of the state apparatus to maximize electoral results[64] to the detriment of the quality of governance, as the Kremlin preferred loyalty rather than efficiency in political appointments.[65] The regime's dependence on buying electoral loyalty, so vividly visible in the 1990s,[66] increased further still in the 2000s and in the 2010s.[67] In sum, such a combination of features of Russia's regime created the main barriers to the authoritarian modernization project.

Finally, ideas and perceptions also affected the authoritarian modernization project in Russia. While Soviet authoritarian modernization was driven by the ideas of Communism and by the ambition of building a new international role model for other societies, the post-Soviet ideational agenda was different in many ways. First, in late twentieth-century and early twenty-first-century Russia, ideas played a relatively negligible role vis-à-vis the material interests of elites and of society at large.[68] Second, for the political leaders who came to power in Russia in the 2000s, the perceptions of "a good Soviet Union"—an updated version of political, economic, and international system of the past, which would demonstrate a good performance and avoid risks of major changes—served as a role model that determined their ideational frame of reference.[69] To some extent, these tendencies also resulted from overreaction by elites and the mass public to the collapse of Communism and of the Soviet Union. But in practice, retrospectively oriented worldviews are hardly conducive to any modernization projects, including authoritarian ones. Perceptions of an existential threat to the political status quo (which were driven by the wave of regime changes in post-Soviet Eurasia, labeled "color revolutions") also impeded modernization plans because of shortening time horizons for elites and because of the need to divert the state's resources to buying the loyalty of elites and the masses alike.[70] In addition, the regime's focus on media manipulation, which serves as a major tool for maintaining contemporary authoritarian regimes (known as informational autocracies),[71] contributed to misperceptions not only among society at large but also among elites who often made ill-suited decisions because of a lack of independent sources of information and inappropriate feedback. For as long as Russia experienced rapid economic growth from 1999 to 2008, these regime-induced flaws of the authoritarian modernization project were partly compensated for by the inflow of money, which was sufficient for keeping the winning coalition together and avoiding major schisms among elites and public demand for changes. In the 2010s, against the background of rising economic problems and major conflict with the West, the risk of regime disequilibrium greatly increased,[72] and the authoritarian modernization project in Russia came under question.

Still, the "myth of authoritarian growth"[73] remained a mainstream of Russia's approach to socioeconomic development and policy-making after the Soviet collapse against the background of strong statist and illiberal components of thinking among Russian elites.[74] No democratic alternatives for modernization projects regarding the agenda of socioeconomic development were discussed seriously, and these issues lie at the heart of policies followed both in the conflict-ridden 1990s[75] and during the period of "imposed consensus" of the 2000s.[76] However, a positive combination of factors brought certain successes using this approach during the wave of policy reforms launched in the early 2000s, which may be regarded as the golden age of Russia's authoritarian modernization project. The overcoming of the protracted transformation recession of the 1990s, the restoration of the coercive capacity of the Russian state, the major recentralization of governance, and the consolidation of the Russian elites, as well as prudent technocratic solutions in certain areas such as tax and fiscal reforms, resulted in numerous advancements in Russia's socioeconomic development in various fields.[77] As one can observe from figures 1 through 4, the period between 2000 and 2005 was very productive for improving the quality of governance in Russia in terms of the rule of law, control of corruption, regulatory quality, and government effectiveness. This improvement largely reflected the effects of policy reforms, which are analyzed in more detail in chapter 4.

Yet one cannot step into the same river twice: the widely proclaimed proposal of modernization made by Dmitry Medvedev during his presidency[78] was just a brief campaign with an emphasis on technological advancements (such as high-tech development and other innovations). This campaign faced major structural and institutional constraints, and during the turbulent political changes of the 2010s it brought partial and controversial results. These results were accompanied by major instances of misbehavior by state officials[79] or even faded away entirely. In fact, the modernization campaign has nearly been forgotten by the Russian public at the moment of writing this book and had rather negligible impact on the dynamics of the quality of governance in Russia. However, the boom of the 2000s is still perceived as a kind of model for the modernization project in Russia, even though it was a context-bounded phenomenon.

Besides these explanations, the attractiveness of the authoritarian modernization project in Russia is also rooted more deeply: the perceptions of the "uniqueness" and "special path" of the country and obsession with status-seeking among Russian elites, intellectuals, and society at large provide fertile grounds for this approach.[80] As one of Putin's former advisors confessed in an interview, in the early 2000s the major arguments in the Kremlin's inner circle for the need for authoritarian modernization were related to the claim of strengthening Russia's international position: "Putin became the author of the 'Russian miracle' despite widespread expectations that Russia would leave the global stage and turn into a second-order country like Indonesia."[81] Although international ambitions often contributed to the rise of entrepreneurship and catch-up development among late-modernizing countries,[82] in Russia's case they also coincided with a desire for major revenge vis-à-vis the West given the loss of great power status after the end of the Cold War and the collapse of the Soviet Union (judged by Putin to be "the greatest geopolitical catastrophe of the twentieth century"). In other words, economic development and related social changes (the increase in incomes, education, and the like) were perceived by Russia's rulers merely as means rather than goals of modernization. These tendencies became explicit after 2014, in the wake of Russia's conflict with the West over Ukraine, which contributed not only to its increasing international isolation but also to a major shift in its domestic agenda. The authoritarian modernization project was not officially curtailed, but its modernization dimension has been reduced to naught amid sluggish economic growth and stagnation of real incomes of Russians. Not only has there been a "tightening of the screws" in the political arena,[83] but economic development priorities have also been supplanted by ambitious geopolitical goals and foreign policy tasks. Policy moves ranging from an import ban on many foreign food products, which caused a steep rise in consumer prices and poor-quality import substitutes, to the law on preferential use of Russian computers and software for state orders and in state-owned companies greatly benefited certain interest groups but were not conducive to the country's development. However, it is too early to discuss whether the myth of authoritarian growth in Russia will be debunked any time soon. Even though these ideas and related policies might no longer be a part of the current agenda, the discreet charm of the authoritarian modernization project is powerful not only because of the endurance of ideas and institutions but also because of the vested interests of those who benefit from this project.

Dilemmas, Challenges, and Constraints

The authoritarian modernization project in contemporary Russia faces several dilemmas, challenges, and constraints. Without attempting to compile an exhaustive catalog, some of the related issues are worth further consideration in light of Russia's experience. In addition to the classic dilemmas of an authoritarian regime's response to rising political demands in the wake of modernization (the "king's dilemma") and a ruler's response to inefficiency of the state bureaucracy (the "politician's dilemma"), one may also consider important challenges that placed unavoidable constraints on this project. They include the challenge of unfulfilled promises (when expectations of progress and rapid catch-up to advanced countries proved to be wrong) and the challenge of mediocrity (despite claims of Russia's greatness, in fact its socioeconomic profile is close to that of an average "normal country").[84]

The "king's dilemma," outlined by Samuel Huntington in his analysis of risks of modernization in traditional monarchies,[85] remains relevant in post-Communist Russia. Economic growth and development, which lie at the heart of the authoritarian modernization project, have contributed to the rise of mass demand for political freedoms (first and foremost, among the urban middle class) as an unintended consequence. The wave of political protests that swept Russia in 2011–2012 was a typical instance of this demand caused by the economic and political changes of the 1990s and 2000s.[86] Thus, the political leadership faced a difficult choice between the continuation of the authoritarian modernization project (increasing the risk of further political disequilibrium) and preservation of their rule at any cost, including the reduction of this project. While hegemonic authoritarian regimes often take the risk of modernization because of their reliance upon a traditional monarchy, dominant party, or military,[87] electoral authoritarian regimes are based upon political institutions that mimic and substitute for those of democracies (such as elections, political parties, and legislatures)[88] and are therefore more vulnerable to political disequilibrium. The reliance of Russia's rulers upon sophisticated techniques of political control such as tools of state dominance over the Internet and umbrella GONGOs (government-organized non-government organizations)[89] is intended to mitigate these risks, but their impact is limited and may result in unintended and undesired side effects in terms of development. These considerations, alongside the short-time horizon of electoral authoritarian regimes, provide more incentives for curtailing the authoritarian modernization project if rulers perceive major domestic and international threats to their political survival—although these threats may be overestimated.

The asymmetric response of Russia's rulers to the 2011–2012 mass protests, which included not only tightening of the screws in domestic politics but also launching a major international conflict with the West over Ukraine, was in a way, also addressed to the king's dilemma. Then Vladimir Putin suddenly shifted his priorities from development to geopolitics and sacrificed the goals of modernization for the sake of international influence and domestic popularity.[90] Although this response provided other risks of disequilibrium than those caused by economic growth and development, from the viewpoint of modernization its consequences were even more devastating than attempts to preserve the political status quo (more typical for the king's dilemma). Policy reforms disappeared from the Russian leadership's list of priorities, and it is difficult to expect that the agenda of rapid growth and development that was so vigorously advocated in the early 2000s will be revitalized any time soon under the current regime's conditions.

The "politician's dilemma" was analyzed by Barbara Geddes in her study of policy reforms in Latin America:[91] the top-down modernization efforts of the political leadership encountered resistance from major interest groups and the notorious inefficiency of the bureaucracy. The essence of reforms can be buried or perverted or alternatively, they can be implemented only through a partial solution where rulers offer some special conditions for their conduct, known as "pockets of efficiency."[92] This dilemma became acute in contemporary Russia, and several failures of major policy reforms clearly demonstrated its salience.[93] Russia's reformers either adjusted their proposals to compromise with bureaucracy and/or interest groups or attempted to bypass standard procedures and find some alternative institutional solutions for conducting certain policies. In both instances, policy successes were rather mixed.

A compromise solution was achieved in the early 2000s in the case of the pension reform policy in Russia, which might have long-term effects for further generations, while its adoption and implementation was able to bring immediate

gains and losses to current political and policy actors. The major conflict between two policy coalitions, the liberal "young reformers," who promoted new
ideas of adoption of an accumulative pension system, and the old-style bureaucracy, which insisted on preservation of the previous status quo mainly because
of its vested interests, resulted in an imperfect compromise between these two
approaches.[94] While the interests of all participants were satisfied, the policy
outcomes were suboptimal, and opportunities for major changes were missed.
In other words, the previous status quo of the inefficient and deficient pension
system has been preserved for the sake of maintaining a balance between the
demands of state bureaucrats, employees, and employers. Yet the problems of the
inefficiency of the pension system continued over time, while the deficit of the
Pension Fund steadily increased. In the end, this solution paved the way to the
unpopular sudden increase in retirement age for Russians in 2018, which has not
been accompanied by structural reforms and has merely reproduced the status
quo at the citizens' expense.[95] Policy compromises with bureaucrats and with
major interest groups (such as old-style trade unions in the case of labor reform)[96]
contributed to the weakening of proposed policy changes, and policy outcomes
were far from the desires of the proponents of modernization. Meanwhile, attempts to bypass regular procedures may contribute to short-term successful policy implementation, but in the medium term these policy innovations may face
major revisions (some of these issues are discussed in chapter 6).

The challenge of unfulfilled promises has been an inherent feature of Russia's
modernization since the early Soviet period. After the Bolshevik Revolution,
Russia failed to catch up to advanced countries in terms of the economic development of its major components such as labor productivity or living standards,
despite the positive effects of industrialization, urbanization, and education;
the main flaws of Soviet modernization were unavoidable and contributed to
the collapse of Communism.[97] The attempt to reform the Soviet system under
Gorbachev was ill-prepared and based on many illusions and misunderstandings
among the elites, so it is no wonder that its failure was perceived by Russian
society as an unfulfilled promise. The turbulent period of post-Soviet reforms
of the 1990s also had a controversial impact on public perceptions, and these
major disillusionments were only partially compensated for during the period of
rapid economic growth between 1999 and 2008. They also contributed to mass
expectations of the "strong state" as the main if not the only provider of material well-being for Russians. The problem is that the end of this boom and the
increasing troubles of the Russian economy further aggravated the perceptions

of unfulfilled promises among elites and masses alike: the failure of Medvedev's modernization campaign and the following wave of protests in 2011–2012 were clear evidence of that. To some extent, large-scale state propaganda in Russia and the tendency toward the country's international self-isolation, although instrumental for the survival of the regime and its rulers, fueled these perceptions, contrary to Abraham Lincoln's famous remark that one cannot fool all the people all the time. The primary danger of lost illusions relates to certain feelings that any modernization efforts in Russia (whether authoritarian or not) may be doomed nearly by default regardless of the contents and mode of conduct of policy reforms.[98] Despite the fact that these feelings are strongly grounded in some interpretations of Russian culture, both historical and contemporary, one should avoid falling into the hopelessness of determinism and not see Russia as a country lacking any prospects for successful modernization.

The challenge of mediocrity results from the belief, quite widespread among many Russians, that Russia is a great and unique country, and it is worthy of extraordinary first-rate recognition by other states and nations because of its major past achievements in various areas, ranging from military victories to cultural glories. This retrospective understanding of Russia's place in the modern world contributes to certain status-seeking efforts but is of limited relevance to a present-day modernization strategy. In many ways, Russia is an average normal country with numerous problems not so dissimilar to mid-developed states and nations. In a sense, the disjuncture between self-perception and reality is similar to the behavior of some teenagers. Drawing parallels with the distribution of pupils in a school class, Russia is neither an "A" student of world development (like Denmark) nor a complete "F" student à la Zimbabwe, but rather something of a "C" student. It is not much different from say, Argentina, one of the fast-growing economies and emerging democracies of the early twentieth century, which recently lost even regional leadership to a more dynamic Brazil after some decades of turbulent regime changes. Like some "C" students, Russia is more or less coping with its current troubles but cannot radically improve its grades. Like many "C" students, Russia simultaneously demonstrates an envy of more successful "A" students and juxtaposition of itself to them: despite the official rhetoric of fear and loathing of the West, Russians prefer to drive a Mercedes or a Toyota, use an iPhone or a Samsung, and want their children and grandchildren to graduate from Oxford or Harvard. The awkward combination of mediocrity and inadequate self-estimation affects not only Russia's ideational agenda but also its institutional performance, as the country does little to improve its quality of governance—again, similarly to some "C" students, who invest little effort in elevating their poor grades.

This list of dilemmas and challenges is hardly unique, having been faced by several autocracies that found themselves between a rock and a hard place when they aimed at modernization and rapid socioeconomic development, on the one hand, and preservation of power of authoritarian rulers, on the other. As Bruce Bueno de Mesquita and his coauthors rightly put it, due to the primacy of politics over policy, autocrats often tend to sacrifice goals of modernization for the sake of their own political survival.[99] Although such a prioritization is natural and such a statement is empirically based on solid evidence from several dictatorships, the connection between authoritarianism and modernization is not always substitutive, but rather, complementary. In other words, some authoritarian leaders pursue modernization-oriented policies simultaneously with building and fortifying their powers and try to achieve their goals in both areas. At first sight, such a dual-track strategy under the auspices of benevolent dictators sounds like a reasonable solution to the numerous problems of authoritarian modernization. However, the above-stated dilemmas and challenges impose certain constraints on implementing this strategy in real terms. It does not mean that autocrats always sacrifice modernization-oriented policies (as the logic of political survival presumes) but the goals and means of these policies undergo major changes. And yes, Russia is not unique in this respect: by the 2020s the authoritarian modernization agenda in Russia has been sacrificed for the sake of political regime stability.[100]

In essence, these challenges and dilemmas put significant constraints on improving the quality of governance in Russia. On the one hand, proponents of an authoritarian modernization strategy aim at a delicate balance between achievements in growth and development and maintenance of the political status quo. On the other hand, attempts at improving the quality of governance may be risky for unity of the winning coalitions because they pose threats to the vested interests of rent-seekers of various kinds. It is no wonder that incentives for major policy changes that may challenge the politico-economic order of bad governance have become limited to short-term campaigns and have weakened over time. While in the early twenty-first century the post-Communist Russian experience may be considered an example of a coexistence of authoritarian modernization and bad governance under a dual-track strategy, after 2014 the agenda of modernization has been wiped away while persistence of authoritarianism remains the goal, thus strengthening the politico-economic order of bad governance.

Authoritarian Modernization in Russia—Mission: Impossible?

It is no wonder that rent-seeking, poor quality of the state regulations and lack of the rule of law impose major barriers to successful implementation of policy reforms. However, unlike many Third World countries, which are widely perceived as hotbeds of stagnation under dictatorships, post-Soviet Russia for a while displays an opposite trend: rapid economic growth in the 2000s served as a major source of building and further maintenance of the politico-economic order of bad governance. At that time, Russia's ruling groups were interested in growth and development not only to increase the amount of rents and to satisfy the appetites of numerous rent-seekers but also because of the need for legitimation of the political regime.[101] Although by the 2020s this agenda was seemingly exhausted, and the word "modernization" almost disappeared from Russian political discourse after Dmitry Medvedev lost his presidential post in 2012,[102] great developmental ambitions (in the form of national projects and the like) remained an important part of policy-making in Russia. The reshuffling of the Russian government in 2020 further revitalized ambitions of a successful implementation of the authoritarian modernization project. Post-Soviet bad governance in Russia implicitly assumes high aspirations by ruling groups. But given the conditions of the Russian state and regime, the agenda of narrow modernization faces major obstacles. Policy reforms that infringe on the interests of influential rent-seekers have often been curtailed, and even those policies backed by powerful supporters may lead to unintended and undesired consequences. These consequences depend not only on specific policies in certain areas, but to a great degree on the hierarchical mechanism of policy-making within the framework of the power vertical, with its aggravation of principal-agent problems (analyzed in detail in chapter 2). Therefore, policy reforms in various areas in Russia have often resulted in privatization of gains and socialization of losses but have not much improved its institutional performance. These outcomes, however, make chances for successful socioeconomic advancement more and more elusive over time. Although the modernization efforts were not entirely in vain, their effects have often been partial, controversial, and short-lived.

To summarize, the political conditions of the authoritarian modernization project in Russia in the 2000s were quite unfavorable to begin with; the combination of electoral authoritarianism and poor quality of governance hindered the success of full-scale simultaneous reforms in various social and economic areas. The reformers could only hope to establish some pockets of efficiency and achieve success in certain high-priority policy areas where the reforms could be more successful, while in other policy areas reforms could either be suspended or fail completely. While an analysis of Russian modernization in the 2000s confirms these expectations, a closer look at the political and institutional environment of adoption and implementation of policy changes in Russia will help to understand the patterns and variations in policy reforms in different areas, analyzed in more detail in chapter 4.

Although considering recent developments in Russia one might argue that the post-Soviet authoritarian modernization project is nearly exhausted and has little chance of continuing in the foreseeable future,[103] it is worth considering its experience further. Modernization as such will be a necessary part of the agenda for Russia's development. Its ideas, institutions, and policies are still to be discussed, even though now there are no signs that a new window of opportunity is about to open. One should learn certain lessons from the trial-and-error reforms and counterreforms of the recent past, accumulate knowledge about their advances and setbacks, and not repeat the same wrong moves. These lessons may be labeled "Mission: Impossible." Similarly to the film series, authoritarian modernization in Russia may include several episodes with recurring protagonists and may be popular among the public. Unlike the films, however, the success of the Impossible Mission Force under a dual-track strategy is highly unlikely.

CHAPTER 4

Opportunities and Constraints

Policy Reforms in the 2000s

WHY ARE SOME SOCIOECONOMIC reforms successful while others are not? To what extent do the political regime and its institutions affect the outcomes of major socioeconomic reforms? Can a reform-minded nondemocratic leader, supported by a team of well-qualified experts, modernize his/her country without the fear of losing in free and fair competitive elections? And what of the conditions supporting (or opposing) the successful implementation of such a narrow program of authoritarian modernization?

The Russian experience of socioeconomic reforms in the 2000s can be perceived as a crucial case of authoritarian modernization in the context of post-Communist social and political changes. In 2000, when Vladimir Putin came to power, the Russian government proposed an ambitious and large-scale program of economic and social reforms in Russia. Some of these reforms were initiated by the liberal economists who had greatly influenced the policy agenda in the 1990s.[1] In the 2000s, they sought to implement their ideas under more favorable circumstances. The 1990s had been marked by a deep and protracted economic transformation recession, a major decline of state capacity, and constant intraelite conflicts; by contrast, the 2000s became a period of high economic growth, recentralization of the Russian government, and large-scale support for Putin's leadership from major political and economic actors and from Russian citizens. Although the policy reforms of the 2000s contributed to the improvement of the quality of governance in Russia, their outcomes have failed to meet the expectations of optimists and pessimists alike. A decade later, the reformers themselves assessed the implementation of their programs, and their leading figures, such as German Gref and Yevgeny Yasin, realized that fewer than half of the proposals had been implemented, and only a few had been successful. (A more precise calculation made in 2016 by the team of the Center for Strategic

Research found that only 36 percent of policy changes had been implemented.)
Several proposed measures stopped at the stage of discussing good policy alternatives, and among those reforms that have been implemented successfully, some
have had a series of unintended and undesired consequences.[2]

It is necessary to explain this diversity of outcomes of policy reforms, considering they occurred nearly simultaneously and within nearly the same economic
and political circumstances. A synchronic comparative analysis allows me to
disregard certain factors such as the impact of the Soviet legacy or public opinion of the Russian people: I do not assume that these factors were unimportant,
but they do not explain why some reforms succeeded and others failed. At the
same time, the widespread statements that tend to explain the troubles of policy
reforms through the resistance of interest groups ("oligarchs," *siloviki*, regional
leaders, and other rent-seekers),[3] the rise of global oil prices, or Putin's interest in
consolidating his personal political power[4] are limited and insufficient. They do
not adequately explain why the tax reform of the 2000s became a success story,
but the reform of the system of social benefits (*monetizatsiya l'got*) faced numerous problems. Why was the reform of the school graduate evaluation system
implemented despite considerable costs, while the reform of the state administrative apparatus and the full-scale reorganization of federal government agencies in fact led to an increased number of bureaucrats and their empowerment?
Putin, oil, and *siloviki* alone are not responsible for the variation in the outcomes
of reforms that were launched almost simultaneously and under similar conditions. This chapter attempts to explain the factors and mechanisms behind the
successes and failures of the 2000s' policy reforms in Russia. I focus on the one
hand on the impact of electoral authoritarianism and the poor quality of the
state on policy changes, and on the other hand on the institutional factors that
affect the vertical and horizontal fragmentation of the Russian government and
the inefficiency of its policies.

Russia's Policy Environment in the 2000s:
Institutions and Incentives

The influence of major political institutions such as the separation of powers
and electoral and party systems on policy-making has been widely analyzed, but
mostly focusing on democratic political regimes,[5] while the effects of authoritarian political institutions on policy outcomes have been underexplored.[6] Under
authoritarianism, parliaments and political parties perform a secondary role
in decision-making at best.[7] The main policy-making agent is the government,

which is appointed and controlled by the authoritarian leadership. In terms of institutional design, present-day Russia is a typical case of the "dual executive" within the framework of a presidential-parliamentary model.[8] The Russian president, as a popularly elected head of state, can appoint and dismiss the cabinet as a whole as well as its individual members. Although the prime minister is approved by the State Duma, he is dependent on a president who can undo any of the prime minister's decisions and can issue presidential decrees that the government must follow. Thus, the Russian institutional design intentionally ensures that the government hold a minimal level of autonomy and perform technical (rather than political) functions. Its role is reduced to implementing the tasks posed by the president and performing routine, daily administrative work in social and economic policy areas.[9]

This model of state governance, codified in the 1993 Constitution, was inherited from both the Soviet model (based on an informal division of labor between the Central Committee of the Communist Party of the Soviet Union and the Council of Ministers) and the Russian Imperial model (based on the monarch's control of both the royal court and the cabinet of ministers). From an authoritarian regime's perspective, this model has both advantages and disadvantages. The main advantage is the opportunity for the president to replace top officials if they are inefficient and/or politically disloyal, or if the president intends to change his policy. In addition, such a model allows shifting the responsibility for policy implementation and switching the blame to the government rather than the president (in the 1990s, Yeltsin used this method quite frequently, reshuffling his government several times). At the same time, citizens' assessment of economic policy performance is an important source of mass support of political leaders;[10] therefore the president is genuinely interested in successful government in terms of its performance. The problem is that the coexistence of the president with a capable and popular government can lead to an erosion of the presidential political monopoly; a successful prime minister can challenge the incumbent in the next electoral cycle as an opposition-backed candidate and/or a potential successor (as shown by the cases of Yevgeny Primakov in Russia and Viktor Yushchenko in Ukraine).[11] The combination of great managerial efficiency and unconditional personal loyalty to the boss is rare among top state officials. As a result, the rise of the principal-agent problem is deeply embedded in this model.

A low level of government autonomy leads to the transformation of the cabinet of ministers from a collective entity of key decision-makers to a technocratic set of officials responsible for implementing the commands of the president and/or prime minister. The president (or in some instances, prime minister)[12] "hires" individuals for executive positions, considering them to be technocratic managers rather than politicians. Hence, the cabinet in this system of governance is neither a group of officials who are politically responsible before the parliament nor a team of professionals who share common policy goals and methods. The prime minister is responsible for coordinating this complicated web of relationships. He is dependent on numerous deputy prime ministers who supervise various state agencies (at times, there have been as many as ten of these deputy prime ministers in Russia). As a result, policy-making under these conditions turns into a complex and often inefficient series of bargains and ad hoc agreements between several state agencies. Top officials must spend countless resources to win intragovernmental struggles.[13] This is why policy-making under these conditions is often perceived by observers as a difficult process.[14]

In Russia's case, policy-making becomes even more complicated due to additional institutional flaws. First, the state agencies responsible for national defence, state security, and foreign affairs have been directly subordinated to the president since 1994 even though their chiefs are also members of the government and should be subordinated to the prime minister as well (later, other state agencies were also added to this list). Second, in order to resolve the principal-agent problem, presidential control has been imposed on the government; this role is performed by the presidential administration, directly subordinate to the head of the state (the Central Committee of the Communist Party performed the same function during the Soviet period). This model intentionally creates parallel governance structures that often compete during the policy process and therefore hinder decision-making.[15] Third, the key ministers and/or deputy prime ministers who are personally linked to the president can influence major policy decisions, bypassing the web of agencies or even bypassing the prime minister. Anatoly Chubais and Boris Nemtsov (two first deputy prime ministers) in 1997–1998[16] and Aleksey Kudrin and German Gref (ministers of finance and of economic development, respectively) in 2000–2004[17] successfully employed this policy strategy. Finally, several presidential decrees are often prepared without the involvement of the governmental officials responsible for certain policy areas. As a result, these presidential decrees sometimes cannot be implemented properly. In addition to horizontal fragmentation (between governmental agencies and other federal executive offices), vertical fragmentation between the federal government and its branches at the subnational level also plays a significant role. In the 1990s, a full-scale decentralization of governance contributed to the capture of territorial branches of federal agencies by the regional elites. In the 2000s, a recentralization of state governance reestablished the federal center's political control over regional authorities but did not establish a division of competences and resources between federal and regional governments. The shift to a hierarchical subordination of territorial governance exacerbated the agency problem in relationships between the center and the regions.[18]

Given these institutional arrangements, one might argue that the Russian executive, even in routine governance, must deal with aggravation of principal-agent problems in relations both between the president and the executive and within the government. This complicates the coordination of different state agencies and their actions and contributes to a protracted policy-making process and/or the making of inefficient decisions. Under these circumstances, the implementation of a full-scale reform program faces serious obstacles. Any bureaucracy is known to be interested in preserving the status quo.[19] Russian political institutions are not capable of overcoming hidden resistance from bureaucrats, especially if and when policy-making requires interdepartmental coordination between different layers of the power vertical and numerous gates of the federal government. If reforms need concerted, large-scale, and highly coordinated action from various segments of the federal and regional bureaucracies, this becomes a major problem for policy changes. The lack of political accountability and the inefficiency of mechanisms of centralized control[20] pushes officials to minimize their efforts to implement policy changes approved by the president. The more significant the involvement of the bureaucracy in policy implementation, the stronger the resistance it experiences from most officials. The policy reformers may be endorsed by a few ideologically driven proponents of these reforms and/or by policy entrepreneurs who expect to achieve personal gains from successful policy implementation.

At the beginning of the 2000s, favorable political conditions for policy reforms appeared to emerge in Russia. Due to rapid economic growth after a long and protracted recession,[21] Putin gained significant popular support. After the 1999 parliamentary election, the Kremlin was able to establish a pro-presidential majority in the State Duma that approved almost all of the Kremlin's initiatives.[22] Strengthening state capacity[23] and recentralizing state governance[24] allowed the Russian government to reduce the influence of rent-seekers in policy-making. But the major driver of policy reforms at that time was Putin's unequivocal support for implementing socioeconomic changes. These circumstances opened a window of policy opportunity[25] that had been closed in the second half of the 1990s.[26]

The concept of the reform program ("the Gref Program" or "Strategy 2010") was developed in the first months of 2000 by the experts at the Center for

Strategic Research (CSR, *Tsentr strategicheskikh razrabotok*). Under Putin's patronage, this center aimed to develop the previous decade's policy proposals. The choice of policy options and Putin's policy positions were influenced by the previous experience of the 1990s. Putin prioritized[27] building a strong and efficient state that would provide long-term economic growth based on financial stabilization and a successful fiscal policy. Improvement of the quality of governance was also listed as one of the priorities of the Strategy 2010 program. Indeed, the weakness of the Russian state and its fiscal crisis are justly considered to be the ultimate cause of policy failures and poor quality of governance in the 1990s.[28] Therefore, major reforms in these policy areas became the key points in the reformers' agenda at the beginning of the 2000s. At the same time, social policy changes that would contribute to societal development in the medium-term perspective were not declared to be top priorities, even though half of Gref's program was devoted to policy changes in these areas. Under electoral authoritarian regimes, social policies are often perceived not as a strategic goal of government but as a means of providing electoral loyalty.[29] The experience of both the 1990s[30] and the 2000s demonstrates that the Russian case is not an exception.

Despite the CSR's role as a think-tank, there was no headquarters that managed or even coordinated various reforms. They were implemented as a set of inconsistent measures controlled by specific ministries. Mikhail Kasyanov, the prime minister from May 2000 to February 2004, did not participate in preparing Strategy 2010. His views often contradicted the policy ideas of key ministers that developed this program.[31] His successor Mikhail Fradkov did not become a significant political actor. In practice, all important decisions (including large-scale reorganization of the Russian government in 2004) were made by the president. In some cases, the responsibilities for reforms were concentrated in one governmental agency, but often they were divided between several ministries and agencies in both the center and the regions. While some reforms required only the one-time adoption of a package of legal acts, others included a sequential chain of actions that required coordination of various actors over a long period of time. Theoretically, one can expect that inconsistent and protracted policy changes will be implemented in an inefficient way,[32] especially under conditions of an electoral authoritarian regime; as such, without immediate positive results in the short term, these reforms may be blocked and ultimately fail.

Thus, the features of the Russian bureaucracy and the institutional design of the executive imposed major constraints on the implementation of reforms in the early 2000s. The possibility of overcoming these obstacles depends, in my opinion, upon three factors: (1) the strategic priority of certain reforms for the

TABLE 3. Factors of Success of Policy Reforms

Factors of policy reforms	Contribute to success if:	Contribute to failure if:
strategic priority of reforms for the political leadership	high	low
concentration and cooperation of agents of reforms during policy adoption and implementation	high concentration of reformers in a single governmental agency; major cooperation among reformers	responsibility for policy changes dispersed among several governmental agencies; limited cooperation among reformers
process of adoption and implementation of policy changes	single-stage reform; short period of adoption and implementation of policy changes	multi-stage reform; long period of adoption and implementation of policy changes

president; (2) implementing a given reform by reformers who are concentrated in a single powerful agency; and (3) reform requiring one-time governmental actions that are implemented within a short period of time (see table 3).

How and why have these factors influenced specific policy reforms and what was the impact of these reforms on bad governance in Russia? To answer this question, I will analyze the experience of policy changes in Russia in the first half of the 2000s.

Successes and Failures of Reforms: Case Studies

Tax Reform: A Major Success

The tax reform implemented in the early 2000s in Russia became a model example of the most successful policy changes of that period. In the 1990s, the emergence of the modern tax system in Russia was accompanied by a weak state capacity, a spontaneous decentralization of governance, political instability, and the obvious imperfections of many legal regulations.[33] As a result, Russian authorities had major difficulties with tax collection causing a major fiscal crisis. The widespread use of numerous tax exemptions, nonmonetary payments in the form of different offsets and money substitutes, and the proliferation of legal, extralegal, and illegal schemes of tax evasion, combined with the high taxation rates and the large number of taxes, made the government's fiscal policies inefficient.[34]

From a formal viewpoint, the tax reform involved the development, adoption, and implementation of the Tax Code, which established unified rules of taxation and fiscal governance in Russia. Its first chapter, which defined the foundations of the country's tax system, was adopted in 1998. But the development of the second chapter took five more years. In 2000–2004, a new set of taxes and tax rates was established that replaced previous ones. As a result, on the one hand, the tax burden on individuals and businesses was drastically reduced (especially due to the changes in the taxation rates of value added tax and profit tax and the introduction of the unified social tax). On the other hand, the fiscal revenues of the state budget increased. This was achieved by adopting a flat rate of personal income tax (13 percent), instead of the "progressive rate" that stimulated tax evasion among relatively well-to-do taxpayers.[35] As a result, between 2000 and 2007, extra revenues for the Russian budget reached an overall level of 1 percent of the GDP (excluding oil revenues).[36]

In addition, the government managed to push a new model of taxation for oil companies through the parliament. First, a subsoil use tax was established with its rate depending on the sector of the economy and the production costs. Second, a progressive rate of oil export duties was introduced, and oil products excises were increased. As global oil prices were rising unprecedentedly after 2003, these policy measures contributed to an immense increase in budget revenues. The increase of tax revenues from the oil sector allowed the government to establish the Stabilization Fund of the Russian Federation—a mechanism for sterilization of budgetary revenues intended to prevent high rates of inflation and to form financial reserves in case of a major decrease in global oil prices. The Stabilization Fund was established despite resistance from certain government ministers and from several MPs (members of the parliament) and lobbyists who were interested in spending extra revenues on current projects instead of saving funds for the future.[37] The prudence of this policy became evident during the 2008–2009 economic crisis when the Reserve Fund of the Russian Federation (which was formed with the use of the Stabilization Fund's resources) covered the Russian budget deficit.

Every aspect of the tax reform had its own influential opponents. MPs from the Communist Party of the Russian Federation fiercely opposed the flat rate of income tax. They considered it a means of tax evasion for the wealthy.[38] Representatives of the state pension and social insurance funds argued against the unified social tax because they lost control over collection of money paid by companies. Finally, oil companies attempted to block the introduction of the subsoil use tax because it greatly increased taxation in that sector.[39] However, despite this resistance from various corners the tax reform was implemented.

The key factor in this success story was Putin's full-scale support of the reformers—Aleksey Kudrin, the minister of finance, and German Gref, the minister of economic development, who relied upon teams that included officials in their respective ministries and numerous experts and advisors. Besides the personal credibility of the reformers, based on the common experience they shared during their service in Saint Petersburg's city administration, Putin considered creating an efficient tax system a priority for his agenda. Thus, he included the introduction of the flat rate of personal income tax in his Budgetary Address to the Russian Parliament, delivered in May 2000. This move consolidated the presidential majority in the State Duma[40] in support of this decision. The decision to introduce the subsoil use tax was more complicated. Russian oil companies influenced the State Duma budgetary committee to a large degree and had support from several MPs. But despite lobbyists' efforts, the government was able to squeeze this proposal through the State Duma. At the end of the day, the oil lobby accepted a consolation prize—the government would be prepared to decrease the subsoil tax rate to zero if the price of oil dropped below $8.00 per barrel; in any event, this did not happen.[41]

Another factor in the success of the tax reform was the concentration of policy-making in the hands of reformers and their supporters. Close connections between Putin, Kudrin, and Gref allowed the two ministers to insulate the decision-making process from their major opponents. Indeed, Putin unilaterally adopted many financial and economic decisions without the participation of the prime minister or the cabinet.[42] For example, a bill on replacing numerous social taxation payments with the unified social tax (a flat rate payroll tax, paid by companies) was submitted to the parliament without the agreement of other state officials, including the heads of the pension and social insurance funds. The stability of the new rules of the game was supported by the long service of the reformers as ministers: Gref left the Ministry of Economic Development in 2007, and Kudrin lost his post as minister of finance in 2011.

Finally, the tax reform was not subjected to a long implementation process. The decision on the flat rate of the income tax was proposed and adopted within one year. Then the Ministry of Finance managed to protect this change from several initiatives to introduce progressive taxation, arguing that the new mode of taxation was efficient because budgetary revenues had increased. However, some elements of tax reform did not survive in the longer term: this was the case with the unified social tax, which provided governmental control over the use of funds but did not increase budgetary revenues as such. As a result, in 2010 Tatiana Golikova, then the minister of Public Health and Social Development, achieved a return to the previous scheme of social taxation payments. After that, the unified social tax was divided into several different social payments managed by the Pension Fund and Social Insurance Fund independently from each other.[43]

Preserving the Stabilization Fund became the government's most difficult task. In 2006, the Investment Fund of the Russian Federation was established within the federal budget, and a certain amount of money from the Stabilization Fund was diverted to the Investment Fund. The new budgetary instrument was intended to accumulate financial resources to fund nationwide infrastructural projects. Soon, those resources were allocated to not only nationwide projects but also regional ones. In 2008, the Stabilization Fund was split into the Reserve Fund and the Fund for National Prosperity. The former performed the same functions as the Stabilization Fund, and the latter aimed to balance the budget of the Pension Fund of the Russian Federation.[44] Although the use of the Stabilization Fund was of great help during the 2008–2009 economic crisis, it did not contribute to the country's long-term development.

Finally, a side effect of successful tax reform was a major improvement in tax administration in Russia in the 2000s and 2010s. Tax officials who had to manage a limited number of clearly defined taxes and follow more transparent "rules of the game," adjusted to new conditions better than many other state agencies. Although they still enjoyed great discretion in dealing with certain categories of taxpayers such as big state-owned companies or small businesses, the degree of arbitrariness largely decreased. Later, technological advancements (such as digitalization) also contributed to the better performance of state tax services. It is no wonder that the former head of the Federal Tax Service, Mikhail Mishustin, was promoted to the post of prime minister of Russia in January 2020.

However, even this success story was limited in scope. Another element of the reform initiated by Kudrin—the development of the principles of performance-based budgeting—did not achieve any significant results.[45] The task of increasing the efficiency of public expenditures could not be resolved by the Ministry of Finance alone (even with presidential support). It required the efforts of several mid-and street-level bureaucrats and other participants in the budgetary process who would have to be suitably motivated and consent to shift their approach for effective use of budgetary spending. As with the case of administrative reform, there was a shortage of such officials in the state apparatus and limited incentives for an advancement of reform among the top political leadership. As a result, this reform failed.

Implementing tax reform demonstrated that the institutional foundations of a success story of policy changes heavily depend on presidential support of a well-formulated policy program. Such a program needs to be conducted by an administratively strong and consolidated team of reformers who can disregard various pressure groups and push through reforms that do not involve lots of participants at the implementation stage. But this case also displays the unique array of factors necessary for policy success. The lack of even one of these factors would lead to the window of opportunity closing for that reform's implementation.

Educational Reform: Mixed Results

In the 1990s, the Russian authorities made several attempts to reform Russian school education. Both the content of school education and the principles of educational governance urgently needed to change. The inefficient use of limited financial resources by the state officials responsible for school and higher education and the lack of an independent system of evaluation for schools and universities were the most important institutional obstacles to developing Russian education. Under these circumstances, the education managers were not interested in improving the quality of education. Secondary schools did not undergo external evaluations of their performance. Final school exams were conducted by the same teachers who taught the courses. To enter university, potential students needed to prepare for entrance exams in addition to taking their final school exams (and many parents paid fees to private teachers out of their own pockets). Most schools located in rural areas could not provide a decent quality of educational services. Educational mobility, even within Russia, was limited by significant costs. This reduced the level of competition for students between universities, especially at the regional level.[46] Attempts to solve these problems in the 1990s faced a lack of funding from the federal budget and resistance from the conservative part of the professional community and political elite.[47]

The fact that a program of educational reform was included in Strategy 2010 opened a window of political opportunity for the reformers. In 2001 the Ministry of Education launched the experiment of introducing the Unified State Exam (*Edinyi gosudarstvennyi ekzamen*, EGE) in certain Russian regions. This mechanism replaced the final examination procedures in secondary schools and combined them with entrance examination procedures in universities. It used a single set of written exams based upon a set of formalized tests. Their results were reflected in final school certificates, while the universities accepted these scores for entrance examinations.

In 2002, as another experiment, the mechanism of state financial obligations to individuals (*gosudarstvennye imennye finansovye obyazatel'stva*, GIFO) was introduced, often called "educational vouchers" in the media. The idea was that after passing the Unified State Exam, a school graduate could be eligible to receive a certain amount of public funds for study at a university to cover tuition fees and provide stipends for living. The size of the state grant would depend on the Unified State Exam score, and the rest of the university's fees should be covered by the students (or, rather, by their parents). This policy measure was designed to contribute to the targeted distribution of public finances among higher education institutions, increase competition between universities to attract the best school graduates, and stimulate a fee-paying model of higher education in Russia.[48] Introducing this model also assumed that study loans would be available for students in the future, in addition to GIFO-based state grants.

The results of these reforms were ambiguous. The GIFO experiment lasted for only three years in a limited number of regions. Upon its negative evaluation by the professional community, the federal authorities abandoned its subsequent implementation and the GIFO mechanism was buried. The Unified State Exam experiment, on the other hand, covered more new regions every year and by 2008 became a nationwide examination. As a result, the State Duma had to amend the law on education in Russia to recognize the Unified State Exam as the only way to complete secondary school and take university entrance exams simultaneously. The opportunity to use the results of the Unified State Exam to apply for several universities at once dramatically increased competition for students in the university education system and improved educational mobility. Still, almost twenty years on, the Unified State Exam has not become recognized by Russian society as a legitimate way to evaluate students by either schools or universities. In the 2010s, Ministry of Education officials discussed the possibility of returning to the previous practice of final examinations in schools and proposed to increase the number of universities that would be able to use additional entrance exams, thus compromising the very idea of the reform. Public opinion of the Unified State Exam is also exceedingly critical.[49]

The educational reforms could not be implemented by their initiators alone. They involved an unprecedented number of participants in the policy process, ranging from members of the State Duma and regional and local officials to university rectors, school directors, and teachers. The complexity of the reforms' implementation and the resistance of numerous interest groups were quite significant. As a result, there was a serious risk of the reforms' failure and a return to the previous status quo; in fact, this happened with the introduction of the GIFO. The Ministry of Education did not initiate this innovation: it was proposed by the experts from the Higher School of Economics who included this policy measure in Strategy 2010 program. However, it caused a furious reaction in the State Duma and was ultimately protested even more passionately than the Unified State Exam. The universities' representatives were also against changing financial arrangements in higher education. As a result, the experiment was considered a failure and abandoned.[50] At the same time, the ministry was interested in implementing the Unified State Exam and was able to overcome equally strong resistance to this innovation through step-by-step implementation of the reform. The experimental status of the new mechanism made it possible to develop and adjust new organizational and substantive arrangements of the examination and reduced the intensity of the debate over the reform, which had not yet been converted into a legal act and therefore, could theoretically be abandoned. When the experiment covered the entire country, its disparate opponents could not make the government and its loyalists in the State Duma prevent its legal formalization. As a result, the policy entrepreneurs from the Ministry of Education could implement this project while insulating the educational reform from the influence of interest groups.

Despite their social significance, educational reforms have never been attributed to Vladimir Putin. He has made several statements in support of Russian education but hardly considers this policy area a priority in his agenda. On the one hand, educational reforms cannot provide an immediate positive effect, regardless of results. On the other hand, Putin sought to keep a distance from the initiators of unpopular policy changes and from decisions made by officials at the ministerial level. At the same time, during the 2000s and 2010s the educational reform was implemented consistently and without significant changes in its content. This indicates that Putin and Medvedev supported these policy measures. In 2011, Andrey Fursenko, then the minister of education, suggested that the Unified State Exam should include only three disciplines—Russian, math, and one of the foreign languages—but President Medvedev rejected this suggestion: "Approaches to conducting the Unified State Exam have been determined, and the exam has proved a reasonable way of testing knowledge."[51]

The Unified State Exam's major problems were to a certain degree caused by the misuse of its results by the government. The reformers initially saw the Unified State Exam as a means of external evaluation of the performance of schools and educational bureaucrats at the local level. But later, the Kremlin used the results of the Unified State Exam as one of the criteria for assessing the performance of regional authorities.[52] As a consequence, the exam scores of school graduates gained administrative and political status. This became one of the reasons for numerous violations during examinations: scandals occur frequently due to the regular leakage of tests and answer keys, the mass involvement of schoolteachers in illegally assisting pupils to pass the tests, and the dubious distribution of the best results among the Russian regions. Thus, scores in the republics of the North Caucasus, despite their notoriously low human capital, were higher than those in Moscow and Saint Petersburg. Only in 2014, when this indicator was removed from the list of indicators of performance of regional governors, did the number of scandals of that kind drop to nearly zero. The efforts of regional and local bureaucrats have been aimed not at increasing the quality of school education but at achieving high scores at any cost. In this way, the functions of the Unified State Exam have been diminished and its role has changed over time.

Nevertheless, the educational reforms can be considered an example of successful gradual and consistent implementation of new institutional arrangements. Initially, these initiatives were implemented as experiments concerning the approbation of new mechanisms in some regions. It was impossible to introduce the Unified State Exam in all Russian regions simultaneously due to both organizational and institutional constraints (lack of experience, high level of uncertainty of outcomes, and high cost of potential failure of the reform) and political ones (most politicians, professionals, and ordinary citizens did not accept the idea of an educational reform). The decision on the Unified State Exam was de facto adopted and implemented by the Ministry of Education. The legislative formalization of the Unified State Exam happened only in 2009, when the State Duma was under the full control of the presidential administration. At the same time, the same strategy contributed to the failure to implement the GIFO system, which could demonstrate reliable results only nationwide and not on the level of individual regions.[53]

To summarize, the institutional changes in educational policy demonstrate the limits of presidential influence on implementing reforms. Even modest presidential support helps the adoption of major decisions and their implementation despite the resistance of various interest groups, especially if the reformers can preserve at least part of their proposals without major concessions to interest groups. But the performance of the mid-range and street-level bureaucracy[54] can reduce the efficiency of implementing top-down ideas.

Administrative Reform: from Bad to Worse

The administrative reform was aimed at solving the problem of inefficiency of public administration, which hindered the country's social and economic development. By the end of the 1990s, a paradox of poor quality of governance was widely observed in Russia: formally, the government had many regulatory powers, but its performance was inefficient.[55] The influence of big business on the adoption and implementation of many important policy decisions led to state capture.[56] At the same time, entrenched state officials formed their clienteles, which included representatives of different businesses and other interest groups.[57] The functions of ministries and state agencies often duplicated one another. The formation of Russian "bargaining federalism" in the 1990s generated politically motivated division of powers between federal and regional authorities.[58] The decline of state capacity and state autonomy raised doubts about the federal government's ability not only to implement any reforms but also to conduct routine daily governance.

Formally, the administrative reform was launched in 2003[59] and officially continues even now. However, the most significant policy measures—(1) the revision of the functions of government agencies; (2) the revision of the so-called redundant functions of the government; (3) the redistribution of other functions between federal and subnational government agencies; and (4) major structural changes to the federal government—were implemented in 2003–2004.[60] After that, the reform was focused on the technologies of improving government services provision, advancement of digitalization, and so forth, but no longer involved politically relevant changes.

In fact, the reform failed to contribute to improving public administration in Russia.[61] The redistribution of powers between layers of government led to a recentralization of governance that more resembled a unitary state.[62] The transformation of the federal government into three types of organizational entities (ministries, federal agencies, and federal services) and the revision of their powers did not contribute to transparent and efficient governance but rather complicated the interactions between the governmental agencies that were responsible for the same policy areas.[63] The only meaningful outcome achieved by these policy changes was a significant increase in the officials' salaries and quantity of civil servants, while the quality of personnel and the motivation of officials, which had been heavily criticized,[64] did not change in practice. Major elements of the reform, such as accountability of public servants, transparency of state agencies and bureaucratic procedures, merit-based recruitment and promotion of state officials, and the like, remain merely on paper. Thus, despite several technological innovations in the everyday practices of interactions between bureaucrats, business people and ordinary citizens, the quality of public services has not much improved. Moreover, in many instances it has become even worse. But why were the results of administrative reform so poor?

One might argue that the administrative reform was on the periphery of presidential attention. Initially, the development of this reform was one of the key items for the Center for Strategic Research.[65] Later, this reform became a priority for the government and the presidential administration. In his annual address to the parliament, Putin paid specific attention to it. In 2003, admitting significant problems in achieving the policy goals, he even promised to provide "needed political impetus" for more active policy in this area.[66] However, Putin did not take the most important step: he did not provide any organizational support for the planned reform. All basic policy measures in this area were coordinated by the governmental Commission for Administrative Reform, which was headed by one of the deputy prime ministers ex officio and worked on an ad hoc basis. Thus, the impact of this coordination center on policy changes was relatively low. In addition, this commission did not possess enough powers to implement reforms; its role was limited to policy proposals. Its scope was restricted to proposing changes in the structure of the government and in the functions of different kinds of governmental agencies. The reform of public service, changes in its personnel, and the revision of other major regulations were delegated to the Commission for Reforming Public Service, headed by Dmitry Medvedev (at that time, the first deputy head of the Presidential Administration). The members of that commission took a conservative approach to reforming public service in Russia.[67] As a result, the policy reform was organizationally divided and full of internal contradictions. All attempts to strengthen the influence of the Commission for Administrative Reform or establish a new strong organization in charge of this reform have failed. For example, in 2004, the Ministry of Finance blocked the adoption of a federal program that could have provided financial resources to implement the administrative reform. At the same time, the proposal to establish an agency in charge of implementation of the reform and allocation of funds was rejected. The implementation of the Conception of the Administrative Reform in 2006–2008 was delegated to the heads of the governmental agencies: in other words, Russian public service had to be reformed by the officials themselves although they were not interested in challenging the status quo and did not have any incentives to implement the reform program.

It is no wonder that the administrative reform greatly contributed to the major rise in quantity of state officials: according to the official data of the Russian State Statistical Committee, while in 2001 their numbers counted to 1,140,600 persons, by 2009 these numbers increased up to 1,674,800 persons (mostly due to reorganizing state agencies and a major increase in the scope of their regulatory functions).[68] In addition, the failure of administrative reform sent a strong signal to Russian elites and society at large that despite the loud rhetoric, the top leadership in Russia was not interested in improving the quality of governance.[69]

The administrative reform aimed at the debureaucratization of the Russian economy and the stimulation of business development coincided with a "statist turn" in Russian economic policy. Since 2004, the promotion of private businesses as major drivers of Russian economy has been replaced by building major state conglomerates in key sectors, ranging from Rosneft and Gazprom[70] to Russian Railways (briefly described in chapter 2). These changes provide contradictory incentives to administrative reform: although state agencies abandoned some of their redundant functions, they also increased their encroachment into the economy by toughening governmental regulations and increasing the regulatory burden on businesses and the noncommercial sector. Thus, a set of measures—for instance, the division of labor between the ministries responsible for policy development and decision-making, the federal services in charge of implementing these decisions, and the federal agencies that provide public services and manage federal property—would lead to an increase in the number of state officials, but it could not improve the quality of governance, instead leading to a major decline. Figures 1 through 4 clearly illustrate such a tendency: in the second half of the 2000s, World Bank's indicators for the rule of law, control of corruption, and regulatory quality in Russia demonstrated a major deterioration. When the shift to the "predatory state" model of state-business relations occurred in Russia during this period,[71] the administrative reform was no longer needed.

One important obstacle to the success of the administrative reform was its long implementation period. Putin had lost interest in this policy area by 2005. Those experts who had initiated the reform were replaced in the Commission for Administrative Reform by the other group of state officials. Finally, the substance of the reform itself was reduced to interminable preparation of new administrative regulations and to making new arrangements for state agencies' online services. At the same time, transparency and debureaucratization of decision-making itself were no longer considered important features of public administration and civil service.

In conclusion, the failure of the administrative reform resulted from the following factors:

1. the lack of drivers of reform, that is leaders who would have enough will and power to implement key decisions despite resistance from major interest groups;

2. dispersed responsibility among state officials and the lack of a politically and administratively strong team who would coordinate the actions of various governmental agencies, which led to inefficiency of reform implementation; and

3. protracted policy changes and the lack of short-term achievements, which decreased presidential interest in this sphere of reform.

As a result, the administrative reform's goals were not achieved, and the quality of state governance and public administration went from bad to worse.

Why Are Reforms (Im)possible?: Social Benefits, Police, Military, and Beyond

The logic behind Russian policy reforms analyzed above is summarized in table 4. Although the cases outlined above obviously do not cover the entire scope of policy reforms implemented by the Russian government within the framework of authoritarian modernization, one can trace the influence of the same factors on policy changes in other areas.

The reform of social benefits implemented in 2004–2005 was not a major priority for the government but was considered a by-product of the redistribution of powers and responsibilities between the federal government and the regions. It ultimately failed due to errors in the budgeting process[72] and inefficient coordination of government agencies at the federal and regional levels.[73] The amount of funds necessary to effectively implement reform proposals was not provided, and the federal authorities put the burden of conducting the reform onto the shoulders of regional governments without designating budgetary transfers that could cover extra costs. This reform contributed to public discontent and to protest rallies in several cities and led to the declining electoral performance of United Russia at the regional elections in spring 2005.[74] As a result, the federal government had to cover significant expenditures, which were much higher than was initially planned. It is no wonder that after this failure, the president and the government argued against implementing any new reforms, including policy changes in other areas: further reforms were shelved, and the very term "reforms" became a taboo in the discourse of state officials.[75] Political and institutional

TABLE 4. Features and Outcomes of Policy Reforms in Russia in the 2000s

Feature	Tax Reform	Educational Reform	Administrative Reform
strategic priority of reform for the political leadership	high	relatively low	initially high, but later low
key agents of the reform	ministers of finance and economic development and their teams	officials in the Ministry of Education	numerous officials in the government and the presidential administration
concentration of agents of the reform during policy adoption and implementation	high	low	low
resistance from interest groups	strong (in some areas), but not coordinated	strong (in all areas), but not coordinated	strong (in all areas)
insulation of reformers from opponents' influence	high (due to presidential support)	limited in some areas; self-insulation in the case of the Unified State Exam experiment	none – the reform was implemented by the major interest groups (the officials) themselves
process of adoption and implementation of policy changes	single-stage; major decisions were adopted and implemented quickly	multi-stage; major decisions were adopted quickly but implemented over many years	multi-stage; major decisions were made and implemented over many years
outcomes of the reform	rapid and positive effects that legitimized reforms	non-immediate and ambiguous effects	insignificant effects
impact of the reform	reduction of the tax burden, stimulation of economic growth, increase of fiscal revenues to the state budget	standardizing a system of evaluation of school graduates (despite numerous defects)	increasing number of officials and rise in their salaries
overall assessment of the reform	(incomplete) success	Unified State Exam - success, GIFO - failure	failure

factors affected the outcome of this reform, alongside technical ones. Although the insulation of the government from interest groups often makes it possible to initiate certain policy changes, it can also aggravate the risk of major policy failures due to inefficient institutional design and/or poor quality of policy implementation.

An even more vivid example of unsuccessful policy change was the police reform initiated under Dmitry Medvedev's presidency, as convincingly analyzed by Brian Taylor.[76] Even though the development of the rule of law and the creation of efficient law enforcement agencies were declared by Medvedev to be his main priorities, the launch of the police reform in 2009 did not bring about any significant effects. This failure was caused, on the one hand, by resistance from influential *siloviki* in the presidential administration and in the government, and on the other hand by Medvedev's inability to build a successful pro-reform coalition among non-*siloviki* officials. The development and implementation of the police reform (including the reduction in the number of law enforcers, personnel changes, and a structural reorganization of agencies) were performed by Ministry of the Interior officials who were the least interested actors when it came to genuine change. Public discussion initiated by the president and his supporters was nominal; alternative proposals were not discussed at all. As a result, the only visible effect of the reform was the change of the title *militsiya* to *politsiya* (police). The numerous reshufflings among the midlevel officials were insignificant, and soon after its start, the reform came to a halt.

In addition, the failure of the police reform demonstrates that policies implemented by an entrenched bureaucracy do not allow for provision of incentives for real change, but often support the status quo. The "new" police remained an agency oriented around presenting appropriate statistical reports irrespective of the real situation regarding crime.[77] The reform of healthcare demonstrates similar tendencies, with a two-fold increase in financial support in the second half of the 2000s failing to lead to improved quality of healthcare services.[78] Although pressure from policy entrepreneurs in some areas (such as the educational reforms) has sometimes contributed to institutional changes, their effects are only partial due to resistance from interest groups and a series of organizational problems. The step-by-step process of implementing certain reforms makes policy changes even more complicated.

Yet not all policy reforms in Russia were doomed to fail. The Russian military analyst Alexander Golts has presented a vivid example of policy advancement in a rather unlikely environment in his perceptive account of successful military reform in Russia in 2008–2012.[79] After a series of replacements of top officials who had done little to restructure the post–Soviet army and attempted to preserve the previous (oversized, inefficient, and costly) status quo in the governance and performance of the Russian military, in 2007 Putin surprisingly appointed Anatoly Serdyukov, then a son-in-law of then prime minister Viktor Zubkov, to be the new minister of defense. His tenure began with the episode of the Russian military conflict with Georgia in August 2008 known as the Five-Day War.[80] This conflict demonstrated that the Russian army was not properly prepared for major ground operations due to technological obsoleteness and poor management and personnel quality. In a sense, even though the Five-Day War has been perceived as a Russian victory, this experience became a major exogenous shock that paved the way to serious reorganization of the military. Serdyukov came to the right job at the right time. He received carte blanche for many actions: he laid off many generals and officers (overall, almost two hundred thousand personnel were cut), reorganized divisions and battalions, restructured the chain of command to make it more modern and efficient, and greatly diminished the number of conscripts in favor of professional military personnel (*kontraktniki*). All of this had been unthinkable for many reformers after the Soviet collapse, but the political will and patronage of the leadership alongside perceptions of the urgent necessity of policy reforms served as major arguments for Serdyukov. To some extent, Serdyukov was able to achieve his goals despite fierce resistance from the military bureaucracy and its numerous lobbyists. However, his reform plans also included the outsourcing of many non-essential services previously performed by the military itself (ranging from construction to catering) away from the insiders of the Ministry of Defense and into the hands of external contractors. He also attempted to review the practices of state procurement for the military to combat overpricing arms and equipment. Such bold moves would inevitably mean a major redistribution of rents and hurt the vital interests of many powerful interest groups.[81] It is no surprise that in 2012 Serdyukov fell victim to a major scandal: an investigation against him was opened amid accusations of adultery with his mistress, Evgeniya Vasilyeva who headed a major department in the ministry. Serdyukov was fired, and his criminal case was closed after a lengthy procedure. Nevertheless, the military reform brought significant fruits, greatly contributing to the more efficient performance of the Russian army during the annexation of Crimea in 2014 and military adventures in Syria since 2015.[82] Some of Serdyukov's reforms, however, were weakened after he was replaced by Putin's long-term associate Sergey Shoigu.[83]

In general, are successful reforms possible within the framework of the authoritarian modernization project? A positive answer should be heavily marked with serious caveats. If a certain reform is the top political priority of a strong and authoritative head of state, if a coherent team of reformers can be insulated from the major interest groups, and if the team implements consistent policy changes quickly and they bring immediate positive results, then this reform is possible even under conditions of poor quality of governance and inefficient institutional design. This combination of favorable conditions is quite rare, and this is why the success story of tax and budgetary reforms in the 2000s remains an exception. But the insulation of reformers from the influence of interest groups as such does not ensure the quality of policy proposals and their implementation: the costs of errors may increase. In addition, authoritarian modernization projects are often implemented by officials who are not interested in policy changes and have little, if any, incentive to promote them. Finally, the failure of some policy reforms can challenge the whole project of authoritarian modernization by undermining the president's incentive to continue major changes. It is unsurprising that after the failure of the "monetization of social benefits," the notion of reform became taboo among the Russian leadership.[84] Later on, reforms were replaced by "national projects," which proposed only an increase in financing without significant structural changes. When Putin returned to the presidential post in 2012, new rounds of large-scale socioeconomic reforms were not discussed, and after the 2014 annexation of Crimea they faded away from Russia's agenda.

From a broad perspective, the Russian experience of authoritarian modernization, as represented in the wake of policy reforms in the 2000s, demonstrates that political leaders, even those who are interested in implementing policy changes, cannot repeat the experience of successful dictators. Those who relied upon an inefficient bureaucracy as the basis of their own winning coalitions[85] are rarely ready to risk a potential political imbalance in the name of possible developmental success. Therefore, their reform strategy is often inconsistent, and the incentives to preserve the status quo are often overwhelming. In the best case, authoritarian modernization can result in a set of temporary and partial policy measures, which may at best bring only partial success in terms of the quality of governance. In the worst case, it turns into a demagogical smokescreen for the preservation of authoritarian power. As one can see, this was the case with the Russian experience in the early twenty-first century: the initial efforts of policy reforms that launched soon after 2000 later turned into words without deeds against the background of aggravation of authoritarian trends in the country. Yet there are no guarantees that possible democratization would create favorable conditions for socioeconomic reforms either; rather, it would provide new challenges. Still, I would argue that there is no reason to believe that policy reforms under the conditions of an electoral authoritarian regime and poor quality of the state can bring great fruits of improved governance in Russia and elsewhere.

CHAPTER 5

The Technocratic Traps of Policy Reforms

OW DOES POLITICS AFFECT policy and vice versa? Why are these two dimensions of political development so often at odds and how this does this relationship affect the quality of governance? Very often, power struggles, the essence of politics, inhibit efficient policies, and this is why numerous projects of policy reforms are implemented only partially and/or in a distorted way or result in unanticipated and undesired outcomes. There are many reasons for contradictions between politics and policy—including political business cycles that put policy changes between elections into question, ideational polarization of political actors whose policy priorities differ widely, and the inability to reach major policy agreements that may block any changes or even lead to policy decisions that make the situation worse than the previous status quo. Examples of the juxtaposition of politics and policy are numerous across countries and time periods. Thus, it is no wonder that many politicians, policymakers, and experts around the globe can endorse the bold statement of Russian economist and former minister of economic development Alexey Uly-ukaev: "The main question of every evolution is constraining political power: how to provide competent decision-making which will depend upon knowledge and experience and not upon voting results, and how to achieve a 'regime of non-interference' of politics in other spheres of public life."[1]

In fact, a "regime of non-interference," if and when it has been achieved in those political and institutional contexts where policy decision-making does not depend upon voting results, has seldom brought positive effects from the perspective of quality of adoption and implementing policy decisions. To a large degree, this disjunction is acute for authoritarian regimes, where voting results do not directly affect possession of political power.[2] Yet major advancements from policy reforms in authoritarian regimes are relatively rare.[3] Moreover, authoritarian leaders sometimes have a vested interest in the inefficiency of their own policies, since it may be used as a mechanism for maximizing political power—the "bad policy as good politics" paradox.[4] As I stated in the preceding

chapters, these leaders and the members of their winning coalitions are beneficiaries of the politico-economic order of bad governance and have little interest
in having it undermined from within. That said, many autocrats are proponents
of efficient policies aimed at rapid and sustainable economic growth and socioeconomic development of their respective states. In democracies, politicians
may also attempt to insulate policy from politics,[5] but the results of reforms in
various policy areas are not always in line with the expectations of supporters of
the regime of non-interference.

The unavoidable and irreconcilable contradiction between politics and policy, widely discussed in the literature,[6] has often stimulated searches for mechanisms to improve the quality of policy intended to limit its dependence on
the directions being taken by politics. Following William Easterly, I will label
these mechanisms "technocratic"—as opposed to political mechanisms, which
imply that decision-making in both politics and policy arenas is conducted by
the same legitimate actors. The goal of this chapter is to analyze the opportunities and constraints inherent to technocratic mechanisms of governance in terms
of policy-making and the effects of policy reforms on the quality of governance
in post-Soviet Russia. In the 1990s competitive and polarized politics were at
odds with market reform policy and were widely perceived as a hindrance to
economic transformation.[7] Conversely, in the 2000s, some policy advancements
in Russia were achieved at the expense of degradation of politics.[8] The insulation
of policy changes from politics has not always led to success,[9] and certain policy
outcomes paved the way for the rise of authoritarian tendencies[10] but brought
mixed results at best during the entire post-Soviet period—illustrating the inherent weaknesses of the political mechanisms for governing the state.

Explaining why following technocratic recipes has brought policy successes in
some cases and not others requires an in-depth analysis of technocratic mechanisms for governing states, one that will reveal the opportunities and constraints
inherent to technocratic policy reforms (described in chapter 4). The argument
of this chapter is that, given the key role of rent-seeking in governing post-Soviet
Russia, attempts at significant policy reform and improving the quality of governance using technocratic mechanisms meet major resistance from interest
groups and parts of the bureaucracy (who often unite their efforts in informal
coalitions). At the same time, the regime of non-interference has left little room
for the emergence of broad and sustainable pro-reform coalitions. This is why
the personal priorities of political leadership have become the main, if not the
only, source of policy reforms. Yet they are often insufficient for successful
achievement of the goals of policy changes and can even turn into an obstacle

to these reforms. The experience of policy changes in the 1990s–2010s in Russia has demonstrated the range of vicissitudes faced by the technocratic model of policy reforms in unfavorable political and institutional environments.

The structure of the chapter is as follows. After theoretical considerations regarding mechanisms of interaction between politicians, bureaucrats, and technocratic policy reformers in nondemocracies, I present an overview of some policy reforms in Russia and their implementation during the 1990s–2010s within the framework of analysis of the regime of noninterference of politics in policy. Possibilities and opportunities for realist alternatives to the technocratic model of policy-making are discussed in the conclusion.

The Technocratic Trap: Dictators, Viziers, and Eunuchs

Technocratic policy reforms are deeply embedded in global history. Most policy changes in the past, both successful and unsuccessful, were conducted in various states and nations within the framework of a technocratic model of policy-making. Political leaders exerted a firm control over politics, and due to domestic and international challenges opted for policy reforms intended to reduce costs and increase benefits, both for their countries and for themselves. But since policy reforms require professional skills and expertise, while their results are unpredictable by definition, it is no wonder that the role of reformers has been delegated to those officials and/or professionals who have certain specialized competences and may be blamed for policy failures in case of undesirable outcomes. In fact, policy reformers in various areas are similar to company managers hired by the owners (in this case, political leaders) to accomplish strictly defined tasks. With that said, policy reformers enjoy a degree of autonomy in their respective areas and are accountable only to their bosses. Political leaders, in turn, benefit from a monopoly on decision-making and policy evaluation, and therefore, can insulate the substance of the reforms from public opinion and, to some extent, from interest groups. Many historical reformers fit this description, ranging from Colbert and Turgot in absolutist France to Witte and Stolypin in Tsarist Russia, and from the "Chicago Boys" in Chile under Pinochet to the Opus Dei technocrats during the last decades of Francoist Spain.

At first sight, this institutional design facilitates the autonomy of technocratic policy-making from politics in both democracies and nondemocracies (even though the nature of politics in these regimes is different). However, it leads to an aggravation of principal-agent problems, and their scope increases with the scale of policy changes. Political leaders are unable to judge the credibility of policy proposals and the quality of their implementation. At best, feedback on policy outcomes reaches the top of the power hierarchy too late (or, conversely, too early in the case of reforms that may bring fruits only in the long term). At worst, especially in authoritarian regimes, this feedback may be heavily distorted and contribute to poor political decisions.[11] Asymmetric relationships between political leaders and technocratic reformers are similar to those between company stakeholders and managers: their interests and incentives differ hugely by definition. The alternative to the technocratic model of policy-making is the political model, which implies that legitimate political leaders and/or parties themselves develop and approve major policy decisions (though these decisions are often based on external expertise) and bear political responsibility for policy outcomes, thus being unable to shift the blame onto technocratic reformers.[12]

However, the mode of interaction between political leaders and technocratic reformers is more vulnerable in terms of principal-agent relations: policymakers concentrate the power resources involved in their own hands, and those resources can be used (or rather, abused) for political purposes. Unlike top managers of companies who cannot overthrow the stakeholders who hired them, top-level technocrats may not only betray political leaders and join the ranks of the opposition, but also even transform from policymakers to politicians and take power for themselves. These risks increase alongside challenges to the political status quo (regardless of policy outcomes), thus raising tensions between political leaders and technocratic policy reformers. Successful and capable technocrats may be even more dangerous for political leaders than their unsuccessful and incapable colleagues, especially in authoritarian settings where power losses and regime changes usually result from intraelite conflicts and breakdowns of informal ruling coalitions.[13] This is why political leaders are often tempted to prioritize the loyalty of technocratic policymakers over their competence. As Georgy Egorov and Konstantin Sonin convincingly demonstrate, the weakening of autocrats' political positions often contributes to the replacement of efficient technocrats ("viziers") with loyal yet inefficient ones, thus decreasing the quality of policy-making.[14]

Examples of betrayal of political leaders by their competent yet disloyal viziers may be considered an extreme version of aggravation of principal-agent problems. Although these practices are relatively uncommon, political leaders will still employ various techniques to prevent the disloyalty of technocratic policymakers without damaging their policy efficiency. In addition to oversight and monitoring of technocrats to reduce information costs, they also promote internal competition between state agencies and informal cliques within the state apparatus and at times constrain technocrats' freedom of decision-making. Also, some policies face a formal and/or informal veto from political leaders (these two options are not mutually exclusive but rather complementary). The windows of opportunity for technocrats regarding policy changes are limited both in terms of the policy areas to which they are granted access and in terms of the scope of their influence on policy outcomes. The weakest link here is not the development of plans and programs of reforms but their implementation by the state apparatus, which is usually not controlled by the technocrats and has little or no incentive for policy reforms regardless of their content. If the quality of the state apparatus is poor, then the technocrats' chances of successfully implementing their plans and programs (even when their hands are completely untied in conducting policy reforms) are slim. Therefore, technocrats limit themselves to partial solutions, diminishing the scope and domains of policy reforms to those specifically protected by political leaders who may grant their patronage to these changes for various reasons. These solutions are less risky in terms of disloyalty of technocratic reformers, but the benefits of the resulting policy advancements for political leaders and their countries are also far from obvious. This is why good intentions of improvements in certain policy areas may contribute to further worsening of the situation.

However, the most important challenge for technocratic policy reforms lies not along the lines of conflict between political leaders and policy reformers and is not even related to the resistance of the bureaucracy to policy changes (whether open or concealed) but arises from the policy influence of interest groups operating both within and outside the state apparatus. The gap between politics and policy-making opens a window of opportunity for "distributional coalitions"[15] and numerous rent-seekers, whereas technocrats' opportunities to build efficient informal (let alone formal) pro-reform coalitions are markedly limited. The struggle between technocratic policy reformers and rent-seekers over policy decisions was at the heart of the turbulent changes in Russia in the 1990s and the 2000s.[16] However, the subordinated status of technocrats makes them vulnerable in terms of politics. Within the framework of the political model, politicians and/or parties may use the popular mandate to launch policy reforms in at least the early stages of political business cycles. Meanwhile, under the conditions of the technocratic model, these opportunities can disappear at any given moment if rent-seekers become more influential in behind-the-scenes lobbying and/or if opponents of the reforms successfully establish coalitions of potential losers from the policy changes.[17] Although insulation of reformers from these influences may reduce the risk of policy changes being curtailed, it also reduces the political support available to technocrats and may provoke them into tacit alliances and compromises with rent-seekers.[18] In essence, technocratic reformers can reach success only when their plans coincide with the priorities and preferences of political leaders. This is why the major political resource of technocrats is their ability to sell policy recipes to political leaders using bright covers and attractive labels whenever those leaders are willing to buy their proposals. Under the conditions of the politico-economic order of bad governance, this venture is questionable to say the least, and it comes as no surprise when the reforms become unsustainable, and are ultimately distorted, diminished, or revised—and not always because of the outcomes of the actual policy. Moreover, policy failures do not so much bury technocrats' reform plans as such but diminish the chances of their implementation by the same teams of reformers.

The combination of negative features that shapes the technocratic model of policy-making are: (1) aggravation of principal-agent problems; (2) risks of disloyalty and attempts at their evasion; (3) limited resources and powers of technocrats against the background of; (4) resistance from interest groups; and (5) limited opportunities for pro-reform policy coalitions. These factors make technocratic reforms unreliable and unsustainable. Under these conditions, technocrats may fall into a trap where their overall role in policy-making diminishes over time, yet they have few opportunities to advance major changes while they still can. Policy areas and zones where positive changes are possible are reduced to a limited number of pockets of efficiency with unfavorable odds of extending them to other policy areas; while the technocrats' discretion is limited to the development of policy programs in the form of advice and consultation without power over the adoption of key policy decisions or control over their implementation.

To put it succinctly, if viziers remain loyal to political leaders but lack major leverages of influence, they may become "eunuchs" of a sort. They often maintain a formally high status that serves as a reward for loyalty and camouflages their inability to exert meaningful influence on policy-making, let alone politics, in their states. In the end, the boundary between technocrats and rent-seekers may be blurred: even if the top echelons of the Russian state agencies are staffed by professionals responsible for problem-solving,[19] their presence does not change the overall picture of bad governance. Rather, technocrats perform important functions of fool-proofing:[20] they may protect autocrats from the most dangerous policy failures, which may result from incompetence and/or their subordinates' excessively voracious rent-seeking appetites (similar to those of Yakunin, described in chapter 2). Yet under conditions of bad governance, policy reforms as such cannot become a magic bullet to diminish the negative effects of this politico-economic order. Technocrats themselves cannot improve the quality of governance, and may be not very interested in doing so, lacking strong positive performance incentives.

These flaws and limitations of the technocratic model are universal and not related to particular countries or historical periods. However, under the conditions of the politico-economic order of bad governance they are aggravated over time.[21] These factors are inescapable and push political leaders, even if they opt for policy reforms, to concentrate their efforts on a narrow front of top-priority reform projects at best and pay less attention to policy changes in other areas. In the worst cases, they are tempted to revise their priorities and to sacrifice reforms to the benefit of the coalition of bureaucrats and rent-seekers. In addition, the dependence of political leaders in Russia on "regime cycles"[22] places priority on those policy changes that may bring relatively quick positive outcomes, while long-term development plans often remain on paper. Due to these factors, even if technocratic reformers enjoy full support from political leaders and overcome resistance from rent-seekers, they are limited in the time and scope of their plans and are often convinced that their cause is hopeless from the very beginning. Policy programs are often subject to self-censorship even at the planning stage, while implementing some reforms becomes filled with bureaucratic tricks, unworkable administrative compromises, and the rejection of key elements.[23]

How does the technocratic model of policy reform in autocracies really work in general and in Russia in particular? Why does it survive regime changes, only adjusting to changing circumstances, and what is its impact on the quality of governance in Russia and elsewhere? Why do technocratic policy reforms bring success in some cases but result in failure in others? How sustainable is the technocratic model and to what extent do political models present acceptable and realistic alternatives? Some of these issues are explored and highlighted in this chapter.

The Origins and Substance of Post-Soviet Technocracy

In May 1992, two major post-Communist policy reformers—Czech prime minister Vaclav Klaus and Russian first deputy prime minister Yegor Gaidar—met in a beerhouse in Prague. According to Gaidar, their discussions about economic policy soon evolved into a heated debate on the politics of transition.[24] Klaus suggested that Gaidar and his team should not limit themselves to policy recommendations but become independent political actors who had to build their political bases of support, compete for political power, establish political parties, and participate in elections. Otherwise, Klaus warned, policy reforms in Russia could be reversed and lead to undesired outcomes. Gaidar, however, was skeptical of Klaus's recommendations and followed them only partially and inconsistently. Overall, Gaidar and the other Russian policy reformers of the 1990s served as viziers who acted under Yeltsin's patronage and (with certain exceptions) did not attempt to play an independent role in politics. Similar tendencies were observed in the 2000s, when technocratic reformers were at the forefront of policy-making in Russia but accepted the Kremlin-imposed formal and informal rules of the game in politics as given facts rather than objecting to these conditions.[25] In the 2010s and later on, technocratic reformers in Russia continued to serve as viziers, despite the dramatic shrinking of their room for maneuver in terms of policy-making. Yet many analyses of policy reforms in Russia and beyond disregard the impact of politics as a key factor in the success and failure of policy changes or attribute secondary importance to this factor.[26]

Of course, it would be unfair to explain the greater success of the economic reforms in the Czech Republic compared to Russia's policy troubles in the 1990s only through the relationship between policy and politics in both countries: their initial conditions and structural problems were also very different.[27] Moreover, Russia in the 1990s was heavily polarized in terms of politics and also experienced numerous intraelite conflicts against the background of a weakening state after the Soviet collapse. These developments left little room for conducting consistent policies, several reforms were compromised, and the decision-making process was chaotic.[28] Even if Russian policy reformers in the 1990s had not restricted themselves to the role of viziers but attempted to themselves set the political agenda, their efforts might have been even less successful in terms of policy outcomes. At best, Russia would have followed a path of "polarized democracy" similar to Bulgaria's where policy was inconsistent and inefficient amid several changes of government.[29] At worst, a defeat of the reformers in the political arena could have aggravated the negative consequences of bad policies similar to those conducted by the Soviet leadership before the collapse of the Soviet Union, thus making the situation in Russia even more chaotic. The technocratic reformers' strategic choice of the role of viziers most probably was the second-best solution. It brought certain short-term benefits for policy changes in the 1990s and 2000s. However, over time, this choice resulted in an increase in social costs for Russia in terms of both politics and policy-making.

What caused the turn of policy-making toward technocracy in post-Soviet Russia instead of choosing a political model? The post-Soviet technocratic reformers in Russia were pragmatic and skeptical of democratic procedures.[30]

Their skepticism was fueled by the experience of Gorbachev's perestroika when politics deeply affected policy-making after major liberalization of the Soviet system. Instead of the emergence of a political model of policy-making, these developments greatly contributed to the economic crisis and the subsequent collapse of the Soviet state.[31] Among the reformers themselves, democratization was perceived as a source of risks stemming from populist policies and as an obstacle to market reforms, while the insulation of government from public opinion and the patronage of a strong leader were considered preconditions for effective policy changes.[32] Due to the major economic crisis and chaotic breakup of the Soviet Union, opportunities to adopt a political model of policy-making were missed. In 1991, the Russian Parliament delegated extraordinary powers to Boris Yeltsin, who established unilateral control over government formation and policy-making, and this decision was enthusiastically approved at that time by Russia's political elite and by public opinion. This move paved the way for further institutionalization of the technocratic model, and the 1993 conflict between Yeltsin and the Russian Parliament, when the latter lost in a zero-sum manner,[33] eliminated opportunities for possible revision of this model.

The technocratic model of policy-making in Russia faced numerous problems related to the notorious inefficiency of the state apparatus and the policy influence of interest groups. The technocratic model presupposes that politics, with its formal actors and institutions, which may affect policy-making (namely voters, parties, and legislatures), should be banished from the policy arena. Yet politics also affects policy-making due to the rise of informal actors—oligarchs, cronies, friends, and followers of political leaders whose policy influence is often much greater than that of formal actors. In the 1990s, the influence of interest groups on policy-making was a side effect of the major decline of state capacity in Russia, growing pains so to speak, of the construction of new states and economies. However, in the 2000s and especially in the 2010s, this process became an indispensable part of bad governance and growing pains transformed into a chronic disease. The increasingly rent-seeking way Russia was governed discouraged policy reforms and reduced them to optional items on the policy agenda. Finally, by the 2020s, policy reforms were excluded from the menu of options altogether, although technocrats still play a major role in fool-proofing, preventing Russia's turn to further decay and degradation in terms of the quality of governance.

Meanwhile, a full-fledged insulation of policy-making from politics was unavailable in many instances: the technocratic model had little chance of realization in a pure form. At minimum, political leaders considered public support to be an important factor in the preservation of their power, thus making politics matter for policy. To a great degree, public opinion in Russia was a function of mass evaluations of policy performance,[34] and despite certain incentives for policy reforms in given areas, poor performance generated short-term risks of declining public support for political leaders due to the social costs of unpopular measures. Even relatively minor bumps on the road, such as the poorly conducted monetization of social benefits in Russia that caused the wave of public protests in 2005,[35] resulted in postponement of policy reforms in various areas. No wonder that later on the very notion of "reform" was rarely used in Russian political discourse and became synonymous with changes that bring numerous negative effects.[36] Moreover, in electoral (rather than in hegemonic) authoritarian regimes, political leaders fear loss of power due to undesired outcomes of elections.[37] These factors provide political leaders with incentives for the extensive use of the state apparatus for political purposes, ranging from delivery of votes for desirable election results to distributing influential posts and rents among allies in informal ruling coalitions. This is why barriers to policy reforms become almost insurmountable.

As a result, post-Soviet technocratic reformers found themselves between a rock and a hard place. On the one hand, political leaders and public opinion expected policy successes; on the other, their policy plans met fierce resistance from interest groups and the state apparatus. This situation contributed to privatizing gains and nationalizing costs: the costs of policy changes were imposed on society, while rent-seeking cronies of political leaders became the main beneficiaries. Technocratic reformers, even if they were able to implement their plans, rarely benefited from policies themselves, but were criticized from every corner, and their achievements could be revised due to changing political circumstances. Still, the need for social and economic development maintained demand for the presence of technocratic reformers in ministries and state agencies and called for more proposals for policy changes.[38] Yet the scope of this demand declined over time, and the supply of reforms became increasingly unwanted. According to an analysis by the Center for Strategic Research, the Strategy 2010 program of policy reforms developed by technocrats was only 36 percent implemented;[39] a follow-up policy program Strategy 2020, to some extent developed by the same expert teams in the early 2010s (and based on its predecessor's policy proposals), was curtailed and only 29 percent of its plans were implemented.[40]

Nevertheless, the same approach to strategic planning was used once again; in May 2018, after his inauguration for his fourth term, Putin signed a new collection of decrees that set strategic goals for Russia until 2024. The contents of these decrees were even less comprehensive and less concrete than those of their predecessors, but the Kremlin proudly announced that Russia was to become one of the top five global economies by 2024. In practice, this round of strategic planning in Russia faced the same institutional problems, such as poor coordination of state agencies and insufficient leverages of manual control from Putin's side. But this time, implementing the strategic plan was related to national projects: eighteen large-scale state programs were approved by the government, and huge funds were assigned to achievement of these goals. However, according to analysis done by the Audit Chamber in early 2020, most of the national projects were conducted in a rather inefficient way, and the state funds were sometimes not even spent [41] or their use did not bring the desired results. Still, the main proponent of the national projects, Putin's economic advisor Andrei Belousov, also known as the leading statist among top economic policymakers, was promoted to first deputy prime minister in 2020. Meanwhile, the economic downturn caused by the COVID-19 pandemic made many of the previously approved national projects irrelevant, and national development goals were once again brought into question. Under these conditions, the constrained political and policy autonomy of the government vis-à-vis the president diminished even further. It came as no surprise that in August 2020 Putin unilaterally and abruptly changed the national development goals he had previously established. Implementing ongoing national projects was simply postponed until 2030, a date that coincided with the end of the following presidential term (allegedly a term to be served by Putin himself). Moreover, the list of Russia's strategic targets was revised, and the much-debated statement about Russia's planned ascendance into the top five global economies suddenly disappeared from it. [42] The approach to the revision of these targets was criticized by some observers, [43] but most important, the validity of strategic planning for Russia's development was questioned, as no one took it seriously as a mechanism of setting goals for the country—at best, these plans could be considered political tools of the Kremlin rather than policy instruments. Considering this experience, the fate of new major policy programs seems uncertain at best.

Judging by the contents of policy reforms initiated by technocrats in Russia in the 1990s, 2000s, and the 2010s, one may identify these reforms as "neoliberal," as initially they were aimed at privatizing state enterprises and at diminishing state involvement in the economy. In fact, Strategy 2010 and other policy programs in Russia were greatly influenced by the neoliberal drive that was a feature of many post-Communist transformations. [44] Moreover, some technocratic reformers, such as Gaidar and members of his team, were actively involved in Russian politics under the banners of liberal parties (Russia's Choice, Democratic

Choice of Russia, and Union of Right Forces) in the period between 1993 and 2003.[45] Ulyukaev, who served as Gaidar's advisor in the early 1990s and took key governmental posts in the 2000s, may be a prime example of a reformer following such a trajectory. That said, these reformers largely remained loyal to the Kremlin, serving as viziers. This is why in the Russian context technocrats were often labeled "systemic" liberals by analysts and observers (as opposed to "non-systemic" liberals, who openly raised their voice against the Kremlin).[46] Yet such an equation of technocrats with economic liberals would be rather incorrect, if not misleading. First, many of the policies proposed by technocrats were not so neoliberal either in terms of content or outcomes, even if they were promoted under liberal slogans. The analysis of reform of Russian electricity in the 2000s conducted by Susanne Wengle convincingly demonstrated that despite the fact that Anatoly Chubais, the leading figure of the camp of Russian liberals, was the main driver of changes, its results were far from the wishes of followers of Friedrich Hayek and Milton Friedman.[47] The former nationwide electricity network, RAO UES, was divided into several subnational monopolies, which in turn, were taken over by major companies such as subsidiaries of Gazprom (in Central Russia) or aluminum giants (in Siberia) so the reform was probably not so much a matter of neoliberalism (or ideology in general) but rather of the business interests of key stakeholders. Second, a number of highly visible technocrats in Russia, such as the former presidential economic adviser Sergey Glazyev or Andrey Belousov, were not liberals at all, and may be better considered economic statists and illiberal politicians.[48] Furthermore, as Joachim Zweynert points out, liberal economic ideas in Russia remain less than popular within the expert community after a quarter century of post-Communism,[49] so labeling virtually all technocratic experts in Russia "liberals" may have little relevance for analysis of their role in policy-making.

Despite the unequivocal rejection of economic growth and development as policy goals of the Russian authorities in the 2020s,[50] one should not infer that the post-Soviet technocratic model of policy-making has been exhausted. On the contrary, it seems that under conditions of bad governance, the technocratic model finds no alternatives in Russia. The key asset of post-Soviet technocrats is their (often high-quality) professional expertise, especially in complex and technically difficult areas such as tax policies[51] or the banking sector,[52] where political leaders cannot govern without reliance upon qualified professionals. In essence, politicians want to avoid major crises in the governance of their respective countries and seek foolproof approaches at least to the economy and finance. In addition, the participation of technocrats in informal ruling coalitions may increase the sustainability of regimes: it allows political leaders to use divide-and-rule tactics vis-à-vis their junior partners[53] and reward successful technocrats who combine both loyalty and competence. The involvement of technocrats in policy decision-making is considered by economic agents (including international businesses) to be a possible barrier against the expropriation of their assets by rent-seeking bureaucrats and against arbitrary changes in the rules of the game. Thus, the promotion of reforms or even the maintenance of the status quo by technocrats serves the legitimation of the politico-economic order of bad governance and brings benefits to political leaders, and sometimes (but not always) to the technocrats themselves. At the same time, political leaders, who may be genuinely interested in policy success, can blame technocrats for undesired costs and unintended consequences of reforms, while positive results of policy changes may open up new opportunities for rent-seekers and increase the aggregate profits of the members of the informal ruling coalitions.[54] Even the potential replacement of competent technocrats with loyal yet incompetent ones (if and when it occurs) does not mean inevitable revision of the technocratic model as such, even though the quality of policy-making may decrease, thus further aggravating numerous problems of bad governance. This is why one must turn from a normative critique of the technocratic model of policy-making to its positive analysis: how it really works and why its political and policy effects are so diverse and often contradictory.

Technocracy at Work: Policy Reforms in the Crossfire

For policy reformers, there is seemingly no task more daunting than conducting major changes within the framework of the political model of policy-making. They face opposition from public opinion, the parliamentary opposition, social movements, media, and interest groups. One can imagine what might happen if major policy changes such as the introduction of the Unified State Exam (EGE)[55] in Russia in the 2000s were advanced by a government politically accountable before a legislature elected via free and fair contest. In that event, an informal coalition of angry parents, dissatisfied educational bureaucrats, and teachers and rectors of most universities would not allow the reformist minister of education to propose the draft bill on the EGE to the parliament, and opposition parties could block the proposal during floor discussions and/or attempt to revise it after the next elections. At best, this reform would be protracted, postponed, and implemented in a different format than initially developed; at worst, it could be completely buried.

Within the framework of the technocratic model, the introduction of the EGE occurred under a completely different scenario. Anticipating huge resistance from opponents of the reform, the Ministry of Education co-opted them into the group in charge of developing the National Education Doctrine (a false target, initially proposed to generate clamor without any real policy impact). At the same time, it pursued a creeping introduction of the EGE under the label of an "experiment," which set its scope to seven years. When the experiment became so widespread over the course of the 2000s that almost all school graduates were required to pass the EGE, the legal codification of this already adopted decision by the parliament become inevitable. However, the initial ideas, which proposed linking EGE results with the amount of state funding of university fees via individual state financial obligations (GIFO), were sacrificed along the way. The rejection of the GIFO was an element of the deal between technocratic reformers and members of the State Duma, in return for pledging loyalty to the EGE; in addition, the reformers themselves had little interest in introducing GIFO, it being a technically complicated venture.

At first sight, this policy outcome could be regarded as a success story for the technocratic reformers: using bureaucratic tricks and administrative maneuvering, they overcame the resistance of various interest groups and the mass public and implemented their project. Yet the EGE faced problems due to the inappropriate incentives of the subnational bureaucracy. EGE results in the regions counted toward evaluation of the performance of regional governors, thus tempting them to achieve better EGE numbers at any cost, including leakage of tests and blatant fraud.[56] Later, however, evaluation rules were changed, and as EGE results became more or less objective, the exam's introduction became irreversible. While the educational mobility of students increased, corruption in school exams declined, and university entrance exams were eliminated, major side effects became visible later. The content and meaning of the EGE degraded over time as the pressure of interest groups such as educational administrators and university managers resulted in fundamental changes. First, anonymous testing was gradually replaced by other mechanisms of evaluation oriented toward the subjective judgments of teachers and more vulnerable in terms of corruption. Second, EGE certificates, initially available for applications to various universities (such that the best school graduates could choose among them), were used for admission to only one college chosen by graduates.[57] At the end of 2016, Olga Vasilyeva, then the minister of education, announced the plan that all Russian universities would regain the right to introduce extra entrance exams in addition to the EGE, thus greatly diminishing its value. Yet, this plan is not fully implemented, however. But since many Russians perceived the EGE nega-tively, and its legitimacy was and still dubious,[58] the revision of the reform and the possible rejection of its achievements could be met with no serious resistance.

Which is a better solution in terms of policy outcomes? First, a long prepara-tory period for the reform, which involves public discussion, mutual adjustment of major stakeholders' positions, step-by-step implementation and further em-bedding; or second, a quick imposition of the reform in the format of a secret operation, bypassing key actors and public opinion, followed by further revisions and ultimate emasculation? Answering these questions requires an in-depth analysis of policy changes in comparative perspective that lies beyond the scope of this book. But in the context of post-Soviet Russia, several policy reforms combined the worst features of the two options and involved appeasing and co-opting stakeholders on the one hand and privatizing gains and socializing losses on the other. In such cases, tactical selective appeasement of stakeholders may give rise to a strategy for policy change where buying the loyalty of veto players turns from a means to an end of technocratic reforms. In that event, not only will policy outcomes become imperfect, but the legitimacy of the re-forms will come under question. The fate of large-scale privatization of state enterprises in Russia in the 1990s is instructive. Privatization was accompanied by co-opting former Soviet enterprise bosses, the so-called red directors, in ex-change for their loyalty and the use of special conditions for privatizing the most attractive assets through loans-for-shares deals. This contributed to the transfer of property rights to a limited number of oligarchs closely linked with political leaders.[59] Although in economic terms this reform was relatively successful and many privatized enterprises performed much better than state-owned compa-nies,[60] the legitimacy of privatization in Russia in the eyes of the mass public was much lower vis-à-vis some other post-Communist states. A large share of Russians endorsed en masse revision of privatization deals.[61] No wonder that the counterreform promoted by the Russian state in the 2000s, namely the creeping nationalization of assets of privatized and private-owned enterprises ("business capture"),[62] was deemed much more legitimate than privatization and reversed the reforms of the 1990s to a great degree. According to data from the Russian Federal Anti-Monopoly Service, by the end of 2016 the Russian state controlled more than 70 percent of all assets in the country's economy.[63]

Thus, reformers who pursue policy changes within the framework of the technocratic model of policy-making are caught in the crossfire of two extreme options. If they try to satisfy powerful interest groups and propose far-reaching compromises for the sake of their co-optation, these compromises may turn out to be so ineffective that the reforms do not achieve their goals. However, should the reformers outwit their opponents in the run-up to the adoption and implementation of policy programs and successfully push through their proposals, the policy changes will not be irreversible. They will potentially be easily undone by counterreforms initiated by interest groups who may restore the situation to the previous point of departure or even make it worse than the original status quo. This is why technocratic reformers often cannot limit themselves to policy-making; they must rely upon political support not only from parties and/or public opinion but also primarily from political leaders. Indeed, political leaders may be interested in successful policy reforms if these strengthen their powers and/or increase their public support. In such cases, the leaders may lead informal pro-reform policy coalitions, whether broad or narrow in nature—the recentralization of state governance in Russia in the early 2000s may serve as a prime example.[64]

However, political leaders' support for technocratic reforms is not a guarantee of policy success; even if this condition is necessary, it is not sufficient. First, leadership changes may put previous policy priorities into question (as happened in Russia with technological modernization, which was set as a top policy priority during Medvedev's presidency). Moreover, if the personal stances of political leaders shift for one reason or another, then policy priorities can even reverse direction. For example, the move by Russia's rulers from economic development goals to geopolitical adventures after the annexation of Crimea in 2014 put Russian technocratic reformers into a semi-peripheral position in terms of policy priorities, which had been changed by Putin almost overnight. However, even if political leaders sincerely support policy reforms over a long period of time, their list of top policy priorities is inherently limited. While they concentrate on supporting several major policy changes, the rest of the items on the policy agenda will remain of secondary importance. The other side of the coin in the success story of tax reform in Russia in the early 2000s, actively backed by Putin,[65] was the failure or at least limited advancement of several other policy reforms.

The support of political leaders is vitally important for technocrats because it gives them leverage for overcoming resistance to policy reforms by powerful interest groups. Sometimes, even this support is not enough; strong and embedded interest groups can divert policy changes in a different direction. This is what happened with police reform in Russia in the early 2010s: despite open and loud public discussion (or perhaps courtesy of this discussion) the outcome of the reform was essentially limited to window dressing and the reshuffling of some personnel.[66] And even if political leaders reduce interest groups' resistance to policy changes, technocrats are rarely able to impose control over the bureaucrats in charge of implementing policy—especially if these policies require interaction and effective coordination of various agencies.[67] It is not by chance that while the Ministry of Finance and the Central Bank of Russia were able to conduct successful macroeconomic policies, target inflation, and implement tax reforms,[68] welfare policies in Russia were conducted in "muddling through" mode and/or merely redistributed federal state subsidies.[69] The main difference was that governing state finance and policy reforms in this area depended on decisions made by a narrow circle of technocrats, and their formal and informal coordination enabled prudent policies; whereas welfare policies required complex coordination not of several persons but of various state agencies on both national and subnational levels. Given the poor quality of the bureaucracy and weak incentives for reforms, it was exceedingly difficult to achieve sustainable coordination, and even the efforts of the technocrats and political leaders were not enough to resolve these issues.

It is thus unsurprising that to technocrats, the most attractive mechanism for implementing policy reforms is the creation of pockets of efficiency—separate organizations with large funding and discretion that can play according to special rules of the game, beyond general principles of state regulations and have more room for maneuvering in conducting policy reforms. For example, implementing large-scale privatization of state enterprises in Russia in the 1990s became possible only because of the establishment of the State Property Committee (Goskomimushchestvo), a powerful vertically integrated agency that had the exclusive right to organize the sale of state assets and was controlled by the team of technocratic reformers led by Chubais.[70] Despite the fact that the central government of Russia in the 1990s had weak leverages of control vis-à-vis regional authorities, Goskomimushchestvo, using the sticks of threats and the carrots of bonuses, was able to conduct a federal program of privatization in most of Russia's regions (with some notable exceptions such as Moscow City and Tatarstan). Moreover, Goskomimushchestvo, using various tricks, was not only able to squeeze legal approval of its proposals through government, parliament, and the presidential administration, but also to acquire broad discretion in its activities, thus becoming a "state within the state."[71] However, after the end of privatization and Chubais's following removal from several top positions in the government, the influence of Goskomimushchestvo and its successor agencies greatly declined. The formal institutionalization of pockets of efficiency may be supplemented by informal mechanisms of their patronage by political leaders who may support their beloved pet projects in various areas. There are many examples of such projects,[72] and some of them have brought certain positive effects. Overall, however, political patronage is vulnerable as a mechanism for promotion of policy reforms because of its informal nature and dependence on political circumstances.

To summarize, one might argue that the imperfect technocratic model of policy-making cannot preserve many reforms (even under favorable political conditions) from partial and inconsistent implementation, emasculation, major revision, or even complete reversal. In the case of the political model, parties and their leaders can correct errors after certain policy failures and relaunch policy reforms under new conditions during one of the subsequent political business cycles. But for technocratic reformers, whose professional credibility depends on their reputation in the eyes of their bosses—namely political leaders—a second chance may never come. This fact produces incentives to use windows of opportunity only to conduct those policy reforms that can bring immediate positive effects. Conversely, policy changes oriented toward long-term advancements may be postponed or result in unworkable compromises. Against the background of the success story of tax reform in Russia in the early 2000s,[73] the failure of the pension reform launched during the same period[74] is a telling example. Changes in the tax system benefited the Russian state and its rulers soon after inception in the early 2000s; whereas the pension reform assumed benefits only in the long run and generated costs for individuals and companies because of the proposed transition to an accumulative pension system and the increase in the age of retirement. Since the technocratic reformers and political leaders who had initially supported the reforms had little interest in adopting and implementing policies that might only bring significant returns decades later, and the bureaucracy as a veto player insisted on preservation of the status quo, debates on pension reform resulted in a compromise aiming to satisfy the major actors. A partial and contradictory 2002 pension reform did not solve any problems but only postponed them, even though the conditions for major changes seem to have become less and less favorable over time. Overall, however, the choice of short-term priorities for policy reform reflected the fact that many post-Soviet leaders have tended to behave, in Olson's terms, as "roving" rather than "stationary" bandits.[75] Their horizons of policy planning have rarely exceeded the next election cycle, while transitions to hereditary succession of power are unlikely.

Thus, the imperfect technocratic model of policy-making faces major and irresistible constraints. On the one hand, technocratic reformers and their patrons among the political leaders prioritize policy reforms with short-term positive effects at the expense of long-term programs. On the other hand, the poor quality of the bureaucracy and the influence of interest groups distort the goals and means of policy changes and negatively affect policy outcomes. Even if technocratic tricks (quasi-experimentation, creating special conditions for reforms under the political patronage of leaders, co-optation, and compromises in the form of sacrificing some reform projects) have brought certain successes, their price may be prohibitively high in terms of irreversibility of policy changes. But even if one admits these flaws and defects of the technocratic model of policy-making, to what extent are alternatives to this model possible, desirable, and realistic, and what are their effects?

Alternatives to Technocracy: No Way Out?

What would happen in Russia if for whatever reasons policy reforms in all areas were abandoned and technocrats only maintained the status quo in crucially important policy fields? Most probably, in the short term neither the political leaders nor the ordinary citizens would notice anything important. They might even breathe a sigh of relief because they were tired of the numerous successful and unsuccessful policy reforms over the last quarter century. The negative effects of the persistence of the status quo bias might be observed only in the medium term and/or after a change of political leadership. Policy reforms and mechanisms for their conduct would eventually be at the center of the political agenda, and alternatives to the imperfect technocratic model of policy-making would be discussed once again.

From the viewpoint of many analysts and the technocrats themselves,[76] the most plausible solution is a correction of the defects of the technocratic model of policy-making aimed at its improvement. One may consider incentivizing bureaucratic performance through competition between agents, constraining the discretion of certain state agencies and revising their powers and, as the most radical solution, the replacement of "bad" political leaders, whose informal ruling coalitions are packed with rent-seekers, with "good" reform-minded and less corrupt autocrats. The problem, however, is that successful policy reforms in autocracies are relatively rare not only because of the personal traits of the political leaders but also because the incentives presented to them have left little chance of fixing the inherent defects of the imperfect technocratic model and transforming it into a perfect one. But even recruitment en masse of the best and brightest professionals into the ranks of policy reformers cannot guarantee that the major problems of the technocratic model will be resolved. Quite the opposite, the poor quality of the bureaucracy and the dominance of rent-seeking interest groups make attempts to improve the technocratic model questionable: they may result in the expansion of (already rigid) state overregulation and in the increase of the discretion of state watchdogs and law enforcement agencies.[77] These changes may create new obstacles to policy reforms instead of the existing ones, or even in addition to them.

But what of the odds of a hypothetical transition from the imperfect technocratic model of policy-making to the political model bringing positive outcomes? In the short-term perspective, these odds are rather dubious. The experience of post-Communist Moldova and Ukraine (especially after 2014) tells us that politically accountable governments, even if they are formed through free and fair elections, are often no better at conducting policy reforms than technocratic cabinets of ministers. In these cases, the risks of state capture from outside, by oligarchic interest groups who compete with one another over rent-seeking, are high, and policy reforms may be blocked even if they are a priority for political leaders. A chain of weak, inefficient, and corrupt cabinets of ministers is not an attractive alternative to the technocratic model. Another risk of such a transition is the aggravation of principal-agent problems within a predatory piranha-like state apparatus[78] and a possible shift toward decentralized corruption, which is justly considered even more dangerous than centralized corruption.[79] In addition, the political model means that politically accountable governments may be hijacked by economic populists who may try to exploit the popular mandate to conduct inefficient policies. It may take Russia to numerous failures from the viewpoint of policy outcomes under conditions of bad governance, and temptations and risks of this kind may increase over time.

However, in the case of present-day Russia, both improvement of the imperfect technocratic model of policy-making and transition to the political model appear unrealistic. Since the political regime in the country is far from being in a full-scale crisis, its incentives are not toward change but toward preservation of the status quo. This is why the main alternative to policy reforms in Russia is further appeasement of rent-seekers and further sluggish development if not stagnation.[80] The sad fate of Ulyukaev, the major proponent of post-Soviet technocracy, may serve as a prime example of this tendency. In November 2016 Ulyukaev, who was minister of economic development at the time, was fired and later sentenced to eight years in jail due to accusations of bribery during the process of privatizing a large block of shares of the state-owned oil company Rosneft. According to media reports, Ulyukaev, who had consistently objected to the government giving preferential treatment to state-owned companies and raised his voice against the proposed mechanism of privatization of Rosneft, was most probably not guilty of these criminal charges. Meanwhile, soon after Ulyukaev's dismissal, the Rosneft block of shares was privatized in a nontransparent and suspicious way: the state-owned Gazprombank offered credit to two foreign investors in exchange for being loaned these shares. Just before this deal, Rosneft-egaz (the holding company that controlled Rosneft shares) had put a large deposit into Gazprombank, so that this money was used to fund the privatization deal. Some observers even compared this model to the infamous loans-for-shares deals of the 1990s.[81] The outcome of this deal was an increase in the influence of Igor Sechin, Putin's close ally and CEO of the Rosneft, who was notorious as a highly voracious rent-seeker even in the rather grim context of Russian crony capitalism. Ulyukaev, who stood for other policy priorities, was sacrificed to the interests of rent-seekers with the consent of Russia's political leadership. This episode (like many others of its kind) was hardly conducive to policy reform.

Ironically, Ulyukaev's own statement, made more than two decades before his downfall, turned out to be prophetic. In the case of the privatization of Rosneft's block of shares (and many others), the decision-making was quite competent and did indeed "depend upon knowledge and experience but not upon voting results." The problem was that the competence, knowledge, and experience of rent-seekers was much more important than the competence, knowledge, and experience of Ulyukaev and the other Russian technocratic reformers. While attempting to avoid the negative effects of politics on policy-making and "to achieve a 'regime of non-interference' of politics in other spheres of public life," technocrats found themselves caught in a trap: policy-making was affected by more negative influences, while politics only aggravated these problems. Under these conditions, the technocratic cure became more dangerous than the disease of bad governance, and it remains to be seen whether Russia will find a more efficacious one.

CHAPTER 6

Success Stories amid Bad Governance

WHILE THIS BOOK DESCRIBES present-day Russia as a case of bad governance, the main objection to this description is related to the fact that Russia (both now and in the past) has demonstrated certain major achievements of state policies in various fields, and some state-directed projects and programs may be labeled success stories in international comparisons. Recent achievements of this kind have been analyzed at the level of several of Russia's regions,[1] of certain sectors of the economy (such as agriculture),[2] and of some state agencies (such as the Central Bank).[3] Their impact is important and visible enough that one should not dismiss these cases merely as minor and negligible exceptions, the specifics of which only confirm the overall rules of bad governance. At minimum, one must pose a question about the causes and mechanisms that allow major successes amid the grim picture of notorious inefficiency, ubiquitous corruption, and widespread rent-seeking involved in governing the Russian state. Moreover, the in-depth deviant case analyses of these outliers will aid in a better understanding of the general trends of bad governance through identification of its limits. In other words, when and under which conditions can the state happily turn from bad governance to good governance, at least for a while, and why may such a wondrous conversion occur in certain cases when in others it does not?

The literature on developmental policies beyond the global West has paid attention to "pockets of efficiency"[4] or "pockets of effectiveness"[5]—state-directed priority projects that are intentionally designed and implemented under special conditions under the patronage of political leaders. Some of these projects have brought not only short-term successes but also major long-term returns and outlived their initial conditions and intentions. However, the list of possible causes of such success stories is quite diverse and includes several organizational, institutional, and technological factors, and quality of management and personnel, which often tend to be considered country-specific and context-bounded.[6] Similar tendencies might be relevant for research on Russia. For example, in his comprehensive overview of innovation projects in pre-Soviet, Soviet, and post-Soviet Russia, Loren Graham focuses on the efforts of certain creative individuals and collective drivers of technological progress vis-à-vis the rigid system of state governance and the political and institutional environment, which was unfavorable for developmental projects.[7] Although it is hard to object to these observations, his focus of analysis leaves unanswered the question of why state policies sometimes paved the way to major breakthroughs (such as the Soviet space project, briefly mentioned by Graham), while other times they resulted only in a waste of resources? The analysis of success stories faces not only the need for conceptual homogenization of a diverse empirical field even within the same country (let alone cross-national research) but also the framing of theoretical and disciplinary scholarly perspectives. For Barbara Geddes, the explanation of pockets of efficiency in Brazil and other Latin American states is driven entirely by institutional accounts;[8] the comparative analysis of Michael Roll mostly focuses on the political leadership and organizational settings;[9] and Graham, in turn, offers a path-dependent perspective on exceptional successes in Russia amid numerous failures.[10] Thus, instead of generalization of analyses of success stories, the research agenda meets with increasing fragmentation.

This chapter does not aim to present universal and comprehensive explanations of success stories in Russia and beyond but proposes a slightly different view on the causes and mechanisms of these phenomena. I argue that effectively implementing priority projects and programs by the Russian state might be understood as the other side of the coin of bad governance. First, the political leadership under conditions of bad governance needs success stories of national development, not only in terms of policies but also as a tool of politics due to their effects on domestic and international legitimation of regimes and leaders. Second, the actual achievements of success stories may perform the functions of both material and symbolic conspicuous consumption in the eyes of elites and masses alike. Meanwhile, political demand for success stories provides certain incentives for policy entrepreneurs among mid-range and top-level bureaucrats who may pursue their upward career mobility and/or priority status and funding while also working toward achieving some broadly defined developmental goals.[11] The problem, however, is that these incentives for policy entrepreneurs are often unsustainable because of their dependence upon patronage from political leaders, making institutionalization of success stories a difficult task. Moreover, given the fact that some success stories are often implemented under special deliberately designed conditions, their multiplicative effects, or trigger effects[12]—that is, the extension of success stories to other projects, organizations, sectors, or regions—are relatively rare. Due to these constraints, some success stories were short-lived, and their returns diminished over time: they not only failed to improve conditions of bad governance but in fact even reinforced the status quo. These tendencies are widespread in contemporary Russia and in its Soviet (if not pre-Soviet) past; they do not contradict the overall pattern of bad governance in the country and may even serve as inherent attributes of this politico-economic order.

The structure of the chapter is as follows. After presenting the case of one of the most well-known success stories in Russia, the Soviet space program, I discuss the role and impact of success stories under conditions of bad governance and emphasize their constraints, which are related to the priorities of the political leadership, the incentives of policy entrepreneurs, and the mechanisms for managing top priority projects against the background of a shortage of resources. Further, I focus on the dilemmas of state policies under bad governance in Russia and highlight the effects of diminishing returns of success stories due to these constraints. The prospects and implications of success stories for Russia's development are considered in the conclusion.

"But We Are Making Rockets"

Before turning to an analysis of the story of success and the story of failure of the Soviet period, one important disclaimer is necessary. As argued in chapter 2, I consider bad governance in present-day Russia to be a product of interest-driven rent-seeking efforts of post-Soviet leaders and elites rather than an effect of various legacies of the past. At first glance, the focus on certain examples from the 1950s–1960s may seem to contradict this argument. However, the rationale of the case studies presented below is a little different. I refer to them in order to explore the issue of the causes of extraordinary achievements amid the overall mediocrity of the government's performance, regardless of the nature of the poor quality of governance. Even though the political system and economic foundations of governing the Soviet Union after Stalin[13] were quite different from those in Russia in the early twenty-first century, it would not be a wild exaggeration to claim that both the Soviet Union and present-day Russia have underperformed in terms of quality of their governance, albeit for different reasons and with different consequences for the respective countries. This is why looking at the relatively rare examples of outstanding overperformance of state-driven programs and projects in different political and institutional contexts may help us to understand why good apples may grow on bad apple trees, even though the trees we are looking at may be of different sorts.

It is hard to find a more salient example of a developmental success story in post-World War II Soviet history than the space program with its exceptional achievements such as the first Sputnik orbital launch (1957) and the first human mission in space, conducted by Yuri Gagarin (1961).[14] This success story was greatly appreciated at the time and is still perceived positively by many Russians: according to a 2008 nationwide mass survey, it was rated as the second most important event in Russian history after victory in the Great Patriotic War of 1941–1945.[15] Indeed, the advancements of the space program served as a profound demonstration of the technological progress of the Soviet Union and contributed to an attractive domestic and international image of the country and its political leadership within the context of the Cold War. However, the success of the Soviet space program was short-lived: the major breakthrough of the 1950s–1960s turned into a plateau in the 1970s–1980s, its material and symbolic returns diminished over time, and subsequent events after the Soviet collapse contributed to Russia's recent shift toward the second echelon of the global space superpowers. What were the causes of this trajectory, and why is the experience of the Soviet space program important for understanding the strong and weak sides of success stories in Russia, both in the Soviet and in the post-Soviet period?[16]

The success of the Soviet space program would have been impossible without the efforts of two key individuals. The chief designer Sergei Korolev (1907–1966) was not only an outstanding organizer of science and technology who effectively coordinated a huge number of individuals and organizations and brilliantly implemented quite a few technologically complex and innovative devices and solutions; he was also (if not above all) a successful policy entrepreneur who was able to persuade Nikita Khrushchev to make the space program as a whole and especially a human mission in space his personal top policy priority.[17] Khrushchev, in turn, desperately needed success stories, especially in the early stages of his leadership when he was pursuing domestic and international legitimation and took major risks that proved to be justified in the case of the space program.[18] Khrushchev was emotional, ill-tempered, and not a very competent leader: he often advanced certain policy innovations that brought only limited success (as in case of the Virgin Lands agricultural program), and even trusted charlatans such as the (in)famous academician Trofim Lysenko.[19] The implementation of the Soviet space program, and especially of human space missions, was an expensive extension of the rocket segment of the arms race, and a possible defeat on this front vis-à-vis the United States (driven by differences in the resource endowment and relative economic weights of the two countries) could have proved sensitive for the Soviets in many ways. However, Khrushchev accepted these risks and provided his personal patronage to the space program and top priority funding for human space missions, despite fierce resistance from the Soviet military.[20]

The outcome of these efforts greatly exceeded the wildest dreams of both Korolev and his political patron Khrushchev. The Soviet Union won twice on the space front because of the successful launch of Sputnik and especially Gagarin's orbital flight against the background of a belated start by their American rivals who had lagged at the beginning of the space program and had been faced with numerous technical problems. The outstanding success of the early stages of the Soviet space program opened new horizons for Korolev and his team: they received carte blanche to implement its new stages, of which the first and foremost was the human mission to the Moon, where the Soviet Union entered competition with the United States known as the "Moon race." As for Khrushchev, the symbolic benefits that he (and the Soviet Union as a whole) received because of the successes of the space program and its demonstrative effects, multiplied by domestic and international propaganda,[21] were highly visible, especially given the increasing scope of the numerous problems the Soviet leadership faced in the early 1960s. However, the symbolic benefits brought to the Soviets by Sputnik and Gagarin only partially compensated for the high political and economic costs of the Berlin Wall, the Cuban missile crisis, the shootings at workers' protest rallies in Novocherkassk, and the need to buy grain from abroad.[22] Even then, these benefits were short-term, and their positive effects were only temporary.

There are no "if" paths of alternative history, and we will never know how the Soviet-American Moon race might have gone had the Khrushchev-Korolev tandem's drive behind the Soviet space program continued. However, the ousting of Khrushchev from the Soviet leadership in October 1964 became a turning point for his top priorities, including the Soviet space program. Soon after that, under pressure from military-industrial lobbyists, the plans for the space program were reviewed in favor of their military component, while costly human space missions lost their priority.[23] In fact, the Soviet Union left the Moon race well before the Apollo program in the United States was implemented in a full-fledged way and before it reached its peak in July 1969 with man's first step on the Moon. The events that followed this departure, such as Korolev's premature death in January 1966, the chain of casualties during human space missions in April 1967 and in June 1971,[24] and Gagarin's death in a plane crash in March 1968, contributed to the space program gradually losing the status of success story for the Soviet Union. On a symbolic level, the struggle for space leadership with the United States was framed as a kind of draw, with the symbolic gesture of the joint Apollo-Soyuz space mission in July 1975. Yet in military terms, the space rivalry with the United States continued, and it became more and more of a heavy burden for the Soviets. In technological terms the Soviet Union was not able to demonstrate new major breakthroughs and put them into mass production; while the United States successfully launched its new Space Shuttle program in 1981, the Soviet response, Buran, did not even reach the stage of human missions.[25]

In essence, up until the collapse of the USSR, the Soviet space program followed a pathway of improving those technological solutions that had been proposed and/or implemented in Korolev's times. More important, the multiplicative effects of the Soviet space program remained limited: the major success story of the Soviet Union on the space front did not contribute to new major success stories in other fields that would have a genuine strong impact on the country's development. The Soviet space program remained a somewhat isolated "pocket of efficiency,"[26] and beyond this narrow field, its influence was relatively weak: no major multiplicative effects[27] were observed—quite the opposite, bureaucratic ineffectiveness became greater and greater over time against the background of the increasing crisis of the Soviet economy.[28] The one-off high returns of the Soviet success story in space declined over time, and its previous achievements increasingly performed symbolic compensatory functions, something visible as early as 1964, the heyday of the Soviet space boom. At that time, the Soviet bard Yuri Vizbor in his song "The Story of Technologist Petukhov" (*Rasskaz tekhnologa Petukhova*) identified himself with Soviet technological and cultural achievements on behalf of the protagonist, who proudly stated: "But we are making rockets . . . and also at the top of the world in the field of ballet" (*zato my delaem rakety . . . a takzhe v oblasti baleta my vperedi planety vsei*). Yet the keyword in this claim is not "rockets": it is "but" (*zato*). It is also worth noting that half a century after Vizbor, in 2014 the keyword "but" performed the same compensatory function after the Russian annexation of Crimea, in the form of the popular slogan "But Crimea Is Ours!" (*Zato Krym nash!*).

To summarize, one might argue that the Soviet space program followed a developmental trajectory that was typical for a number of other success stories in Russia and beyond: (1) top policy prioritization by political leaders who actively supported new projects and programs and offered full-scale patronage to policy entrepreneurs; (2) quick achievement of visible results because of the high concentration of resources, with a number of symbolic returns; (3) limited multiplicative effects; (4) change in policy priorities (sometimes because of changes of leaders and/or top managers of these projects and programs); and (5) subsequent loss of the status of success story.

In many ways, the success story of the Soviet space program remains outstanding against the background of other technological advancements that were not converted into major achievements due to the lack of high-level patronage and/or other policy priorities of political leadership. Benjamin Peters in his in-depth analysis of the failure of Soviet Internet presents impressive evidence of what may happen to promising ideas if they do not receive strong enough political support.[29] He focuses on the sad fate of Soviet mathematician Viktor Glushkov, the major promoter of building a "unified information network," the potential predecessor of, if not alternative to, the present-day Internet. Glushkov, a director of the Kiev Institute of Cybernetics, proposed the development of an All-State Automated System of Management (OGAS) that could pave the way to making a nationwide computer network as the main tool of governing the Soviet Union. However, Glushkov's patrons in the Soviet bureaucracy were second-order state officials at the level of ministries and the Central Statistical Agency, while the top leaders, Brezhnev and Kosygin, remained indifferent to his project at best. In addition, the powerful Soviet minister of finance, Vasily Garbuzov, openly opposed OGAS, and in the end Glushkov fell victim to interagency rivalry. The OGAS proposal was never implemented, so the Soviet Union, which in the 1960s was very much at the state-of-the-art global level in this field, gradually lagged behind the West over the subsequent decades, and this gap was never overcome. The Soviet model of governance, with its hierarchy of the power vertical, greatly contributed to such an outcome; unlike the space program, the Soviet Internet did not turn into a success story.

Yet this trajectory of success story is not limited to the context of the Soviet experience of the 1950s–1980s, as one may compare the Soviet space program with the more recent experience of the Skolkovo innovation center in the 2010s: Skolkovo went through the same stages but in a more rapid way and with much smaller effects. During the presidency of Dmitry Medvedev this project served as a major symbol of the widely advertised plan for Russia's technological modernization, was at the center of the president's attention and was given priority funding by the state and business actors despite the great skepticism of some key stakeholders.[30] The project aimed to achieve a breakthrough for Russia in the field of high technology, and was intended to build a new success story of international technological collaboration based on active involvement of global corporate and science leaders, ranging from Intel to MIT. However, the implementation of this project was limited in space (only a single suburban area near Moscow) and in time (only during Medvedev's presidency) and oriented toward short-term public effects in the manner of a showcase, rather than toward long-term commercial benefits and technological advancements.[31] It is no wonder that after 2012, when Medvedev lost his presidential position, the Skolkovo project stalled and lost its priority status, its funding declined as the Russian authorities no longer required major donations to Skolkovo from big business, and its initially planned role as a major driver of high technology and economic growth was all but forgotten. Subsequent developments, such as the deterioration of Russia's relations with the West, the stagnation of the Russian economy and the devaluation of national currency, further weakened the already limited effects of the Skolkovo project. In 2013, the Russian law enforcement agencies launched a criminal investigation against the Skolkovo Foundation, accusing its top management of misuse of funds,[32] while the Kremlin's preferences in the field of high tech shifted to yet another pet project, namely the "Innovation Valley" of Moscow State University, which was conducted in collaboration with the Innopraktika Foundation, led by Katerina Tikhonova, who was labeled in the media as allegedly being the daughter of Vladimir Putin. This foundation has received major contracts from other large state companies and state agencies, but its activities remain highly nontransparent, with little by way of results visible yet. Some critics have observed that the replication of Skolkovo-type innovation projects in Moscow and other regions may be driven not by the goals of technological development but rather by intentions of diverting state funds into private pockets.[33] Although the decline of Skolkovo was much more rapid and dramatic than that of the Soviet space program, they represent typologically similar phenomena of former success stories.

While analyses of pockets of efficiency as mechanisms of development conducted in Asia, Africa, and Latin America[34] have underlined the key role of their institutionalization and long-term impact, Russia's success stories are largely short-term ventures, ones that face major difficulties in their institutionalization and especially impersonalization. Over time, these "success stories" tend to lose their initially high-profile positions and undergo what has been labeled "bastardization" in the chapter 2 of this book—a systematic worsening in performance in the process of implementation and subsequent decay.[35] One should note, however, that this chapter deals with real success stories, which are broadly understood here as achievements of outstanding overperformance of state-directed development programs and projects, highly visible nationally and/or internationally for at least a certain period. It is not concerned with various substitutes for real successes, such as Potemkin village-like fake demonstrative projects, or numerous examples of fraud (such as the "cotton affair" in late Soviet Uzbekistan, doping scandals in sports, and the like). Real success stories are meant to promote Russia's development in various fields, but they are often implemented partially and inconsistently. This is why we have to understand why Russia's success stories have not always reached their goals and have resulted in short-term achievements and how the mechanisms of their implementation are related to the overall logic of the politico-economic order of bad governance in Russia.

Actors, Institutions, and Incentives

The key ingredients of successful developmental projects and programs in the public sector in Russia and beyond are top priority support from the political leadership, effective efforts by policy entrepreneurs (ministers, governors, city mayors, university rectors, company managers, and the like), and the competent provision of these projects with material, financial, and personnel resources. However, all of these components often bring contradictory results. The incentives for both the political leadership and policy entrepreneurs are mixed at best, and resources, even if their concentration is high enough to achieve some success stories, are insufficient for subsequent multiplicative effects and further dissemination of best practices.

The political leadership under conditions of bad governance is interested in success stories for two main reasons. First, as stated above, some policy achievements help to legitimize the political status quo: despite the well-known argument that bad policy is almost always good politics,[36] many political leaders are interested in the economic growth and development of their countries, and Russia is not an exception. Second, even though rent-seeking is the main goal and substantive purpose of state governance in Russia, this fact does not prevent leaders and elites from pursuing developmental goals that may also contribute to rent-seeking. Several major state-led projects and programs accompanied by large-scale embezzlement of funds (such as the 2014 Sochi Olympics) may illustrate this combination of rent-seeking and developmental goals.[37] These projects are not limited to rent-seeking and are also aimed at bringing some returns in terms of development, although these returns are often relatively small because of the high costs imposed by corruption. Similar to the political leaders' demand for successful technocratic managers, who have to provide effective policies in key sectors of the economy and finance (analyzed in chapter 5), these leaders also need policy entrepreneurs who are capable not only of routinely implementing top-down directives but also of successfully advancing their own initiatives. Pet projects and programs directly supported by political leaders become the main sources of several success stories, paving the way for investment of major resources (both public and private) into these ventures and opening possibilities for special state regulations of given projects and programs well beyond the general practices and routines of decision-making. Such rules of the game were typical both for the Soviet space program and for the Skolkovo project. The conditions of informal deals between patrons (political leaders) and their clients (policy entrepreneurs) imply top priority resource endowment and carte blanche for policy entrepreneurs on virtually all initiatives in their respective fields in exchange for promises of quick and highly visible policy successes. However, the list of such top priorities for any given political leader is limited practically by definition, and this is why policy entrepreneurs are often forced to compete with one another for scarce state resources and for meaningful attention from political leaders. Moreover, a change in the leaders' policy priorities (let alone a change in leaders themselves) threatens to put an end to these projects and programs (as happened with the Skolkovo project) or at least put a large question mark over success stories (as happened with the Soviet space program).

One of the central problems of the politico-economic order of bad governance in Russia is the lack of incentives for long-term development among political leaders. As I noted in previous chapters of this book, their time horizon is limited by the terms and conditions of personalist rule and by the risk of losing power, while the chances for dynastic succession are low,[38] and this is why political leaders tend to behave similarly to "roving" rather than "stationary" bandits.[39] In doing so, they choose those policy priorities that may bring quick and visible returns accompanied by a number of demonstrative effects, even at the expense of achieving long-term strategic goals. This approach may contribute to policy successes in some fields but decreases the chances of successfully implementing policy changes in other areas. The experience of Russia's policy reforms in the 2000s (analyzed in chapter 4) and subsequent implementation of strategic policy programs in the 2010s[40] suggests that while the incentives of political leaders are oriented toward short-term successes, these incentives also affect policy entrepreneurs.

Top managers and major implementers of key state projects and programs, even if they are willing and able to improve performance in their respective fields, are not sure that their intentions will be implemented given frequent personnel replacements, the ever-changing formal and informal rules of the game, and the shifting priorities of the political leadership. These circumstances also determine the incentives for would-be policy entrepreneurs. At best, they invest major efforts into short-term projects with limited reach at the expense of long-term outcomes and consequences, or in the worst case, they prefer personal enrichment over the developmental success of their sectors, organizations, or territories. The problem of creating an appropriate set of incentives to shape the behavior of state officials remains unresolved as the political-economic order of bad governance in Russia places a large question mark over the incentives. Unlike Russia, present-day China provides certain incentives for policy entrepreneurship among top-and mid-level bureaucrats. Such incentives are provided by the institutional systems for career advancement of the Communist Party's regional leadership based on performance evaluation, including interregional mobility of personnel and such major prizes as chances of obtaining jobs in the Central Committee. Chinese provincial officials have to put effort into the successful socioeconomic development of their territories, while their fierce internal competition for career advancement diminishes the risks of systematic misreporting and fraud given the mutual policing among bureaucrats.[41] For Russia's regional leaders, however, the incentives are rather different—as Ora John Reuter and Graeme Robertson convincingly demonstrated, Russia's governors more often lose their jobs for poor political performance and failure to deliver votes than for poor economic performance in terms of developing their areas.[42] To summarize, if a Chinese regional boss may achieve success by building new roads and hospitals and combatting air pollution, his Russian counterpart has to inflate voter turnout and crack down on regional protests. These different incentives aggravate rent-seeking behavior in Russia and are hardly conducive to development; in a sense, they also underline the inefficiency of electoral authoritarianism in Russia compared to its hegemonic version in China.

It is no wonder that incentives for policy entrepreneurship in Russia are so heavily distorted, and not only due to insufficient positive incentives for improving policy performance and limited chances for upward career mobility in the public sector. The effects of negative incentives, driven by the set of formal and informal rules of the game and practices of their enforcement within the framework of the "overregulated state" in Russia,[43] are even more important in this respect. The combination of high density and low quality of state regulations in various sectors and policy fields on the one hand, and of its arbitrary and selective enforcement by the state apparatus on the other, is inimical to policy entrepreneurship. The Russian state reasonably expects that without top-down pressure the lower layers of the power vertical will not invest enough effort to effectively implement state policies. This is why the government delegates wide-ranging and sweeping powers to regulatory agencies responsible for monitoring and auditing any organization in various sectors. Furthermore, the government has established multiple indicators to report on and impose severe sanctions for noncompliance, at all levels of governance. In other words, instead of involving regulatory agencies in the activities of both state-led and private organizations only in cases of extraordinary misconduct (the "fire alarm" model), the Russian state has imposed comprehensive monitoring and tight control over all organizations (the "police patrol" model).[44] To some extent, such an approach results from an overreaction by the political leadership to rent-seeking behavior of officials in the state apparatus and public sector. Its excessive conduct contributes to a major rise in agency costs, distorted practices of oversight and monitoring among various agencies, and the increasing dysfunctionality of courts, police, and other state organizations.[45] These practices of the "overregulated state" provide incentives for overproduction of reports in many state and private organizations, and response to possible attacks from state agencies has even changed to be the primary function of their activities. The overregulated state stimulates top managers at all layers of the power vertical not to policy entrepreneurship and improvement of performance in their fields, but rather to risk aversion and avoiding possible punishment for any formal or informal violations of rules, which are highly likely in the case of development-oriented initiatives. This is why top managers do not aim to establish new pockets of efficiency without strong support and the patronage of the political leadership. The problem is that the number of beneficiaries of patronage is limited by its very nature, and the pool of potentially successful policy entrepreneurs is shrinking over time. Moreover, patronage is a necessary condition of success stories, but it is far from being sufficient. For example, the significant development of a major Russian bank, Sberbank, which greatly improved the quality of its service and performance, was a side effect of the appointment of German Gref, a close ally and trusted expert of Vladimir Putin, as its CEO.[46] At the same time, chapter 2 presented the case of another close ally of Putin, Vladimir Yakunin, who upon being appointed as CEO of another major Russian company, Russian Railways, changed the company strategy and turned it into a major channel for rent extraction. The strengthening of the hierarchy of the power vertical has contributed to the fact that the investment of resources into the projects lobbied for by several top managers has brought insufficient returns and/or resulted in a

massive misuse of funds. As a result, these tendencies make the power vertical
even more stable and rigid at the expense of developmental goals.

Finally, the shortage of material, financial, and personnel resources available
to top managers of state-directed projects and programs remains a major barrier
to achieving new success stories. Russia was and still is a second-order country
in terms of its degree of socioeconomic development, and its stated intentions to
become a global space leader (in the case of the Soviet space program) or a leading international center of high technology (in the case of Skolkovo) were hardly
feasible in the long term. Top managers, in turn, respond to these constraints
by using an overconcentration of resources. The costs of success stories are high,
implementing top-priority projects requires mobilizing almost all available specialists, and meeting deadlines turns into a sequence of hasty activities, often at
the expense of quality of implementation. Despite the high costs, overconcentrating resources may sometimes help achieve one-off successes, but the problems
stated above can become aggravated over time. Successes, once achieved through
overconcentrating resources, become more difficult to maintain, especially given
the competition between projects within the country and in the international
arena (as in fact happened with the Soviet space program). In essence, overconcentrating resources bleeds other projects and programs that lack priority status.
This is why plans of secondary importance may be ignored or forgotten because
of little interest from the top leadership (as the failure of OGAS tells us). Multiplicative effects become even less feasible, and negative incentives for outsiders,
who now have no chance to produce success stories, become even stronger. As a
result, the success of the few causes the failures of the many: overconcentrating
resources leads to draining the pool of potential targets for disseminating best
practices beyond pockets of efficiency.

To summarize, one might argue that success stories in Russia (and several
other countries) face numerous barriers, both structural ones caused by a shortage of resources and institutional ones related to agency-driven incentives under
conditions of bad governance. Nevertheless, in cases where there is a winning
combination of the policy priorities and patronage of political leaders and strong
and effective policy entrepreneurs who can achieve quick and visible performance in their projects and programs, even these institutions and incentives may
contribute to certain success stories despite unfavorable conditions. Yet the same
institutions and incentives may close the path to multiplicative effects of success
stories and dissemination of their best practices beyond narrow fields prioritized
by the authorities. Rather, as the experience of both the Soviet space program
and the Skolkovo project suggests, success stories may lose their excellence over

time and no longer maintain their special status. The Russian state and its top officials create with their own hands the same syndrome of unfavorable conditions for implementing top priority projects and programs that were outlined by Loren Graham in his historical analysis of barriers to innovation in Russian businesses[47]—excessive costs of projects, inefficient state regulations, and weak potential for multiplicative effects. This is why many success stories in Russia are not exceptions that still conform to the overall rules of bad governance, but rather an integral part of this politico-economic order. The high achievements of success stories do not only legitimate political leaders and their patronage. Their demonstrative effects and compensatory functions also legitimate the mechanisms of these achievements against the background of the numerous pathologies and ineffectiveness of the Russian state. However, one should not consider success stories to be only short-term initiatives by political leaders that have negligible impact on the development of the country and/or sectors of its economy and territories.

The Anatomy of Success: The Higher School of Economics

A number of factors that have contributed to the achievement of certain success stories in Russia are not particularly country-specific, whether within the context of post-Communist transformations[48] or in other parts of the globe.[49] Overall, effective policy entrepreneurs, thanks to the patronage of the political leadership, are able to maintain organizational autonomy of their projects, programs, organizations, or territories, and due to quickly achieving positive outcomes, attract more resources and effectively invest them into new successes. These actions lead to increasing returns and successful maintenance of organizational autonomy and further institutionalization and organizational continuity despite changes in top management and the political leadership. However, in Russia's case, this recipe works imperfectly given the contradictory features of authoritarianism and bad governance; and this is why some success stories should be analyzed with a number of reservations.

One case of systematic construction of a success story in post-Soviet Russia that may be considered exemplary in this respect is the Higher School of Economics (HSE; a National Research University since 2009).[50] The university was established from zero in November 1992 when acting Prime Minister Yegor Gaidar signed a decree on the creation of a new economic training center for personnel working under the conditions of a market economy. The founding rector, Yaroslav Kuzminov, established the core of the HSE's team in relatively short order and attracted almost all the prominent market-oriented economic experts and many officials from the government.[51] The figure of Yevgeny Yasin, an authoritative economist of the older generation who served as minister of economy in Russia and later took the post of academic director of the HSE,[52] was representative of this recruitment pattern. In 1999–2000, Kuzminov and other representatives of the HSE were at the center of the development of the Strategy 2010 program of socioeconomic reforms adopted by the Russian government, and subsequently the informal status of the HSE was greatly elevated.[53] It became the major brain trust of liberal reformers,[54] and policy-oriented projects ordered by the government and other state agencies became a visible part of the HSE's activities and an important source of its revenues.[55] Under the influence of the HSE, a number of policy innovations were launched in various fields, such as implementing the Unified State Exam.[56] Kuzminov became a prominent public figure, often considered a prospective candidate for various posts in the government, but kept his job at the HSE; however in 2014, he was elected to the Moscow City Duma (a legislative assembly), and in 2015 became a cochair of the Moscow branch of United People's Front, a major pro-Putin organization. Kuzminov's wife, Elvira Nabiullina, served as minister of economic development and then as a chair of the Central Bank of Russia; in other words, their personal union was intertwined with top-level political connections. Kuzminov was also at the center of a network of economic experts closely linked to the Russian government and often labeled "systemic liberals" in the media. He was the codirector of development of a new governmental program, Strategy 2020,[57] and actively participated in preparing several of Putin's decrees on issues of socioeconomic development. At the same time, top state officials served as the HSE's trustees, regularly gave talks at its annual conferences, and supported this organization in various forms, ranging from state contracts to new office buildings. While the HSE initiated several state-directed projects and programs, it also became one of its major beneficiaries, both directly and indirectly.

In fact, Kuzminov turned out to be a successful policy entrepreneur: he invested resources effectively into the market advancement of the HSE and attracted various new sources for development of the organization, including tuition fees and contracts from businesses and from the state agencies. In the 2000s, the HSE grew extensively, taking over several educational establishments, expanding its regional campuses in Saint Petersburg, Perm, and Nizhny Novgorod, and incorporating several buildings in Moscow and later in Saint Petersburg. From its beginnings as a small, specialized training program in economics, it became one of Russia's largest universities:[58] its scholarly profile went beyond social sciences and humanities and included math and computer science. These achievements contributed to a great increase in its international visibility,[59] which attracted several international academic stars as heads of its projects and laboratories (who stated their HSE affiliation in their academic publications) and resulted in effective incentives for its lecturers and researchers. These incentives included juicy carrots such as HSE internal grants and individual bonuses for publication in leading international journals and other achievements, and hard sticks such as short-term contracts that allowed university managers to easily replace inefficient and/or undesired personnel. This combination enabled the HSE to attract both leading scholars and prospective young researchers who had previously worked in other institutions in Russia and abroad and to get rid of scholars with poor publication records. Even HSE's academic critics recognized its achievements.[60] To summarize, a high degree of autonomy, effective organizational leadership, and skillful patronage became the major pillars of the HSE's success.

Against the background of a worsening domestic and international political and economic climate, especially after 2014, the success of the university, which is based on the principles of international integration, academic freedom, and self-governance, has faced increasing challenges. HSE has followed a "too big to fail" strategy throughout its extensive growth as an organization, which has reduced some of the risks. However, the political risks for a "liberal" university under the auspices of top state officials, who formed the HSE Board of Trustees, have remained high. Major contradictions have become visible since the summer of 2019. At that time, the HSE Department of Political Science merged with the Department of Public Administration, with simultaneous termination of the job contracts of some professors of the former political science department, who had gained a strong reputation as liberal political analysts and vocal critics of Russia's authorities.[61] This process was initiated by HSE vice rector Valeria Kasamara (a political scientist herself), who argued that the university should stay beyond politics in terms of partisanship; her claim, however, was perceived as a call for self-censorship.[62] Furthermore, Kasamara herself balloted as an independent candidate for the Moscow City Duma, endorsed by the city hall, while the denial of registration to opposition candidates caused mass protests. Among several protesters arrested, a young libertarian activist and Kasamara's own undergraduate student at the HSE, political scientist Yegor Zhukov, soon became a symbol of these contradictions.[63] In the end, Kasamara lost the election to an opposition-backed candidate, and Zhukov soon received a probation and was released from prison. In response, in early 2020, the HSE changed its internal regulations, cancelled support for several student initiatives, and requested that its scholars and staff avoid mentioning HSE affiliation in their public rhetoric and activities that go beyond their immediate professional duties. Soon after that, under the guise of ongoing reorganizations, HSE terminated job contracts for several of its publicly visible professors and lecturers who openly criticized Russia's authorities and their policies, especially in the media. These political compromises, however, did not help the HSE preserve the previous status quo. In the end, in July 2021, Kuzminov resigned from the rector's post and passed HSE leadership to his successor Nikita Anisimov, a former rector of the Far Eastern State University. To what extent this departure marked the end of the HSE as a success story remains to be seen.

Overall, the HSE success story was to a great degree related to Kuzminov's personal performance,[64] and given the increasing challenges and declining time horizon for further planning, the chances of the institutionalization and impersonalization of this success story have diminished over time. Even though any conclusions about this success story would be premature, one must admit that the HSE's success was exceptional and has contributed only to a limited multiplicative effect on other higher education establishments in Russia, and the state resources that the HSE has (deservedly) attracted for its development have not been received by other state universities. But does this mean that the handful of success stories under bad governance are always doomed to remain isolated islands of high-quality development amid a sea of mediocrity, while the managers of other state-directed projects and programs are forced to keep muddling through?

The "5–100" Project: Why Successes Are Rare

To some extent, the project of multiplying success stories and disseminating best practices in higher education, as attempted by the Russian authorities in the 2010s, helps understand why success stories are so rare in Russia and beyond. The "5–100" state project aimed to promote five Russian universities into the top 100 of the global rankings of higher education organizations by 2020.[65] This project was approved by the president and government of Russia; it involved a number of Russian state universities, as selected by a special commission, receiving state subsidies for the purpose of their development, which could then help with their advancement in international rankings. The main driver of the project, launched in 2012 after Putin's presidential decree and officially approved in 2013, was the Ministry of Education and Science, led by Dmitry Livanov, an active supporter of reforming science and education in Russia and especially of internationalization of Russian scholarship.[66] The "5–100" project also generated ideas that were included in the government's Strategy 2020 program developed by Kuzminov and his team, and in turn, aimed to disseminate the best practices of the HSE.[67] This direction was chosen as a top policy priority by Russia's political leadership because of a winning combination of several factors. First, at that moment, Russia's leaders were still pursuing a strategy of authoritarian modernization (outlined in chapter 3) that included successful growth and development as an objective of governing the country (at least, at the level of rhetoric), and advancing higher education perfectly fit these goals. Second, the "5–100" project was not invented out of the blue but served as a logical extension of the establishment of federal and national research universities in Russia in the 2000s, which were considered "growth poles" in the higher education sector.[68] Third, the elevation of Russian universities to the heights of global rankings could have visible demonstrative effects and could perform the function of conspicuous consumption of symbolic goods by the Russian leadership and elites. It could also perform compensatory functions, outweighing the major notorious defects of Russian higher education, which range from widespread corruption to poor quality of university governance, research, and teaching.[69]

The start of the "5–100" project was promising. The Russian state assigned fifty-seven billion rubles for its implementation in 2013–2017 and added slightly more funds later. The Ministry of Education and Science, with the help of an international board, selected twenty-one state universities to participate in the project, including the HSE and the Moscow Institute of Steel and Alloys (Livanov had served as rector of this institution before taking his ministerial post). All these universities presented roadmaps to implement the "5–100" project, which involved a significant rise in the proportion of international students and scholars, a major increase in the quantity and quality of academic publications (particularly in international scholarly outlets), and several other steps. However, two leading institutions, the Moscow State and Saint Petersburg State Universities, were deliberately excluded from the project. The formal argument was related to the fact that these universities already occupied top positions in global rankings, but this move also made it possible to exclude their influential rectors from being involved in the venture (which was especially true in the case of Viktor Sadovnichiy, the notoriously isolationist rector of Moscow State University). Putin's patronage of the project enabled it to maintain its budget (relatively high by Russia's standards), despite cuts in some of the ministry's expenditures at the end of 2014. However, the advancement of Russian universities in global rankings soon faced major challenges.

First and foremost, the "5–100" project was too short-term in terms of its time horizon: it was measured in years rather than in decades, like the Project 211 and Project 985 in China, which aimed to achieve similar goals of global advancement of Chinese universities.[70] But such a long planning horizon was unrealistic for Russia, because the political leadership does not consider potential benefits in such a distant future. The fact that the achievement of the project's goals by 2020 was perceived as impossible by top managers and participants in the project greatly affected all incentives—the community of leaders of Russian higher education was interested not in achieving the final results but in demonstrating partial and temporary advancements at the level of interim reporting. The scope of funding for the "5–100" project was also insufficient for its ambitious goals, especially because its resources were spread among more than twenty recipient universities. Finally, the mechanism for implementing the project and the requirements imposed on universities by the Russian state did not involve irreversible structural and institutional changes to university governance, let alone an increase in their organizational autonomy aimed at successful long-term development of these institutions after the end of the project. It is no wonder that some of the universities included in the "5–100" project perceived it as a one-off massive inflow of state funds, a kind of sizeable gift, which should be met with appropriate reporting on publications and internationalization and nothing more. Even when some university-level policy entrepreneurs initiated innovative ventures, they faced a shortage of resources, limited time horizons, and multiple tensions with scholars and administrators. This is why, for example, the ambitious School of Advanced Studies at Tyumen State University (one of the beneficiaries of the "5–100" project) has encountered major schisms and conflicts, and it is highly doubtful whether it can fulfill its great promises.[71]

In addition to these problems, the project faced challenges of a different kind. After 2014, the policy priorities of Russia's political leadership shifted from developmental goals to geopolitical adventures. The project, aimed at international integration of Russian higher education, poorly fit these new priorities. In 2016, Livanov, the major driver of the "5–100" project, was fired from his ministerial post, while his successors had limited bureaucratic influence and demonstrated little interest in their predecessor's initiatives. Later, however, in the wake of reorganizing state agencies, the project came under the auspices of the Ministry of Science and Higher Education, and in early 2020, Valery Falkov, the former rector of Tyumen State University, was appointed as a minister. Overall, however, the success of the "5–100" project was mixed at best; although advancement of the Russian universities in global rankings was visible,[72] it was insufficient to achieve the project's goals. However, the HSE and some other institutions greatly improved their positions in the rankings for several disciplines. In some cases, however, efforts to improve global rankings at any cost brought undesired effects, such as contracts between Russian universities and consulting firms that were themselves involved in making international university rankings: this was justly considered a conflict of interest.[73]

The prospects for further extension of the "5–100" project in somewhat different format (also known as Priority 2030)[74] look rather questionable. While one should not deny the major progress made by some Russian institutions of higher education, especially regarding internationalization and publications, and the emergence of some university-driven initiatives beyond the HSE, these achievements have not resulted in qualitative changes to the landscape of Russian higher education (at least, as of yet) and have not given rise to a cumulative effect of successful development of the sector. None of the universities involved have demonstrated achievements comparable with those of the HSE, and its best practices have been disseminated only with significant difficulties.

The experience of "5–100" has demonstrated the problems with transferring success stories beyond their initial contexts. The dissemination of best practices is one of the instances of policy diffusion that are aimed at institutional isomorphism, "a constraining process that forces one unit in a population to resemble other units that face the same set of environmental conditions."[75] Scholars have outlined three types of diffusions that lead to this outcome, namely coercive, mimetic, and normative. Coercive diffusion, promoted by the state, has the strongest effect on the behavior of individuals and organizations, especially in authoritarian settings. Yet coercion is hardly an effective means of achieving success stories, especially when negative incentives are weak (there are no repressions in Russia for inefficient top managers in the public sector even in cases of total failure), and its long-term positive incentives are questionable. Mimetic diffusion, when the top leadership chooses role models from a menu of possible options, is also problematic given the low organizational autonomy of state-led projects and programs. Finally, normative diffusion emanates from sources that are perceived to be "legitimate and reputable."[76] These sources of isomorphism are complementary, but under conditions of bad governance, none of them contribute appropriately to dissemination of best practices. The normative sources and role models for top managers are not successful policy entrepreneurs, but rather successful rent-seekers; in the public sector, they dream of behaving like Yakunin rather than like Gref. Without top-down pressure, the dissemination of best practices by top managers of companies and organizations may result in their prosecution by the overregulated state, especially if they achieve success. Furthermore, coercive diffusion rarely coincides with resource endowment, which is necessary to achieve and maintain success stories, and this is why these pressures may lead to short-term campaigns or attenuate the best practices, which may result in less-than-best consequences. Moreover, state-led projects and programs that lose priority status and/or funding become vulnerable to the threat of normative and mimetic diffusion from role models of rent-seeking and passive adjustment to ever-changing state regulations and producing meaningless reporting. In such situations, coercive diffusion from the state toward former (or failed) success stories, alongside personnel reshuffling, may contribute to their bastardization and make it irreversible.

This skeptical account should be read with certain caveats: the cases analyzed in this chapter are based in certain policy fields and may be regarded as affected by their peculiarities, and this is why any generalization of conclusions from the achievements and the shortcomings of success stories will be only possible upon further research. This does not mean that sustainable success stories and/or dissemination of best practices in the public sector in Russia are impossible or doomed to be isolated islands that do not meaningfully affect the overall dismal picture. However, the overall role of success stories in Russia's development should be reconsidered, not only here and now but in a longer-term perspective.

On the Use and Abuse of Success Stories

The (in)famous argument that Russia is a "normal country"[77] has been objected to on various grounds. Among them, the claims widely used in public discussions concern Russia's numerous global achievements in different fields ranging from arts to sports. Yet if one were to consider normality as a statistical rather than a substantive phenomenon, then the average scores would not take any outliers into account. Similar to a school class, where the only A-student will barely affect overall grades given a majority of C-students, the extraordinary achievements of certain success stories do not make the country great against the background of modest progress in other fields. Moreover, most of these great Russian successes were achieved in the distant past, and they cannot serve as a free pass once and forever. Still, constant references to success stories, especially in the public discourse on Russia, to a certain degree tend to smooth out overall discontent with the country's mediocre performance and drive discussions on its causes and effects onto the periphery of the attention of elites and masses alike. This is why overemphasizing success stories at the expense of interest in the political, economic, and social environment beyond them has contributed to the continuity of bad governance and even legitimated this politico-economic order. In reality, certain success stories were achieved not because of the overall conditions of bad governance but because these projects and programs were implemented under special conditions. In a sense, the compensatory functions of some success stories in Russia and beyond may be also considered as manifestations of mediocrity syndrome in the country.[78]

In fact, Russia, an average country of the twenty-first century, has most probably exhausted the potential of its infrastructural and personnel resources for success stories on the global scale comparable with those of the Soviet space program. It is highly likely that Russia's current and possibly future success stories are doomed to be limited to certain niches. But insofar as the institutions and incentives that emerged in the Soviet and in post-Soviet periods encouraged high demand for success stories among political leaders and society at large, we might expect a recurrent tendency of state-led programs and projects aimed at such achievements. At best, these success stories can bring only partial and temporary successes, and at worst, they may come to naught (as happened with Skolkovo) or even lead to the opposite result, as with the Sochi Olympics and their numerous doping scandals.[79]

However, attempts to diminish the pernicious effects of bad governance, if and when they occur in Russia, may contribute to a decline in purposeful state sponsorship of success stories for several reasons, including a shortage of the infrastructural and personnel resources that are necessary for achievements of this kind. The question is to what extent this shift in using resources will enable the Russian authorities to change the very paradigm of development and switch from an orientation toward a small number of extraordinary and highly visible achievements to the improvement of quality of socioeconomic development? Such a move may lay foundations not for separate success stories with weak multiplicative effects at the expense of everything else, but for gradual advancement of the country toward better performance. The lack of change in the paradigm of development increases the risk that Russia's success stories in the twenty-first century will remain matters of the past—in all likelihood, forever.

CHAPTER 7

The Politics of Bad Governance

Russia in Comparative Perspective

B Y THE EARLY 2020S, Russia has seemingly entered the mature stage of its bad governance. Its authoritarian regime has been consolidated, while rent-seeking and corruption within the framework of the power vertical and the overregulated state are perceived as the only mechanisms for governing the Russian state—not only by state officials but also by a significant portion of Russian society at large.[1] There is a dismal consensus among most observers that bad governance under durable authoritarianism in Russia will persist for decades (if not forever) and book titles such as "Will Putin's System Survive until 2042?"[2] have become nearly ubiquitous. At best, scholars express some hope for the long-term effects of economic growth, which alongside generational changes, may lay down favorable conditions for democratization in Russia some decades from now.[3] Economic experts, however, express skeptical opinions about Russia's prospects for sustainable growth and development in times of low oil prices and international sanctions, especially given the priorities of the country's leadership.[4] Even the political scientists' cautiously positive outlook reminds one of a statement by the nineteenth-century Russian poet Nikolay Nekrasov who predicted the bright yet distant future of Russia in his *The Railway* (1864): "Alas! That the day of our joyful tomorrow // I shall not witness—and neither shall you."[5]

In a broader perspective, these expectations reflect global concerns about the future of democracy and good governance worldwide amid the rise of authoritarian populism, which is harmful for politics and governance alike.[6] However, the current dismal consensus among scholars over prospects for democracy and good governance in the world (and especially in Russia) is not entirely new. In a way, it looks like a replica of the previous dismal consensus of the 1970s. This was the time when the negative consequences of the Vietnam War and

Watergate were considered major threats to the Western world much more than the effects of Brexit and the Trump presidency are today, when the dead end of stagflation was perceived as a predictor of the coming decline if not complete collapse of capitalism, and when almost nobody believed that Communism would end relatively soon. During these years, prominent scholars published alarmist reports about the irresolvable global crisis of democracy and capitalism, and overwhelming determinism dominated in skeptical accounts of the future of freedoms in developing countries[7]—all things that sound much too familiar to present-day observers. In the late 1980s, these fears turned into major hopes and high expectations, most probably demonstrating a dramatic if ill-thought-through shift from unreasonable pessimism to unreasonable optimism. These lessons from the 1970s and how the dismal consensus was overcome over the next decade—both in political and in scholarly terms—may be useful for re-assessing the current state of governance in Russia and some of its post-Soviet neighbors and its further prospects against the background of declining quality of governance in various parts of the globe. To what extent are the sources and mechanisms of bad governance in Russia outlined in the previous chapters of this book country-specific and context-bounded, as opposed to representing an ongoing global trend? How does Russia's post-Soviet experience of bad governance look in a broader comparative perspective? Which lessons may be learned from attempts to constrain bad governance in various countries, and may some of these lessons be learned in Russia? Why and how may bad governance in Russia prove its resilience vis-à-vis major exogenous shocks such as the epidemic of COVID-19 that struck all over the world in 2020? And what might we expect for the future of Russia in terms of the quality of governance? This chapter will not provide comprehensive answers to all these questions but intends to put them into a research agenda. It is an important exercise given the recent boom of studies of Russian politics and governance in the United States and beyond.[8] The need for new frameworks for analysis of bad governance in Russia in a comparative perspective instead of the present-day dismal consensus is also important for further development of a research agenda and may have implications beyond the region of Eurasia.

I will start with some considerations on where governance in Russia is now and what we might expect for the future, using the conceptual lenses of "political decay" outlined first by Samuel P. Huntington[9] and more recently by Francis Fukuyama.[10] Then I will discuss recent attempts to diminish the most pernicious effects of bad governance in some countries and why some of these attempts have generated more positive effects than others. In the concluding sections, I will consider the role of bad governance in Russia's response to COVID-19 and possible developments of political changes in Russia and their influence on the quality of governance.

Bad Governance and Political Decay: beyond Russia

Within the intellectual tradition of modernization studies, political development is juxtaposed with political decay, the process that leads to increasing inefficiency of social and political institutions: over time, either these institutions lose their role as rules of the game in a given society or, more often, following these rules contributes to further degradation of societies in terms of development.[11] In a way, long-standing institutions can be considered structural constraints on the behaviour of individuals, including political and economic actors. In such a long-term perspective, the focus on institutions in the process of political decay mostly concentrates on their major flaws stemming from an outdated nature and excessive rigidity (usually inherited from the past), which may not respond appropriately to new challenges. In the historical perspective of *longue durée*, such an account may be correct. However, for a short-term horizon there is a tendency to consider institutions (primarily, formal rather than informal institutions)[12] as given facts without an in-depth analysis of their genesis and evolution. Meanwhile, the analysis presented in this book offers a perspective on the role of institutions in political decay through the lenses of an agency-driven process of institution-building. In this respect, bad governance as an intentional outcome of this process may be regarded as an instance of political decay, albeit from a different perspective to those previously offered by scholars of modernization.

Political decay as a consequence of agency-driven processes is not unique to Russia; in fact, many self-interested rulers would like to govern their domains without the significant constraints imposed on them both in democracies and in non-democracies. In the turbulent times of the twenty-first century, they have often gained excellent opportunities to reach these goals and establish a politico-economic order of bad governance in various states and nations. In particular, the wave of popular discontent with the status quo, which gave birth to various populist movements and political leaders across the globe from Europe to Latin America, has contributed to their drive toward bad governance in pursuit of self-interest.[13] Regardless of their origins (scholars differ greatly in their analyses of causes of contemporary populism),[14] these leaders tend to distort existing institutions and/or rearrange them in order to exploit public resources for private purposes. Numerous examples ranging from Venezuela under Hugo

Chavez and Nicolas Maduro[15] to Turkey under Recep Tayyip Erdogan[16] are quite telling in this respect. If such leaders face little or no resistance from other political and economic actors and from society at large, they may follow the path of the Russian leaders in building and strengthening bad governance. This does not necessarily mean that present-day Russia intentionally acts as a role model for other countries and exports bad governance abroad as a part of its foreign policy strategy,[17] but there is no doubt that a number of politicians all over the world only dream of enjoying the scope of discretion available to Vladimir Putin.

In many ways, the recent experience of Donald Trump's presidency could be regarded as an attempt to impose elements of bad governance on the United States.[18] In placing his family members and personal cronies in key positions in the state apparatus, using American diplomacy as a tool for obtaining *kompromat* (compromising materials)[19] on his political rivals, obstructing justice, and turning state regulations into weapons for his political dominance. However, Trump has faced strong resistance from various corners of society. American politicians, bureaucrats, media, and civil society actors have opposed his intentions and somewhat diminished the possible negative impact of Trump's strategy: as of yet, they have not been able to build new major barriers against making bad governance but have also not let him eliminate all existing ones. This is why Trump's effects on the quality of governance in the United States were less devastating than they could have been in many other countries under similar leadership. In the end, Trump's poor handling of the pandemic crisis caused by COVID-19, as well as other instances of his misbehavior, contributed to his loss in the 2020 presidential contest. Given the resilience of many long-standing institutions (including fair elections, constitutional checks and balances and federalism) and the pluralism of political and economic actors, American politics prevented poisoning of its governance in the most dangerous forms, similar to those in Russia—although the experience of Trump presidency was costly for the United States in many ways.

But what can happen when institutions that can present barriers to bad governance are weak and insufficiently resilient, while resistance to populist politicians is insufficient? The recent experience of Hungary might be a prime example of such a path toward political decay. Although this country underwent the collapse of Communism and went through the process of democratization and market reforms relatively peacefully, it faced major challenges in the aftermath of the 2008–2009 global economic crisis.[20] Soon after that, the post-Communist political elite was heavily discredited and the economic strategy of global integration via implementation of neoliberal policies[21] lost its appeal in the eyes of

major actors and society at large. Against this background, Viktor Orban and
his centre-right party Fidesz gained popular support because of their fierce criticism of the previous developments in Hungarian politics and won a majority in
the parliament in 2010. Since that time, the Hungarian political landscape has
changed dramatically. Orban conducted judicial counterreforms, making judges
solely dependent upon political appointments, imposed strict state control over
the major media, put severe constraints on foreign-funded NGOs, and initiated harsh pressure on the Central European University (CEU) established and
funded by Hungarian-born global billionaire George Soros—in the end, CEU
was forced to relocate from Budapest to Vienna. While actively using national-
ist and anti-European rhetoric to boost his popularity, Orban effectively chan-
neled European funds to strengthen his power base, and overall enjoyed many
benefits from his strategy of financial nationalism[22] and other illiberal populist policies.[23] It comes as no surprise that Fidesz-related businesses obtained
major benefits from Orban's rule, while the quality of governance in Hungary
in the 2010s deteriorated, especially with regard to corruption and the rule of
law.[24] Despite numerous mass protests against monopolizing power and other
antidemocratic moves by the government, Orban retained strong leverages of
control. Although in 2019 an opposition-backed candidate managed to win the
Budapest mayoral election, the new regulations imposed by the Hungarian government made him powerless, as all resources were transferred into the hands of
government-appointed officials. Naturally, in the wake of the initial COVID-19
outbreak in April 2020, Orban effectively seized the moment to increase his
formal and informal powers and widen the scope of his control over key sectors
of the Hungarian economy.[25]

The Hungarian scholar Balint Magyar labels the politico-economic order
established in Hungary after 2010 the "mafia state."[26] This pejorative term was
mostly coined to be eye-catching for readers, and its validity as an analytic tool
may be objected to on various grounds.[27] However, the phenomenon itself may
be regarded as one instance of agency-driven efforts to build and consolidate
bad governance. Despite numerous peculiar features of the Hungarian case, described by Magyar in great detail, Hungary's path toward bad governance is not
so dissimilar to that of Russia (in fact, Magyar himself extended his analysis to
some other post-Communist countries).[28] Even though in the 1990s and 2000s
Hungary was perceived by many sympathetic observers as a poster child for successful development and European integration, it was not able to obtain strong
enough immunity against intentionally creating bad governance. Although in
the Hungarian case the populist style of Orban and Fidesz served as a tool for

demolishing barriers against bad governance, while in Russia Putin's policies were largely antipopulist,[29] these differences tell us more about the instruments for the creation of bad governance than about its actual mechanisms.

One should consider that political decay caused by bad governance should not be equated to the collapse of the state, at least in the relative short term. Rather, political decay may launch a long-term downward trajectory of economic and societal development over time.[30] The main problem with this trajectory is that it has proved to be resistant to correction: once the politico-economic order of bad governance is built and consolidated, all moves toward overcoming it will become more and more difficult. At a certain point, this downward trajectory may become irreversible despite all efforts, causing a lock-in effect. This basically means that the countries poisoned by bad governance may find no way out: this is why the parallel with chronic diseases, outlined earlier, might be relevant for those countries that are deeply affected by bad governance over a long period of time. Even though their leaders and elites may realize that the pernicious effects of bad governance are dangerous not only for the futures of their countries but may also harm their own interests, they tend to avoid the use of the bitter medicine of major political and institutional changes, especially in a nondemocratic context. William Easterly vividly describes this paradox in his analysis of countries of sub-Saharan Africa.[31] From this perspective, contemporary Russia may be considered a prime example of imperfect recipes for improving the quality of governance without major changes.

Bad Governance in Russia: No Way Out?

By the early 2020s, preservation of the political status quo for as long as possible and avoidance of any threats of regime changes in Russia became the key element of the Kremlin's political strategy. The ongoing process of tightening the screws in Russia's domestic politics (started after the 2011–2012 wave of mass protests) reduced the risks of the regime's implosion due to public discontent,[32] and despite some bumps on the road in terms of undesired results at subnational elections, the Kremlin was more or less insulated from unpleasant surprises from the Russian voters. The slow pace of economic development in Russia and international sanctions have not significantly changed this picture: like many authoritarian regimes across the globe,[33] Russia was not heavily sensitive to the near stagnation of its economy (slightly above 1 percent annual growth between 2014 and 2019) and a decline in real incomes of its citizens. Even unpopular policy decisions, such as the major increase in retirement age for Russians, adopted in

2018,[34] only resulted in a temporary decline in Putin's approval rate and did not shake the existing political equilibrium.

It is no wonder that under these circumstances, the extension of Putin's stay in power for an indefinite period became the number one priority task for the Kremlin. In January 2020, Putin announced a major revision of the Russian 1993 constitution in his annual state of the nation address. Initially, the handful of proposed amendments was rather vague, but it implied further empowering the president at the expense of the government and the legislature. The most decisive constitutional amendment was proposed in March 2020 and stated that upon the introduction of the new set of amendments, previous presidential terms in office were nullified, and the limit of two six-year terms should apply only after the next presidential elections scheduled for 2024. In fact, these constitutional changes, approved by the legislature, mean that Putin could stay in power until 2036.[35] Such a constitutional rearrangement in Russia is hardly unique among personalist autocracies across the globe,[36] as several rulers in Africa or in post-Soviet Eurasia have used similar institutional tricks to ensure their stay in power for indefinitely long periods of time.[37]

Unsurprisingly, the Kremlin's intention to prevent political changes in Russia at any cost further contributed to political decay in the country, thus leading to aggravation of already acute problems with the quality of governance. Nevertheless, Russia's leaders did not ignore these problems completely and often raised these issues as priorities for their agenda. They offered several recipes to improve the quality of governance in Russia, which may be summarized as a combination of three major directions, or 3D: deregulation, digitalization, and decentralization. However, these recipes in themselves and their actual implementation seem like imperfect approaches to countering bad governance in Russia.

Deregulation as an instrument for improving the quality of governance in Russia is vigorously advocated by liberal economists, especially in the aftermath of the 2008–2009 global economic crisis.[38] The problem, however, is twofold. First, despite the loud rhetoric of state officials who call for a "regulatory guillotine,"[39] the outcomes of many revisions of numerous by-laws and governmental decrees are selective, partial, and insignificant as of yet: entrenched bureaucrats and special interest groups have little incentive to revise the existing status quo. In terms of policy reforms, the insulation of the Russian government from the influence of societal actors, cultivated since the early 2000s,[40] has demonstrated its dark side. Major policy changes, though necessary, can be conducted in Russia only by those state actors who pursue their own self-interest and may deliver unintended policy outcomes.[41] For example, it was hard to expect that deregulation in Russian academia would be conducted effectively by the same actors who previously contributed to its overregulation and imposed dubious practices of oversight and evaluation.[42] Moreover, as deregulation remains a matter of discretion on the part of the regulators themselves, these efforts may even result in perverse effects such as "regulatory capture."[43] Very telling in this respect is the experience of RZhD, which almost unilaterally imposed high commuter services tariffs onto the shoulders of regional budgets, while being endorsed by the Russian government (as described in chapter 2). In 2020, the Russian government proposed a bill that involved a sweeping elimination of all previous environmental regulations, except for those approved by the government. This proposal could bury state requirements for environmental accountability of businesses and norms of disclosure of negative environmental effects of economic activities, ruin any fair methodology for assessing ecological damages, and severely limit the regulatory functions and monitoring of state environmental watchdog agencies. Only after a series of alarming calls from environmental activists,[44] approval of this proposal has been postponed and later on stopped at least for a while. In fact, however, this happened not because of the ultimate importance of environmental issues for the government, but rather because the overall framework of the regulatory guillotine had not been sufficiently prepared, and the process of interagency negotiations within the state bureaucracy took more time than was initially expected by its initiators. That said, it is highly likely that the environmental concerns will not stop the regulatory guillotine or change its major directions. Even the most socially efficient deregulation can at best reduce some of the risks for policy entrepreneurship crated by the negative incentives within the power vertical. However, it cannot in itself provide positive incentives for improving the quality of governance, given prioritization of loyalty over efficiency and the lack of transparent meritocratic mechanisms for rewards and career advancements within the Russian state.

Digitalization became a new buzzword among Russian state officials and technocratic experts in the mid-2010s. The advancement of algorithmic governance (driven by artificial intelligence rather than by self-interested humans) is widely perceived as a mechanism for constraining the rent-seeking aspirations of special interest groups and for improving the effectiveness of government. Furthermore, techno-optimists, such as German Gref (currently, CEO of the largest Russian bank, Sberbank), consider online platforms to be an instrument of accountability that may serve as a viable alternative both to the power vertical and to representative democracy.[45] The evidence, however, is far from these optimistic expectations. On the one hand, against the background of isolationist trends in Russian politics and the obsession of Russia's leadership with threats to its sovereignty, digitalization faces numerous political constraints that have contributed to many attempts at the "nationalization of the Russian Internet."[46] Successes on this front have been modest, to say the least. In 2012, Rostelekom, the state communication monopoly, launched the major project of making a national Internet search engine, "Sputnik," which was intended by the Kremlin to be a state-controlled alternative to Google. However, despite it investing more than two billion rubles from state funds into this project, Sputnik received less than 1 percent of all search inquiries in Russia, and the project was finally closed in September 2020.[47] On the other hand, the government is faced with pressure from special interest groups that tend to adjust algorithmic governance to serve their own purposes. Andrei Isaev, an influential State Duma member from United Russia, summarized the essence of such an approach. He openly stated in front of journalists in August 2019: "If you, an official, come to an Internet company to resolve a concrete issue, and he (its representative) responds: 'hey, there is an algorithm, so I can't change anything,' then you should ask him to change the algorithm."[48] As one can see, this approach is hardly compatible with the ideas of effectiveness and impartiality promoted by crusaders of digitalization.

The increasing use of digital technologies for purposes of surveillance and political control, most notably in China, has contributed to the development of major concerns regarding the rise of "digital totalitarianism"[49] in many autocracies, including Russia. Ironically, bad governance has hindered technological developments in this direction in Russia, as many high-tech initiatives of this kind are used as smokescreens for rent-seeking and corruption, and in the end attempts by Russian authorities to impose various sophisticated mechanisms of control over citizens have had only partial effects at best.[50] For example, the Kremlin failed to stop the use of popular messenger Telegram, launched by the Russian IT entrepreneur Pavel Durov, who fled the country after vicious attacks on his previous projects from state-affiliated companies, endorsed by state security services. State regulators ultimately prohibited the use of Telegram and tried to block it across the country but failed to do so despite a series of attempts (at least, as of yet).[51] Rather, these attempts resulted in the Streisand effect, as Telegram became increasingly popular among Russian users and anonymous channels in this messenger were employed as a means of communication among Russian elites.[52]

Still, the effects of politically driven digitalization can be observed in Russia, albeit in different forms than in China. They were heavily criticized in the aftermath of the September 2019 Moscow City Duma elections, when in one of the single-mandate districts, electronic voting via a web portal contributed to a shift in the outcome. According to the offline mode of voting, the independent candidate Roman Yuneman won with a solid margin over his major opponent, university rector Margarita Rusetskaya, who was openly endorsed by city hall. Yet online voting brought quite the opposite results: Rusetskaya won a landslide majority when votes were counted via the web, and in the end, she gained a seat in the legislature. Meanwhile, the web portal was hacked, and faced many technical glitches, so the integrity of online voting has been questioned by election observers.[53] Similar trends were discussed in the aftermath of 2021 State Duma elections, when electronic voting results not only totally contradicted the results of offline voting, but also contributed to dubious electoral victories of candidates of major pro-Kremlin party, United Russia, in eight single-member districts of the city of Moscow.[54]

In a similar vein, Carolina Schlaufer, Daria Gristenko, and Andrey Indukaev analyzed opportunities for and constraints of the "digital governance" model in Russia, using the evidence from the Moscow-based project Active Citizen, which was developed by the city government as an instrument of communication with Muscovites.[55] Despite noticeable success in aggregating citizens' requests, online platforms still constrain citizens' empowerment, as advanced digital tools are used only in limited policy domains and certain types of participation because the agenda-setting of e-participation is tightly controlled by the Moscow City government.[56] Even though in most instances the effects of digitalization on governance in Russia may have less salient political connotations, the fundamental problem remains the same: algorithms and online services can improve the quality of governance only if these mechanisms are complementary to impartial and effective offline good governance, but *not* if they aim to substitute for it.

Last and important, decentralization remains the most problematic part of the current Russian agenda for improving the quality of governance in the country. These problems are related to the consequences of the major political, economic, and administrative recentralization that Russia underwent in the 2000s.[57] Following this shift, the autonomy of most of Russia's regions and localities was greatly reduced, as they became heavily dependent on the central government both in economic and in administrative terms. This is why many projects and programs aimed at advancing regional socioeconomic development are all but doomed to be overcentralized. Alexander Libman and Andrey Yakovlev demonstrated the limits of this centralized approach in their research on the performance of a newly established ministry in charge of developing the Russian Far East.[58] Despite the strategic importance of this region and the need for a major inflow of resources into the Far East due to urgent demographic, infrastructural, and other problems, the positive effects of this effort by the federal government remain limited, to say the least. One temporary solution is the promotion of specialized policy and geographical areas that enjoy preferential treatment and a certain degree of decentralization and deregulation granted by the central authorities. However, the major challenge policy-makers encounter is a trade-off between sufficient local knowledge and the capacity to lobby the ministry's interests efficiently in the federal center. This is an uneasy balance, and indeed actual policy success heavily depends on not only personal style and connections but also the political priorities of the central government. Policy stability and continuity under personalist autocracies are constantly threatened since international and domestic priorities may change at any time depending on the autocrat's will, as happened in 2014 after the annexation of Crimea.

Given the consequences of recentralization amid Russia's sluggish economic growth, only a handful of Russia's relatively wealthy regions, being less dependent on federal funding and driven by proactive leadership, can afford their own large-scale development programs and major innovation projects.[59] The housing renovation program in the city of Moscow may be considered one of the few examples that attract major public attention; it was aimed at resolving housing problems for many Muscovites and promoting gentrification of urban areas in the Russian capital. This program faces major problems due to the dominance of special interests of developers and construction companies, nontransparency, and political constraints of the Moscow City government.[60] The Moscow renovation program offers an example of how different institutional and participatory formats are used to accommodate the variety of business and bureaucratic interests and pursue an ambitious developmental plan despite complex problems and resistance from Muscovites. If the poor quality of governance serves as an obstacle to successful development in Moscow, with its plentiful financial resources and relatively high degree of autonomy for the city government, it is no surprise that in many not-so-wealthy regions and municipalities these problems are much more acute.[61]

What about bottom-up influence on subnational governance from the mass public? Most recently, the Russian government actively promoted projects on participatory budgeting and other forms of public engagement in various localities. While critical observers dubbed these tendencies "participatory authoritarianism,"[62] promoters of participatory budgeting in Russia argued that even small-scale local funding caused certain grassroots enthusiasm and offered local activists new opportunities for improving their communities on the basis of joint responsibility of municipalities and local citizenry.[63] However, in-depth assessments of public participation in local governance are more skeptical, revealing major problems with the role of the local public in urban policy-making.[64] If, under democratic arrangements, the coproduction of public goods results from the joint efforts of the local government and civil groups, the paradox of civic activism and self-management under nondemocratic and nontransparent rule is that even if successful, the lion's share of the public goods production costs is shifted to the local communities. In other words, local communities often provide better governance than local governments, thereby decreasing political pressure on the state and municipalities. These controversies may reflect a more fundamental issue of grassroots mass participation in the absence of local (as well as of nationwide) democracy: public engagement may promote good governance only by being complementary to mechanisms of electoral accountability and separation of power at the local level, not substituting for them.

The 4D solution, which may go beyond recipes of deregulation, digitalization, and decentralization and put political democratization as the number one item on the agenda of improving the quality of governance in Russia, remains off the current menu of Russian authoritarianism. This is why all other recipes for countering bad governance in the country may be considered partial and temporary solutions at best—without major political changes there is no means of improvement. Yet even a possible democratization of Russia's political regime and subsequent attempts at full-scale revision of its politico-economic order cannot guarantee a diminishment of bad governance in the country, as the recent experience of some other post-Communist countries suggests.

Combatting Bad Governance: Rethinking the Post-Communist Experience

As one can see from the previous chapters, the creation of bad governance in Russia after the Soviet collapse exemplified intentional poisoning of the state by rent-seekers who became beneficiaries of the emerging politico-economic order and attempted to consolidate it in a long-term perspective. The turbulent period of "triple transition"[65] after the collapse of the previous order in the 1990s made such state capture easier,[66] thus paving the way for further aggravation of bad governance in the 2000s and 2010s. However, although numerous other post-Communist countries faced somewhat similar problems after the collapse of Communist regimes, their trajectories of governance differ widely. While weakening of the states amid the economic transformation recession had visible negative effects on quality of governance in the early 1990s, later some of these countries were able to overcome these growing pains over time, while others struggled with protracted and complicated diseases. What does this experience tell us about the possible ways of overcoming bad governance both in the short and in the long term?

Overall, analyses of post-Communist reforms in Eastern Europe have demonstrated that large-scale renewal of the state apparatus and high elite circulation *ceteris paribus* contribute to the success of structural reforms and improving the quality of governance.[67] But in post-Soviet Eurasia immediately after the Soviet collapse these opportunities were missed or did not emerge at all. In particular, the incomplete democratization in Russia at the start of the 1990s was curtailed after the "democrats" took power in 1991; this resulted in a narrowed recruitment pool of elites and the preservation of the old guard in the state apparatus in key ministries, to say nothing of subnational governments.[68] It is unsurprising that newcomers to the Russian government in the 1990s found themselves isolated and facing many obstacles in the pursuit of policy reforms.[69] Many of their policies were compromised from the beginning and did not improve the quality of governance either as a whole or in individual policy areas.[70] Moreover, they were not aiming to open new windows of opportunity for political recruitment and elite circulation and served as the junior partners in a new winning coalition of regime supporters. The entrenchment of ruling groups, the sluggish vertical mobility of elites, and the narrowing of their recruitment pools played an important role in the preservation of bad governance: under these conditions, incentives to effectively govern the economy and the state were undermined.

In their case study of the success story of Estonia after the Soviet break-up, Neil Abrams and M. Steven Fish present a perceptive account in their analysis of relationships between post-Communist regime dynamics and the quality of governance.[71] They observe that the end of the Communist regime and Estonian independence opened a window of opportunity for a radical restructuring and large-scale cadre renewal not only among ruling groups but also within the apparatus of the state as a whole. The changes in Estonia's elite were more radical than those in other Baltic countries,[72] and rejecting the use of a "good Soviet Union" as a role model served as a driver for structural reforms. The impact of the sizeable Russian-speaking minority (who shared a more positive perception of a Soviet Union as a paradise lost)[73] on politics and policy-making in Estonia was severely constrained after the Soviet collapse.[74] It is hard to say whether such a deliberate exclusion played a positive role in building barriers against making bad governance. Policy changes in Estonia involved borrowing and implementing best practices of state governance from advanced Western countries (and its Nordic neighbours in particular), paved the way for successful market economic reforms, and helped overcome bad governance. Moreover, after the Soviet collapse Estonia successfully used certain advantages of its relative backwardness[75] in terms of infrastructure and institutions, and effectively used advanced technological solutions such as digitalization, alongside deregulation, to improve the quality of governance.[76] Thus, one might argue that the positive impact of democratization on the quality of governance was achieved not only through elite competition, but also as a mechanism for restructuring the state apparatus by means of elite circulation and the breakdown of previous power hierarchies.[77] This was a solution that preemptively diminished the pernicious effects of bad governance.

As long as major political changes are postponed, combatting bad governance may turn into an increasingly difficult task requiring extraordinary efforts of political leaders in terms of overhauling previous elites and restructuring the state apparatus. The experience of Georgia is telling in this respect. The 1990s featured devastating political decay, aggravated by severe economic troubles, elite turmoil, and the loss of two breakaway territories, Abkhazia and South Ossetia.[78] The overthrow of the highly corrupt and unpopular regime during the Rose Revolution in 2003 provided a chance to launch large-scale policy reforms. The new leader, Mikheil Saakashvili, brought a number of new people, including young professionals, into key positions in the state apparatus and contributed to implementing several structural changes in major policy areas, ranging from the economy to education and police.[79] Some of these reforms, aimed at deregulating the economy and transparency of services,[80] resulted in major improvements, such as reducing red tape and petty corruption, and an increase in government effectiveness. These advancements were used by Saakashvili to promote Georgian policy reforms (and of himself) in the eyes of his domestic audience and international donors and present his achievements as a success story.[81] However, as Ketevan Bolkvadze correctly points out, even this example demonstrates the limits of the effects of elite changes: Saakashvili and his entourage pursued those policy changes that they expected to increase their own power. It is no wonder that administrative reforms in Georgia soon reached a saturation point. When the new self-interested elites under Saakashvili faced challenges from their political opponents, further policy changes were curtailed.[82] In the end, in 2012 Saakashvili lost the election, having been accused of numerous wrongdoings (including large-scale illegal police violence) during his election campaign, and soon after fled the country due to the threat of criminal prosecution. Still, the results of policy reforms under

Saakashvili were not reversed in full, and some policy changes continued after his departure, though their pace and scope slowed down to a certain degree.[83] Improving the quality of governance in Georgia was partial; however, without major elite changes and a certain political will from the leadership, even this relatively modest advancement could not be realistic for Russia.

But if post-Communist elites become entrenched, then regime changes, though often seen as democratic breakthroughs, do not always undermine bad governance, and indeed may even aggravate its pathologies. The case of Ukraine may serve as a prime example of this paradox. During the entire post-Soviet period, this country exemplified "pluralism by default" due to a configuration of elites driven by embedded regionalism and unavoidable competition between interest groups.[84] President Yanukovych's attempt to impose his political monopoly and grab the most possible rents greatly contributed to his overthrow in 2014.[85] Setting aside the subsequent chain of events, which involved the annexation of Crimea and a bloody conflict in Donbass, the "revolution of dignity" of 2014 resulted in the emergence of a competitive "neopatrimonial democracy" in Ukraine.[86] However, democratic elections as such have not improved the poor quality of governance by default. Rather, state capture from inside by Yanukovych and his cronies was replaced by state capture from outside by competing oligarchs.[87] The new Ukrainian president, Petro Poroshenko, was a wealthy oligarch himself, and his political career was largely opportunistic. More important, despite the call to purge former representatives of Yanukovych's regime, little elite turnover was visible, especially in the state apparatus. In particular, structural and personnel changes in Ukrainian courts,[88] and in several law enforcement agencies, were delayed indefinitely. The belief that post-Yanukovych Ukraine had merely replaced one group of crooks and thieves with another, while bad governance remained nearly the same, was not a wild exaggeration. In July 2019, Poroshenko lost his presidential re-election bid to a new leader, Volodymyr Zelensky, a former stand-up comedian, who became widely known after starring in the TV series *Servant of the People*, where he played the role of a school history teacher who was elected president of Ukraine. In a sense, the TV dream came true, as over three quarters of Ukrainian voters endorsed Zelensky during the run-off, and his newly established party bearing the name "Servant of the People" soon acquired a parliamentary majority after the new elections. There was certainly a popular demand for major elite changes, but the new government and the presidential administration were largely unsuccessful and conflict-ridden, and soon replaced by new nominees who have also failed to demonstrate a strong performance. The pace of reforms remains slow and does not affect the core of bad governance.

In a similar vein, Scott Radnitz, in his analysis of regime changes in Kyrgyzstan in 2005 and 2010, argues that elite-driven mass mobilization preserves the predatory and rent-seeking nature of governance, even in cases where it results in replacing ruling groups.[89] Politicizing the governing economy and the state and incentives for bureaucrats' loyalty at the expense of their effectiveness are typical for a number of competitive democracies in almost the same way as for electoral authoritarian regimes. In short, the political competition of elites, which lies at the heart of democratization, is not a panacea for overcoming bad governance, at least in the short term. In certain circumstances, such competition à la pluralism by default, may only aggravate corruption and unrule of law,[90] and the chain of weak and ineffective governments may become hostages of competing cliques of elites and oligarchs.[91] From this viewpoint, one might argue that democratization should be perceived as a necessary yet insufficient condition for improving the quality of governance. At minimum, major elite changes and a deep reshuffling of the entire state apparatus, alongside long-standing and systematic efforts to improve the quality of governance driven by the political will of domestic actors, and thorough oversight by the international community are key ingredients to combatting bad governance in post-Communist countries and beyond. Without all of these ingredients, these countries may experience major setbacks in the quality of governance, as the experience of Hungary, described above, demonstrated.

Under such circumstances, even the rotation of corrupt and ineffective rulers after free and fair elections only contributes to the preservation of the politico-economic order. At best, governments can resolve the most acute problems by muddling through, while the principles of bad governance remain unchallenged: corrupt and ineffective governments, seeking rent extraction, may put an end to any attempts to constrain bad governance for decades, if not centuries. As bad governance itself serves as an obstacle to sustainable economic growth and development, there is a high probability that over time the corruption and ineffectiveness of governments may be reproduced repeatedly. In this scenario, post-Communist countries could be doomed to durable bad governance in the same way as the states of sub-Saharan Africa (despite obvious differences in degree of socioeconomic development).[92]

A Perfect Storm: The Pandemic Crisis and Bad Governance in Russia

The COVID-19 pandemic that hit the globe in 2020 has been a sudden and simultaneous stress test for all countries. It has clearly exposed both their strengths and weaknesses in terms of policy-making in many areas and in many layers of governance, thus becoming a perfect storm for assessments and evaluations of numerous issues of the quality of governance in the country. In general, the success and failure of various countries have been explained through the mutual impact of state capacity (with regard to infrastructural power of the state),[93] legitimacy, political leadership, and public health policies.[94] For many, including developed countries, the existing conditions of their national health care systems turned out to be the weakest link, if not the bottleneck, as hospitals across the globe struggled to cope with excess pressures during a surge of infections (especially in some European countries like Italy that had high shares of aged residents, the most vulnerable to the pandemic). Some political leaders, such as Jair Bolsonaro in Brazil or Donald Trump in the United States, responded to the pandemic challenge sluggishly, and behaved inconsistently, ineffectively, and often irresponsibly vis-à-vis pandemic threats. In certain countries, such as Sweden, alternative strategies of pandemic response chosen by politicians and state officials have also contributed to their dubious performance. In Russia, however, all these components of reaction to the pandemic were greatly affected by the consequences of the bad governance presented and analyzed in the previous chapters of this book.

From the viewpoint of structural conditions, Russia had strong potential for a relatively efficient response to the pandemic crisis. A relatively low population density, large distances between major cities, and not particularly high domestic and international transport connectivity (except for major hubs and transborder areas) created the possibility for a slow spread of the virus across the country. A relatively developed public health infrastructure and large number of medical personnel also made a successful performance possible. Moreover, COVID-19 reached Russia fairly late relative to other major European states, so Russia had enough time to prepare for the crisis. In addition, Russian citizens were much more tolerant of the numerous pandemic-related restrictions imposed by the state than their European counterparts and did not strongly object to the government's actions. However, in 2020–2021, Russia rose to the list of top developed countries in the world in terms of excess mortality rate, which was mostly driven by COVID-19.[95] According to some expert statements, by the end of 2021 excess mortality in Russia exceeded one million, although this data (based upon population registers) may be rather incomplete.[96] In essence, the political priorities of Russia's leadership, alongside the policy effects of bad governance, greatly contributed to such an outcome.

At the exact time when COVID-19 reached Russia, its leadership prioritized other issues than dealing with the pandemic, as it was driven by the nature of Russia's political regime. At that moment, a large-scale revision of the Russian constitution was in full swing, with a handful of amendments approved by the parliament on March 10, 2020, designed to allow Putin to retain power in Russia until 2036. As the regime built its legitimacy in the eyes of its citizens on the basis of voters' support for an undemocratic leader, a quasi-plebiscitary "popular vote" was set for April 22, 2020, to formalize these changes with a demonstration of citizens' approval of the constitutional amendments and of the continuity of Putin's rule.[97] It comes as no surprise that constitutional amendments turned out to be priority number one for the Kremlin. Had the pandemic not happened, this plan would most likely have been successfully implemented. Not surprisingly, the coronavirus was initially perceived by the presidential administration as just a minor bump on the road to the main goal. However, the scale of the infection surge forced the Kremlin to postpone the upcoming approval of constitutional amendments until a later date. This unexpected and unwanted change in the Kremlin's political strategy and its search for new legitimation of Putin led to Russia's late and largely inefficient response to the pandemic challenge. To put it bluntly, Russia effectively failed the coronavirus test for the sake of the regime's continuity. The lives and health of Russian citizens were not prioritized by authorities: as doctor Alexander Myasnikov, the spokesperson in charge of state information management during the pandemic, openly stated in his speech on Russian TV: "Those who are supposed to die will die."[98] This reasoning was not based only on cynicism but also reflected the strategic considerations of the authorities. As human losses themselves did not challenge the preservation of the political regime and the mechanisms of governance, they were considered to be of secondary importance at best. The Kremlin perceived risks not from the pandemic as such but rather from the political disequilibrium it could cause.

As a result, politics was prioritized over policy-making, and the potential risks of anti-regime mobilization and avalanche-like decline in Putin's public support were perceived in the Kremlin as more serious threats than the direct (COVID-19 victims) and indirect (economic recession) impact of the pandemic. No wonder that the major package of anti-crisis measures adopted in Russia in late March 2020 included, *inter alia*, criminalization of fake news regarding the pandemic and imposition of strict control over the spread of unwanted information on the ground—doctors and nurses across Russia were at risk of being fired, if not prosecuted, and shared information with journalists and observers only under conditions of anonymity.[99] At the same time, the rise of the "information autocracy"[100] (in other words the regime that is based upon extensive use of lies as a tool of dominance)[101] has proved to be a double-edged sword under the conditions of the pandemic. It provides strong incentives for intentional distortion of information and production of Kremlin-desired good numbers at all layers of the state hierarchy, ranging from regional governors and city mayors to directors of local hospitals and the like.[102] When the meaninglessness of official Russian statistics on the number of infected people and of pandemic-related casualties was demonstrated by experts, who used advanced quantitative techniques of analysis, these disclosures caused a furious reaction from Russian state officials, and vicious counterattacks against international media.[103] The response of the Russian state was a further change in regulations aimed at further decreasing official numbers and obscuring the real picture.[104] From this perspective, Russia's rulers followed the role model of the "good Soviet Union," outlined previously, as Soviet officials tended not to disclose bad news regarding major disasters[105] and often even failed to gather certain statistical data if indicators demonstrated negative tendencies.[106] Although the reliance upon distorted information was not helpful in combatting the pandemic, the power vertical that prioritized loyalty over efficiency, most probably pursued other goals than the health of Russian citizens, and the media provides evidence of Russian state officials passing the blame in the midst of the pandemic.[107]

The overregulated state in Russia provides yet another set of incentives for inefficient combatting of the pandemic. The awkward combination of high density and poor quality of state regulations in the field of public health has provided negative incentives for directors of hospitals as well as for doctors and nurses on the ground. They have had to minimize risks of being fired by their superiors, if not prosecuted by law enforcement, for any real or imagined wrongdoings. The ongoing ill-designed "optimization" of public health facilities in Russia aimed at making huge conglomerates of big hospitals at the expense of local medical centers (especially in small towns and rural areas) has only aggravated the situation.[108] This is why loyally following any directives from their superiors, who in turn are interested in whitewashing statistics and portraying a rosy picture of successfully combatting the pandemic, remains the only available strategy for almost every worker in the Russian public health system.

At the same time, the Russian state leadership has become flawed both in personal and in institutional terms on the medical front. Unlike in many developed countries, responsibility was transferred not to the Ministry of Health or any other specialized state agency in charge of medical affairs, but to the state watchdog agency Rospotrebnadzor, primarily responsible for numerous regulations in the consumer market. This agency (which set sanitary norms and had broad discretion over punishment for their violation) had previously gained a notorious reputation for being involved in the ban on food imports from "unfriendly" countries such as Georgia. While public health agencies are based on a two-tier system of subordination (most hospitals are subordinated to and funded by subnational authorities, and the federal ministry performs functions of coordination), Rospotrebnadzor is based on the strict top-down hierarchy of its own power vertical, and was perceived by the government as an organization that could implement top-down orders without consulting with other agencies. This is why the government nominated the head of Rospotrebnadzor, Anna Popova, to be in charge of all regulatory actions taken by the state during the pandemic. The territorial branches of this agency became veto actors in the regions regarding the pandemic, as governors were requested to get its approval on all related actions, and it gained discretion and funding without bearing any responsibility for public health performance. According to journalists' reports, Popova received carte blanche from the top leadership, and her political patron, the deputy prime minister Tatyana Golikova, counseled Popova at the beginning of the pandemic to act such that, in their words: "Everything will be all right and afterwards you will not be ashamed [before superiors]."[109]

In the wake of the pandemic outbreak, many necessary steps came with delays and were guided by the political motivations of Russia's authorities. The first stimulus package for the economy was approved only in May 2020, used about 1.5 percent of the GDP (which was highly insufficient by the standards of developed countries),[110] and mostly focused on support for large state companies rather than small and medium businesses. As for compensations for Russian citizens, they were fairly limited. Rather than making any bold moves in the wake of the outbreak, Putin refused to announce a state of emergency or a major lockdown; instead, he officially declared a "week off" in March 2020 and then extended it several times up until May 2020 (the same trick was repeated in May 2021, during the new outbreak of the pandemic). Ultimately, the authority to combat the coronavirus was de facto entrusted to the chief executives of Russia's regions. They gained rights and responsibilities to handle problems caused by the pandemic, including regulating work, travel, and services, preparing medical facilities for the influx of patients, and the like.

Administrative decentralization in itself could have been a justified measure during the pandemic. Russia is a diverse country, and the scale of the problems caused by the coronavirus varied greatly between the provinces. Yet the entire mechanism of governance in Russia was insufficient for the country to provide an effective response to the pandemic crisis at the regional level. First and foremost, many provinces had limited amounts of resources to resist the pandemic, while the transfers from the federal budget reached regional coffers with a major delay. Second, the conditions of the overregulated state caused a failure by both federal and regional governments to provide the resources needed to deal with the consequences of the pandemic (due to the risk of being accused of misusing state funds). Third, the power vertical was not designed to deal with such crises, as apart from delivering required voting results at any cost and avoiding mass protests, the regional and local officials' objective was to achieve targets imposed in a top-down manner, measured as percentage points of performance indicators against previous years.[111] Therefore, it is hardly surprising that during the pandemic the governors of some Russian regions provided official reports to the Kremlin of nearly unchanged numbers of cases and (mostly unsuccessfully) attempted to hide excess mortality data.[112]

As to more substantive measures for combatting the pandemic, the Russian authorities put major efforts into developing Russia's own COVID-19 vaccine. Thanks to overconcentrating resources necessary to develop and produce a vaccine, and a rush to launch it, Russian authorities proudly registered a vaccine, labeled Sputnik V (official title Gam-COVID-Vac) on August 11, 2020, earlier than other similar products by global pharmacological companies such as Pfizer or Johnson & Johnson. Such a prompt approval of Sputnik V was met with criticism in the mass media and discussions in the expert community about whether approval was justified in the absence of robust scientific research confirming safety and efficacy.[113] However, in February 2021, an interim analysis from the trial was published in *the Lancet*, the major global medical journal, indicating 91.6 percent efficacy without major side effects.[114] In many ways, Sputnik V's launch was perceived by Russian authorities as a grand success story. However, its trajectory became not so dissimilar to some other success stories in Russia, as analyzed in chapter 6. First, amid the pandemic, Russia attempted to use the supplying of new anti-COVID medicine as a tool of aggressive "vaccine diplomacy," demanding major concessions from member states of the European Union for priority supply of the vaccine. Russia's vaccine-related pressure on governments in countries like Slovakia and the Czech Republic, aimed at changes in their policies toward Russia, caused major political scandals.[115] Some other countries faced delays in procuring Russian vaccines. In the end, Russian attempts to conquer international vaccination markets had limited success, as Sputnik V failed to get quick approval by American and European regulators. Second, and most important, the domestic campaign of vaccination largely failed. Russia had officially started vaccination with Sputnik V as early as December 2020 (the use of foreign vaccines was not permitted in Russia). However, by late December 2021 only 45 percent of Russians had received at least one dose of the vaccine—a much lower share than in most developed countries.[116] The Russian authorities paid little attention to persuading citizens to be vaccinated, while the state propaganda aimed at discrediting the European and American experience of combatting the pandemic (including vaccination efforts abroad) intentionally or unintentionally spread many nonsensical ideas about the pandemic and therefore disoriented many ordinary Russians. Only in June 2021, when the new outbreak of COVID-19 caused a new spike in the number of victims, did the government seek to increase the vaccination rate at least among public sector employees and service sector workers. To what extent these belated measures will help to combat the pandemic in Russia remains to be seen.

Meanwhile, the "popular vote," conducted on July 1, 2020, was probably the most massive and shameless instance of fraudulent voting in Russia's post-Communist history. Using various means, ranging from large-scale workplace mobilization of voters (mostly public sector employees)[117] to routine ballot box stuffing and delivering entirely fake results, the Kremlin reached its target. According to official data, the turnout was about 65 percent of Russian voters, and almost 78 percent of them voted for the constitutional amendments, although mass surveys demonstrated a much lower degree of approval,[118] and some experts argued that about thirty million votes were added to the real numbers.[119] Still, even this fraudulent procedure has not shaken the legitimacy of Russia's regime, at least as of yet. Before the "popular vote," the Kremlin's mouthpieces openly declared that their goal was to cement the status quo for as long as possible and to demonstrate to all Russians that everything in the country will remain the same, so that "after Putin there will be Putin," as the speaker of the State Duma summarized the message.[120] It is hard to predict to what extent these dreams of averting major political changes in Russia forever will come true, but the long-term continuity of Russia's current political regime will almost inevitably result in further political decay and aggravating the numerous vices of bad governance analyzed in this book.[121]

Concluding Remarks: Is Bad Governance Forever?

In 1348, Ambrogio Lorenzetti, the author of the *Allegory of Bad Government* (presented on the cover of this book), fell victim to a pandemic—like many residents of Siena and other medieval cities in Europe, he died of the bubonic plague. But almost seven centuries from that time, his frescoes remain on the walls of the Palazzo Pubblico in Siena and still serve as a powerful reminder of the causes and effects of good and bad governance across space and time—be they discussed in medieval Siena, in contemporary Russia, or anywhere on the globe. Neither the city portrayed by Lorenzetti nor the numerous cities and towns of Russia are doomed to be governed badly because of their unfavorable structural conditions. Quite the opposite, these polities exhibit various manifestations of bad governance because their rulers, similarly to the main character of Lorenzetti's fresco, behave like tyrants and tend to minimize any constraints on arbitrary rule. In the absence of domestic and international constraints, tyrants rarely have strong incentives to govern their domains in an effective and efficient way, and this is why numerous vices of bad governance, so vividly presented in the fresco, often become a constituent core of mechanisms of governance in various states and nations.

Judging from this perspective, contemporary Russia represents a pure case of intentional building of bad governance on the ruins of the Soviet system after its collapse and troubled transformation. This outcome was not predetermined by Russia's legacies of the past, nor was it an effect of the individual characteristics of Putin and other Russian leaders. Rather, Russia's rulers were able to pursue their own self-interest and reach their goals, while rulers of many other countries were not able to do so for various reasons. The consolidation of authoritarianism in Russia during the first two decades of the twenty-first century undoubtedly entrenched bad governance and exacerbated its major effects, such as corruption and rent-seeking. However, bad governance in Russia does not necessarily lead the country to immediate total disaster and major failures in all key policy fields. The mechanisms of governance built in Russia in the twenty-first century imply elements of fool-proofing, and many prudent technocratic solutions have enabled an aversion of the worst risks. Moreover, under certain circumstances, success stories of strong government performance have demonstrated major achievements in different policy fields, but even though these successes often became limited and unsustainable over time. This is why neither hopes nor fears of inevitable collapse of bad governance are relevant to Russia, at least as of yet. Rather, Russia has exhibited a pattern of durable bad governance, or low-level equilibrium, which may not be shaken even if sooner or later the country faces major political regime changes. Democratization is a necessary yet insufficient condition for overcoming bad governance, as the recent experience of Ukraine suggests.

What are the lessons that might be learned from the experience of bad governance in contemporary Russia? First and foremost, political foundations lie at the core of mechanisms for governing the state, and personalist authoritarian regimes provide fertile grounds for building bad governance, especially if these regimes prove to have a certain durability, as in Russia's case. Second, regardless of loud rhetoric, the dreams of authoritarian modernization have not been significantly converted into reality, as political leaders rarely invest systematic efforts into improving the quality of governance unless they face major domestic and/or international challenges and constraints. Third, irrespective of Russia's foreign policies, its practices of bad governance have a high chance of turning into a role model for many rulers of other countries who would like to govern their states in a similar way to Putin. Finally, one must admit that while bad governance may initially emerge in any given country and be further aggravated by conscious poisoning by politicians, it will not disappear by itself without tremendous and systematic efforts by the political class and society at large, and the success of such efforts is relatively rare. For these reasons, bad governance is most likely to turn from growing pains of post-Communist state-building into its chronic diseases, which may be not fully curable.

All metaphors, which are so widely used in social sciences, are imperfect as they are only partly congruent with complex realities, and the medical metaphor of the causes and effects of bad governance employed in this book is no exception. In the world of medicine, a patient who behaves irresponsibly about his or her disease, that is, ignores professional recommendations, refuses medical treatments, and worsens his or her health using alcohol and smoking, usually dies prematurely. But in the world of twenty-first century politics, states and societies, unlike individuals, are immortal—for good or ill, they are not dying at all, not disappearing from the global map by themselves nor being conquered by other powers. Rather, the miserable countries affected by the chronic disease of bad governance may endlessly continue their mediocre, hopeless, and meaningless existence under these worsening conditions, and over time be left with fewer and fewer chances for their recovery. This is the real threat for Russia and for other countries that are not immune to bad governance. After a certain stage of decay, the declining quality of governance may reach a point of no return. If so, then it will not be possible to improve the Russian state by any available means. Rather, the question for scholars and experts may be how to eliminate it without causing major harm to the human beings in the country and across the globe. To what extent such a question may become a major item on Russia's agenda in the foreseeable future remains to be seen.

Preface and Acknowledgments

1. Samuel P. Huntington, *Political Order in Changing Societies* (New Haven, CT: Yale University Press, 1968), 1.

2. See the two-volume book by Francis Fukuyama: *Origins of Political Order: From Prehuman Times to the French Revolution* (New York: Farrar, Strauss, and Giroux, 2011); and *Political Order and Political Decay: From the Industrial Revolution to the Globalization of Democracy* (New York: Farrar, Strauss, and Giroux, 2014). See also Daron Acemoglu, James A. Robinson, *The Narrow Corridor: How Nations Struggle for Liberty* (New York: Penguin, 2019).

3. See *Worldwide Governance Indicators* (Washington, DC: World Bank, 2021); http://info.worldbank.org/governance/wgi/, accessed May 31, 2021. See also Jan Teorell, Aksel Sundström, Sören Holmberg, Bo Rothstein, Natalia Alvarado Pachon, Cem Mert Dalli, *The Quality of Government Standard Dataset*, version January 2021 (Gothenburg: Quality of Government Institute, 2021), https://www.gu.se/en/quality-government/qog-data/data-downloads/standard-dataset, accessed May 31, 2021.

4. For an anthropological study of these issues, see Alena V. Ledeneva, *Russia's Economy of Favours: Blat, Networking, and Informal Exchange* (Cambridge: Cambridge University Press, 1998).

5. See Albert O. Hirschman, *A Bias for Hope: Essays on Development and Latin America* (New Haven, CT: Yale University Press, 1971).

Chapter 1

1. For example, in 2019, Russia ranked 137th of 180 countries in the annual Corruption Perception Index. See *Corruption Perception Index* (Berlin: Transparency International, 2020), https://www.transparency.org/cpi2019, accessed September 7, 2021. In 2020, the composite evaluation of the Rule of Law Index by the World Justice Project ranked Russia 94th out of 128 countries. See *World Justice Project Rule of Law Index 2020* (Washington, DC: World Justice Project, 2020), https://worldjusticeproject.org/sites/default/files/documents/WJP-ROLI-2020-Online_0.pdf, accessed September 7, 2021. The

average indicator for corruption control in Russia in the 1996–2015 period, according to the World Bank, was –0.86 on a scale from –2.5 (lowest possible grade) to +2.5 (highest possible grade). See *Worldwide Governance Indicators* (Washington, DC: World Bank, 2021), http://info.worldbank.org/governance/wgi/, accessed September 7, 2021.

2. Among numerous journalist investigations, one of the most impressive is the Panama Papers, a series of reports about global high-profile corruption and money laundering provided by the Organized Crime and Corruption Reporting Project, https://www.occrp.org/en/, accessed September 7, 2021. For evidence on Russia, see: Roman Anin, Olesya Shmagun, Dmitry Velikovsky, "The Secret Caretaker," https://www.occrp.org/en/panamapapers/the-secret-caretaker/, April 3, 2016, accessed September 7, 2021; Paul Radu, "Russia: The Cellist and the Lawyer," https://www.occrp.org/en/panamapapers/russia-the-cellist-and-the-lawyer/, April 26, 2016, accessed September 7, 2021; Roman Anin, "Russia: Banking on Influence," https://www.occrp.org/en/panamapapers/rossiya-putins-bank/, June 9, 2016, accessed September 7, 2021.

3. See Sergey Aleksashenko, *Putin's Counterrevolution: How Putin's Autocracy Undercut Russia's Economy and Chances for Democracy* (Washington, DC: Brookings Institution Press, 2018); Anders Åslund, *Russia's Crony Capitalism: The Path from Market Economy to Kleptocracy* (New Haven, CT: Yale University Press, 2019).

4. The most visible examples were presented in a series of investigative reports produced by the Anti-Corruption Foundation, led by the key figure of the Russian opposition, Alexei Navalny. See "On vam ne Dimon," https://dimon.navalny.com, accessed September 7, 2021—a 2017 documentary film about the corruption of then-prime minister of Russia Dmitry Medvedev, which reached more than seventeen million views in a month after release. See https://www.youtube.com/embed/qrwlk7_GF9g?hl=en&cc_lang_pref=en&cc_load_policy=1, accessed September 7, 2021. In 2021, the Russian courts jailed Navalny and labeled the Anti-Corruption Foundation an "extremist" organization.

5. See Andrey Zvyagintsev, *Leviathan* (2014), https://www.imdb.com/title/tt2802154/, accessed September 7, 2021. The film won numerous major awards, including Best Screenplay at the 2014 Cannes Film Festival and Best Foreign Language Film of the 72th Golden Globe Awards.

6. See Andrey Zaostrovtsev, "Authoritarianism and Institutional Decay in Russia: Disruption of Property Rights and the Rule of Law," in *Authoritarian Modernization in Russia: Ideas, Institutions, and Policies*, ed. Vladimir Gel'man (Abingdon: Routledge, 2017), 73–94.

7. See Brian Taylor, *The Code of Putinism* (Oxford: Oxford University Press, 2018), 159–160.

8. For a detailed account of Lorenzetti's frescoes from the perspective of art history, see Patrick Boucheron, "'Turn Your Eyes to Behold Her, You, Who Are Governing, Who Is Portrayed Here': Ambrogio Lorenzetti's Fresco of Good Government," *Annales. History, Sciences Sociales* 60 (2005/06): 1137–1199. I am indebted to Gilles Favarel-Garrigues for this reference.

9. For an account from the perspective of political theory, see Quentin Skinner, "Ambrogio Lorenzetti: The Artist as Political Philosopher," *Proceedings of the British Academy* 72 (1986): 1–56.

10. See *The Quality of Government Institute*, University of Gothenburg, https://qog. pol.gu.se/, accessed September 7, 2021.

11. For detailed consideration of the meaning of these frescoes, see Quentin Skinner, "Ambrogio Lorenzetti's Buon Governo Frescoes: Two Old Questions, Two New Answers," *Journal of the Warburg and Courtauld Institutes* 62 (1999): 1–28.

12. Among numerous accounts of Russia's post-Communist transformations, see Lilia Shevtsova, *Yeltsin's Russia: Myths and Reality* (Washington, DC: Carnegie Endowment for International Peace, 1999); Andrei Shleifer, Daniel Treisman, *Without a Map: Political Tactics and Economic Reform in Russia* (Cambridge, MA: MIT Press, 2000); Michael McFaul, *Russia's Unfinished Revolution: Political Change from Gorbachev to Putin* (Ithaca, NY: Cornell University Press, 2001); Anders Åslund, *Russia's Capitalist Revolution: Why Market Reforms Succeeded and Democracy Failed* (Washington, DC: Peterson Institute for International Economics, 2007); Vladimir Gel'man, *Authoritarian Russia: Analyzing Post-Soviet Regime Changes* (Pittsburgh, PA: University of Pittsburgh Press, 2015), especially chapter 3.

13. For analyses of the problems with the rule of law in post-Communist Russia, see, in particular, Vadim Volkov, *Violent Entrepreneurs: The Role of Force in the Making of Russian Capitalism* (Ithaca, NY: Cornell University Press, 2002); Jordan Gans-Morse, *Property Rights in Post-Soviet Russia: Violence, Corruption, and the Demand for Law* (Cambridge: Cambridge University Press, 2017); Kathryn Hendley, *Everyday Law in Russia* (Ithaca, NY: Cornell University Press, 2017); Maria Popova, "Putin-Style 'Rule of Law' and the Prospects for Change," *Daedalus* 146, no. 2 (2017): 64–75; Taylor, *The Code of Putinism*, especially chapter 5.

14. Among the voluminous literature on the subject, see, in particular, Bo Rothstein, Jan Teorell, "What Is Quality of Government? A Theory of Impartial Government Institutions," *Governance* 21, no. 2 (2008): 165–190; Bert A. Rockman, Sung Deuk Hamn, "The Notion of Good and Bad Governance in Comparative Perspective," *Korean Journal of Policy Studies* 26, no. 2 (2011): 1–16; *Good Government: The Relevance of Political Science*, eds. Sören Holmberg, Bo Rothstein (Cheltenham: Edward Elgar, 2012).

15. See David Buchan, "Soviet Export of Technologies," *Financial Times*, September 14, 1984.

16. For an important and insightful analysis, see *Ranking the World: Grading States as a Tool of Global Governance*, eds. Alexander Cooley, Jack Snyder (Cambridge: Cambridge University Press, 2015), especially chapters 1 and 7.

17. For the classical notion of the use of "deviant case analyses" for theory-building in comparative politics, see Arend Lijphart, "Comparative Politics and Comparative Method," *American Political Science Review* 65, no. 3 (1971): 682–693.

18. Francis Fukuyama, "What Is Governance?" *Governance* 26, no. 3 (2013): 350.

19. See Mark Bevir, *Democratic Governance* (Princeton, NJ: Princeton University Press, 2010); *Good Government: The Relevance of Political Science*.

20. For a comprehensive overview, see *The Oxford Handbook of Governance*, ed. David Levi-Faur (Oxford: Oxford University Press, 2012).

21. See *Worldwide Governance Indicators*; Jan Teorell, Aksel Sundström, Sören Holmberg, Bo Rothstein, Natalia Alvarado Pachon, Cem Mert Dalli, *The Quality of*

Government Standard Dataset, version January 2021 (Gothenburg: The Quality of Government Institute, 2021), https://www.gu.se/en/quality-government/qog-data/data-downloads/standard-dataset, accessed September 7, 2021.

22. See Bo Rothstein, "Good Governance," in *The Oxford Handbook of Governance*, ed. David Levi-Faur (Oxford: Oxford University Press, 2012), 143–154.

23. For definitions and criteria of measurement, see *Worldwide Governance Indicators*.

24. See *Elites, Institutions, and the Quality of Government*, eds. Carl Dahlström, Lena Wängnerud (London: Palgrave Macmillan, 2015); Carl Dahlström, Victor Lapuente, *Organizing Leviathan: Politicians, Bureaucrats, and the Making of Good Government* (Cambridge: Cambridge University Press, 2017).

25. According to Guillermo O'Donnell, these principles are: "1. All laws should be prospective, open and clear; 2. Laws should be relatively stable; 3. The making of particular laws . . . must be guided by open, stable, clear, and general rules; 4. The independence of the judiciary must be guaranteed; 5. The principles of natural justice must be observed (i.e., open and fair hearing and absence of bias); 6. The courts should have review powers . . . to ensure conformity to the rule of law; 7. The courts should be easily accessible; 8. The discretion of crime preventing agencies should not be allowed to pervert the law." See Guillermo A. O'Donnell, "Polyarchies and the (Un)Rule of Law in Latin America: A Partial Conclusion," in *The (Un)Rule of Law and the Underprivileged in Latin America*, eds. Juan E. Mendez, Guillermo A. O'Donnell, Paulo Sergio Pinheiro (Notre Dame, IN: University of Notre Dame Press, 1999), 317.

26. See *Russian Modernization: A New Paradigm*, eds. Markku Kivinen, Brendan Humphreys (Abingdon: Routledge, 2021), especially chapters 1 and 7.

27. See Ella Paneyakh, "Zaregulirovannoe gosudarstvo," *Pro et Contra* 13, nos.1–2 (2013): 58–92: Ella Paneyakh, "The Overregulated State," *Social Sciences* 45, no. 1 (2014): 20–33.

28. See Nicholas Sharron, Victor Lapuente, "Does Democracy Produce Quality of Government?," *European Journal of Political Research* 49, no. 4 (2010): 443–470; Andrey Melville, Mikhail Mironyuk, "'Bad Enough' Governance: State Capacity and Quality of Institutions in Post-Soviet Autocracies," *Post-Soviet Affairs* 32, no. 2 (2016): 132–151.

29. See, for example, *Corruption and Governance* (Washington, DC: World Bank Group, n.d.), http://webcache.googleusercontent.com/search?q=cache:TlSOP14Xq18J:lnweb18.worldbank.org/eca/eca.nsf/Sectors/ECSPE/E9AC26BAE82D-37D685256A940073F4E9%3FOpenDocument+&cd=1&hl=en&ct=clnk&gl=fi, accessed April 14, 2020.

30. On "conceptual stretching," see Giovanni Sartori, "Concept Misformation in Comparative Politics," *American Political Science Review* 64, no. 4 (1970): 1033–1053; David Collier, James P. Mahon, "Conceptual 'Stretching' Revisited: Adapting Categories in Comparative Analysis," *American Political Science Review* 87, no. 4 (1993): 845–855.

31. See Alina Mingiu-Pippidi, *The Quest for Good Governance: How Societies Develop Control of Corruption* (Cambridge: Cambridge University Press, 2015); Richard Rose, Caryn Peiffer, *Bad Governance and Corruption* (Cham: Palgrave Macmillan, 2019).

32. See Douglass C. North, John J. Wallis, Barry R. Weingast, *Violence and Social Orders: A Conceptual Framework for Interpreting Recorded Human History* (Cambridge: Cambridge University Press, 2009).

33. See Daron Acemoglu, James A. Robinson, *Why Nations Fail: The Origins of Power, Prosperity, and Poverty* (New York: Crown Business, 2012).

34. On informal institutions, see *International Handbook of Informal Governance*, eds. Thomas Christensen, Christine Neuhold (Cheltenham: Edward Elgar, 2012); *The Global Encyclopedia of Informality*, 2 vols., ed. Alena V. Ledeneva (London: UCL Press, 2018).

35. See Elinor Ostrom, *Governing the Commons: The Evolution of Institutions for Collective Action* (Cambridge: Cambridge University Press, 1990), 53.

36. On "power pyramids," see Henry E. Hale, *Patronal Politics: Eurasian Regime Dynamics in Comparative Perspective* (Cambridge: Cambridge University Press, 2014), especially chapter 6.

37. On types and causes of corruption, see Andrei Shleifer, Robert W. Vishny, "Corruption," *Quarterly Journal of Economics* 108, no. 3 (1993): 599–617; Daniel Treisman, "The Causes of Corruption: A Cross-National Study," *Journal of Public Economics* 76, no. 3 (2000): 399–457.

38. See O'Donnell, "Polyarchies and the (Un)Rule of Law in Latin America: A Partial Conclusion," 303.

39. See Margit Cohn, "Fuzzy Legality in Regulation: The Legislative Mandate Revisited," *Law and Policy* 23, no. 4 (2001): 469–497.

40. See Ronald Wintrobe, *The Political Economy of Dictatorships* (Cambridge: Cambridge University Press, 1998); Bruce Bueno de Mesquita, Alastair Smith, *The Dictator's Handbook: Why Bad Behavior Is Almost Always Good Politics* (New York: Public Affairs, 2011).

41. See Gel'man, *Authoritarian Russia*, chapter 2; *The New Autocracy: Information, Politics, and Policy in Putin's Russia*, ed. Daniel Treisman (Washington, DC: Brookings Institution Press, 2018); Timothy Frye, *The Weak Strongman: The Limits of Power in Putin's Russia* (Princeton, NJ: Princeton University Press, 2021).

42. "Institutions . . . are created to serve the interests of those with the bargaining power to devise new rules," Douglass C. North, *Institutions, Institutional Changes, and Economic Performance* (Cambridge: Cambridge University Press, 1990), 16.

43. See Acemoglu, Robinson, *Why Nations Fail*, especially chapter 3.

44. See North, Wallis, Weingast, *Violence and Social Orders*, especially chapter 1.

45. See Robert D. Putnam, *Making Democracy Work: Civic Traditions in Modern Italy* (Princeton, NJ: Princeton University Press. 1993)

46. See Joel S. Migdal, *Strong Societies and Weak States: State-Society Relations and State Capabilities in the Third World* (Princeton, NJ: Princeton University Press, 1988); *Trust and Governance*, eds. Valerie Braithwaite, Margaret Levi (New York: Russell Sage Foundation, 1998).

47. See Bo Rothstein, *The Quality of Government: Corruption, Social Trust, and Inequality in International Perspective* (Chicago: University of Chicago Press, 2011).

48. See Edward Banfield, *The Moral Basis of a Backward Society* (Glencoe, IL: Free Press, 1958); Allen Hicken, "Clientelism," *Annual Review of Political Science* 14 (2011): 289–310; Hale, *Patronal Politics*, especially chapter 3.

49. See Putnam, *Making Democracy Work*; Avner Greif, *Institutions and the Path to the Modern Economy: Lessons from Medieval Trade* (Cambridge: Cambridge University Press, 2006); Rothstein, *The Quality of Government*.

50. Among the voluminous literature on Russia and post-Soviet countries, see, in particular, Åslund, *Russia's Capitalist Revolution*; Gerald Easter, *Coercion, Capital, and Postcommunist States* (Ithaca, NY: Cornell University Press, 2012); Alena V. Ledeneva, *Can Russia Modernise? Sistema, Power Networks, and Informal Governance* (Cambridge: Cambridge University Press, 2013); Karen Dawisha, *Putin's Kleptocracy: Who Owns Russia?* (New York: Simon and Schuster, 2014); Hale, *Patronal Politics*; Brian D. Taylor, "The Transformation of the Russian State," in *The Oxford Handbook of Transformations of the State*, eds. Stephan Leibfried, Evelyne Huber, Matthew Lange, Johan D. Levy, John D. Stephens (Oxford: Oxford University Press, 2015), 637–653.

51. See Åslund, *Russia's Capitalist Revolution*, especially chapter 8.

52. See Dawisha, *Putin's Kleptocracy*; Åslund, *Russia's Crony Capitalism*.

53. See Balint Magyar, *Post-Communist Mafia State: The Case of Hungary* (Budapest: Central European University Press, 2016).

54. See Ledeneva, *Can Russia Modernise?*, especially chapter 1.

55. See Hale, *Patronal Politics*, chapter 3.

56. See Stefan Hedlund, *Russian Path Dependence: A People with a Troubled History* (London: Routledge, 2005).

57. For a classical account from this perspective, see Richard Pipes, *Russia under the Old Regime* (New York: Scribner, 1974).

58. For comparative historical analyses, see Charles Tilly, *Coercion, Capital, and European States, AD 990–1992* (Oxford: Basil Blackwell, 1992); North, Wallis, Weingast, *Violence and Social Orders*; Francis Fukuyama, *The Origins of Political Order: From Prehuman Times to the French Revolution* (New York: Farrar, Straus, and Giroux, 2011); Francis Fukuyama, *Political Order and Political Decay: From the Industrial Revolution to the Globalization of Democracy* (New York: Farrar, Straus, and Giroux, 2014).

59. See Mancur Olson, "Dictatorship, Democracy, and Development," *American Political Science Review* 87, no. 3 (1993): 567–576.

60. The list of heavily corrupt and completely inefficient leaders in sub-Saharan Africa, such as Mobutu Sese Seko in Congo (Zaire) (1965–1997) or Robert Mugabe in Zimbabwe (1980–2017), is quite extensive. Among leaders in post-Soviet Eurasia,

Saparmurat Niyazov in Turkmenistan (1985–2006), as well as his successor, Gurban-guly Berdymuhamedow, who rules the country until 2022, may belong to this category.

61. For a critical account, see William R. Easterly, *The Tyranny of Experts: Economists, Dictators, and the Forgotten Rights of the Poor* (New York: Basic Books, 2014).

62. See Max Weber, "Politics as a Vocation," in *From Max Weber: Essays in Sociology*, eds. H. H. Gerth, C. Wright Mills (New York: Oxford University Press, 1946), 77–128.

63. See Charles Tilly, "War Making and State Making as Organized Crime," in *Bringing the State Back In*, eds. Peter Evans, Dietrich Rueschemeyer, Theda Skocpol (Cambridge: Cambridge University Press, 1985), 169–187; Tilly, *Coercion, Capital, and European States*.

64. See Michael Mann, "The Autonomous Power of the State: Its Origins, Mechanisms, and Results," *European Journal of Sociology* 25, no. 2 (1984): 185–213.

65. See Douglass C. North, Barry R. Weingast, "Constitutions and Commitment: The Evolution of Institutions Governing Public Choice in Seventeen-Century England," *Journal of Economic History* 49, no. 4 (1989): 803–832; for a theoretical and comparative analysis, see North, Wallis, Weingast, *Violence and Social Orders*.

66. See Steven Levitsky, Lucan A. Way, *Competitive Authoritarianism: Hybrid Regimes after the Cold War* (Cambridge: Cambridge University Press, 2010).

67. Among the voluminous literature on the subject, see in particular: *Democracy in Decline?*, eds. Larry Diamond, Marc F. Plattner (Baltimore: Johns Hopkins University Press, 2015); Steven Levitsky, Daniel Ziblatt, *How Democracies Die* (New York: Broadway Books, 2018); Yascha Mounk, "The Undemocratic Dilemma," *Journal of Democracy* 29, no. 2 (2018): 98–112.

68. For a detailed account of varieties of authoritarian regimes, see Barbara Geddes, Joseph Wright, Erica Frantz, *How Dictatorships Work: Power, Personalization, and Collapse* (Cambridge: Cambridge University Press, 2018). For a comparison of quality of governance in various types of authoritarian regimes, see Nicolas Charron and Victor Lapuente, "Which Dictators Produce Quality of Government?," *Studies in Comparative International Development* 46, no. 4 (2011): 397–423.

69. For analysis of these issues in a comparative perspective, see Alexander Libman, Michael Rochlitz, *Federalism in China and Russia: Story of Success and Story of Failure?* (Cheltenham: Edward Elgar, 2019).

70. Dani Rodrik, "The Myth of Authoritarian Growth," *Project Syndicate*, August 9, 2010, http://www.project-syndicate.org/commentary/the-myth-of-authoritarian-growth, accessed September 7, 2021.

71. For this argument, see Bueno de Mesquita, Smith, *The Dictator's Handbook*, especially chapter 3.

72. See William Golding, *Lord of the Flies* (London: Faber and Faber, 1954). The real story that inspired Golding's novel was just the opposite: teenagers, who serve as the main characters of the book, demonstrated a high capacity and willingness to cooperate for the common good. See Rutger Bregman, *Humankind: A Hopeful History* (London: Bloomsbury, 2020), chapter 2.

73. For the first such interpretation of the novel among political scientists, see Samuel P. Huntington, "Political Development and Political Decay," *World Politics* 17, no. 3 (1965): 416.

74. See Bueno de Mesquita, Smith, *The Dictator's Handbook*.

75. See Taylor, "The Transformation of the Russian State."

76. See Joel S. Hellman, "Winners Take All: The Politics of Partial Reform in Post-communist Transitions," *World Politics* 50, no. 2 (1998): 203–234.

77. See Hale, *Patronal Politics*, especially chapter 11; Gel'man, *Authoritarian Russia*, chapter 2; Lucan A. Way, *Pluralism by Default: Weak Autocrats and the Rise of Competitive Politics* (Baltimore: Johns Hopkins University Press, 2015), especially chapter 6.

78. See North, *Institutions*, 16.

79. On "performance legitimacy" under authoritarianism, see Samuel P. Huntington, *The Third Wave: Democratization in the Late Twentieth Century*, Norman: University of Oklahoma Press, 1991), 55.

80. For a comparative analysis, see Jason Brownlee, "Hereditary Succession in Modern Autocracies," *World Politics*, 59, no. 4 (2007): 595–628.

81. See Olson, "Dictatorship, Democracy, and Development."

82. See Dawisha, *Putin's Kleptocracy*.

83. On protests in Russia in the 1990s and in the 2000s, see Graeme B. Robertson, *The Politics of Protests in Hybrid Regimes: Managing Dissent in Post-Communist Russia* (Cambridge: Cambridge University Press, 2011); Samuel A. Greene, *Moscow in Movement: Power and Opposition in Putin's Russia* (Stanford, CA: Stanford University Press, 2014).

84. On the impact of international actors on economic policies and regulatory frameworks in Eastern Europe, see, in particular, Hilary Appel, Mitchell Orenstein, *From Triumph to Crisis: Neoliberal Economic Reform in Postcommunist Countries* (Cambridge: Cambridge University Press, 2018).

85. On the impact of Western linkages and leverages on regime-building in various regions of the world, see Levitsky, Way, *Competitive Authoritarianism*, chapter 2.

86. See Bueno de Mesquita, Smith, *The Dictator's Handbook*, chapter 1.

87. See Melville, Mironyuk, "'Bad Enough' Governance."

88. See Fabian Burkhardt, "Foolproofing Putinism," *Ridl.io*, 2021, March 29, https://www.ridl.io/en/foolproofing-putinism/, accessed September 7, 2021.

89. For a detailed account, see Andrei Yakovlev, "Composition of Ruling Elite, Incentives for Productive Usage of Rents, and the Prospects of Russia's Limited Access Order," *Post-Soviet Affairs* 37, no. 5 (2021): 417–434.

90. For these parallels, see Gel'man, *Authoritarian Russia*, 25–26.

91. For some accounts of governance during the last decades of the Soviet Union, see, in particular, Jerry F. Hough, Merle Fainsod, *How the Soviet Union Is Governed* (Cambridge, MA: Harvard University Press, 1979); Timothy J. Colton, *The Dilemma of Reform in the Soviet Union* (New York: Council of Foreign Relations, 1986); Yegor Gaidar, *Collapse of an Empire: Lessons for Modern Russia* (Washington, DC: Brookings Institution Press, 2007).

92. For a detailed account, see William A. Clark, *Crime and Punishment in Soviet Officialdom: Combatting Corruption in the Soviet Elite, 1965–1990* (Armonk, NY: M. E. Sharpe, 1993).

93. For different assessments of Soviet economic policies during perestroika, see Anders Åslund, *Gorbachev's Struggle for Economic Reform* (Ithaca, NY: Cornell University Press, 1991); Vladimir Mau, "Perestroika: Theoretical and Political Problems of Economic Reforms in the USSR," *Europe-Asia Studies* 47, no. 3 (1995): 387–411; Chris Miller, *The Struggle to Save the Soviet Economy: Mikhail Gorbachev and the Collapse of the USSR* (Chapel Hill: University of North Carolina Press, 2016).

94. Among different accounts of the Soviet collapse, see, in particular, David Kotz, Fred Weir, *Revolution from Above: The Demise of the Soviet System* (London: Routledge, 1997); Gaidar, *Collapse of an Empire*; Stephen Kotkin, *Armageddon Averted: The Soviet Collapse, 1970–2000* (Oxford: Oxford University Press, 2008); Serhiy Plokhy, *The Last Empire: The Final Days of the Soviet Union* (New York: Basic Books, 2015).

95. See Volkov, *Violent Entrepreneurship*, chapter 5.

96. For detailed descriptions, see Chrystia Freeland, *Sale of the Century: The Inside Story of the Second Russian Revolution* (Boston: Little, Brown, 2000); David Hoffman, *Oligarchs: The Wealth and Power in the New Russia* (New York: Public Affairs Books, 2002).

97. See Kathryn Stoner-Weiss, *Resisting the State: Reform and Retrenchment in Post-Soviet Russia* (Cambridge: Cambridge University Press, 2006).

98. See Volkov, *Violent Entrepreneurship*, chapters 5 and 6.

99. On the "triple transition," see Claus Offe, "Capitalism by Democratic Design? Democratic Theory Facing the Triple Transition in East Central Europe," *Social Research* 58, no. 4 (1991): 865–892.

100. See Yakov Pappe and Yana Galukhina, *Rossiiskii krupnyi biznes: pervye 15 let, Ekonomicheskie khroniki 1993–2008* (Moscow: State University—Higher School of Economics, 2009); Thane Gustafson, *Wheel of Fortune: The Battle for Oil and Power in Russia* (Cambridge, MA: Belknap Press of Harvard University Press, 2012).

101. See Vladimir Gel'man, "Leviathan's Return? The Policy of Recentralization in Contemporary Russia," in *Federalism and Local Politics in Russia*, eds. Cameron Ross, Adrian Campbell (London: Routledge, 2009), 1–24; Gulnaz Sharafutdinova, "Subnational Governance in Russia: How Putin Changed the Contract with His Agents and the Problems It Created for Medvedev," *Publius* 40, no. 4 (2010): 672–696.

102. See Volkov, *Violent Entrepreneurship*, chapter 6.

103. See Theda Skocpol, "Bringing the State Back In: Strategies of Analysis in Current Research," in *Bringing the State Back In*, eds. Peter Evans, Dietrich Rueschemeyer, Theda Skocpol (Cambridge: Cambridge University Press, 1985), 3–37.

104. On post-revolutionary stabilization, see Arthur Stinchcombe, "Ending Revolutions and Building New Governments," *Annual Review of Political Science* 2 (1999): 49–73.

105. For a detailed account of economic changes in Russia, see *The Oxford Handbook of the Russian Economy*, eds. Michael Alexeev, Shlomo Weber (Oxford: Oxford University Press, 2013).

106. See Aleksashenko, *Putin's Counterrevolution*, chapter 1.

107. See also *Authoritarian Modernization in Russia: Ideas, Institutions, and Policies*, ed. Vladimir Gel'man (Abingdon: Routledge, 2017).

108. For some descriptions, see Aleksashenko, *Putin's Counterrevolution*, especially chapter 6; Åslund, *Russia's Crony Capitalism*, chapter 2.

109. Adam Przeworski, *Democracy and the Market: Political and Economic Reforms in Eastern Europe and Latin America* (Cambridge: Cambridge University Press, 1991), 86.

110. For comparative analyses of Russia's subnational politics, see Ora John Reuter, Graeme B. Robertson, "Subnational Appointments in Authoritarian Regimes: Evidence from Russian Gubernatorial Appointments," *Journal of Politics* 74, no. 4 (2012): 1023–1037; Noah Buckley, Ora John Reuter, "Performance Incentives under Autocracy: Evidence from Russia's Regions," *Comparative Politics* 51, no. 2 (2019): 239–266.

111. For a comprehensive account, see *Zastoi-2: Posledstviya, riski i al'ternativy dlya rossiiskoi ekonomiki*, ed. Kirill Rogov (Moscow: Liberal'naya missiya, 2021).

112. See Gel'man, *Authoritarian Russia*, chapter 5.

Chapter 2

1. See Alexei Navalny, "Khroniki genotsida russkikh," *navalny.com*, December 24, 2014, https://navalny.com/p/4036/, accessed September 7, 2021.

2. For various accounts of reforms in the railway sector in Russia since the 2000s, see Russell Pittman, "Blame the Switchman? Russian Railways Restructuring after Ten Years," in *The Oxford Handbook of the Russian Economy*, eds. Michael Alexeev, Shlomo Weber (Oxford: Oxford University Press, 2013), 490–513; Konstantin Gaaze, "Reformy po krugu: president vernul elektrichki, kotorye sam otmenil," *Forbes.ru*, February 5, 2015, http://www.forbes.ru/mneniya-column/vertikal/279533-reformy-po-krugu-prezi-dent-vernul-elektrichki-kotorye-sam-otmenil, accessed April, 18, 2020; Farid Khusainov, *Zheleznye dorogi i rynok* (Moscow, Nauka, 2015), 64–117. For a critical assessment, see Alexei Navalny, "Problema elektrichek, likbez ot FBK," *navalny.com*, February 5, 2015, https://navalny.com/p/4107/, accessed September 7, 2021.

3. The regional budgets bear responsibility for implementing Vladimir Putin's May 2012 decrees that called on regional authorities to achieve a major rise in public sector employees' salaries without an increase in budgetary revenues, so many other expenditures (including subsidizing commuter trains) were inevitably cut.

4. See Navalny, "Problema elektrichek."

5. I am indebted to Farid Khusainov for clarifications of these issues.

6. See Pittman, "Blame the Switchman?"

7. See Nikolay Petrov, "Nomenklatura and the Elite," *Russia in 2020: Scenarios for the Future*, eds. Maria Lipman, Nikolay Petrov (Washington, DC: Carnegie Endowment for International Peace, 2011), 499–530.

8. See Yakunin's personal web page on the official site of the Faculty of Political Science at the Moscow State University, http://polit.msu.ru/teachers/yakunin/, accessed September 7, 2021. Yakunin's major 470-page coauthored monograph, which portrayed vicious attacks by the West on the Russian statehood and called for Russian counterattacks, may be regarded as a prime example of a conspiracy theory. See Vladimir Yakunin, Vardan Bagdasaryan, Stepan Sulakshin, *Novye tekhnologii bor'by s rossiiskoi gosudarsnennost'yu*, 3rd ed. (Moscow: Nauchnyi ekspert, 2013).

9. See *22 Ideas to Fix the World: Conversations with the World's Foremost Thinkers*, eds. Piotr Dutkiewicz, Richard Sakwa (New York: New York University Press, 2013), chapter 9.

10. See Navalny, "Problema elektrichek."

11. See Brian Taylor, *The Code of Putinism* (Oxford: Oxford University Press, 2018), chapter 5. For a general account of state-business relations in Russia, see Andrei Yakovlev, "The Evolution of Business-State Interaction in Russia: From State Capture to Business Capture?" *Europe-Asia Studies* 58, no. 7 (2006): 1033–1056; Andrei Yakovlev, "State-Business Relations in Russia after 2011: 'New Deal' or Imitation of Changes?" in *The Challenge for Russia's Politicized Economic System*, ed. Susanne Oxenstierna (Abingdon, NY: Routledge, 2015), 59–76.

12. See Mikhail Bushuev, "Zachem byvshii glava RZhD Yakunin poluchil nemetskuyu rabochuyu vizu," *dw.com*, August 21, 2018, https://www.dw.com/ru/зачем-бывший-глава-ржд-якунин-получил-немецкую-рабочую-визу/a-45157830, accessed September 7, 2021.

13. See Farid Khusainov, "Negromkii yubilei. Programme strukturnoi reformy na zheleznodorozhnom transporte—20 let," *vgudok.com*, May 20, 2021, https://vgudok.com/lenta/negromkiy-yubiley-programme-strukturnoy-reformy-na-zheleznodorozhnom-transporte-20-let, accessed September 7, 2021.

14. For a detailed historical account, see *The Economic Transformation of the Soviet Union, 1913–1945*, eds. R. W. Davies, Mark Harrison, S. G. Wheatcroft (Cambridge: Cambridge University Press, 1994), chapter 8.

15. See Pittman, "Blame the Switchman?"; Khusainov, *Zheleznye dorogi i rynok*, 71–92.

16. In particular, the leader of the Russian opposition Alexei Navalny achieved his nationwide name recognition because of numerous disclosures of high-profile corruption among top officials and state managers, presented in much detail on his website, www.navalny.com, accessed September 7, 2021. See "On vam ne Dimon," https://dimon.navalny.com/, accessed September 7, 2021.

17. For a detailed overview, see *The Oxford Handbook of the Russian Economy*, eds. Michael Alexeev, Shlomo Weber (Oxford: Oxford University Press, 2013). See also chapter 4 of this book.

18. See Douglass C. North, *Institutions, Institutional Changes, and Economic Performance* (Cambridge: Cambridge University Press, 1990), 16.

19. See Milan Svolik, *The Politics of Authoritarian Rule* (Cambridge: Cambridge University Press, 2012), especially chapters 3 and 4; Barbara Geddes, Joseph Wright, Erica

Frantz, *How Dictatorships Work: Power, Personalization, and Collapse* (Cambridge: Cambridge University Press, 2018), especially chapters 4 and 5.

20. See Andreas Schedler, *The Politics of Uncertainty: Sustaining and Subverting Electoral Authoritarianism* (Oxford: Oxford University Press, 2013).

21. See Marc Morje Howard, Philip G. Roessler, "Liberalizing Electoral Outcomes in Competitive Authoritarian Regimes," *American Journal of Political Science* 50, no. 2 (2006): 365–381.

22. For overviews, see Grigore Pop-Eleches, "Historical Legacies and Post-Communist Regime Change," *Journal of Politics* 69, no. 4 (2007): 908–926; Jody La Porte, Danielle Lussier, "What Was the Leninist Legacy? Assessing Twenty Years of Scholarship," *Slavic Review* 70, no. 3 (2011): 637–654.

23. See Michael Bratton, Nicolas van de Walle, "Neopatrimonial Regimes and Political Transitions in Africa," *World Politics* 46, no. 4 (1994): 453–489; Gero Erdmann, Ulf Engel, *Neopatrimonialism Revisited: Beyond a Catch-all Concept* (Hamburg: German Institute for Global and Area Studies, 2006), GIGA Working Paper no. 16, https://core.ac.uk/download/pdf/71729549.pdf, accessed September 7, 2021.

24. See Richard Pipes, *Russia under the Old Regime* (New York: Scribner, 1974).

25. See Kenneth Jowitt, "Soviet Neotraditionalism: The Political Corruption of a Leninist Regime," *Soviet Studies* 35 no. 3 (1983): 275–297.

26. See Herbert Kitschelt, Zdenka Mansfeldova, Radoslaw Markowski, Gabor Toka, *Post-Communist Party Systems: Competition, Representation, and Inter-Party Cooperation* (Cambridge: Cambridge University Press, 1999), 21–24.

27. See Henry E. Hale, *Patronal Politics: Eurasian Regime Dynamics in Comparative Perspective* (Cambridge: Cambridge University Press, 2014), especially chapter 3.

28. See Alena V. Ledeneva, *Can Russia Modernise? Sistema, Power Networks, and Informal Governance* (Cambridge: Cambridge University Press, 2013), especially chapter 1.

29. See Stefan Hedlund, *Russian Path Dependence* (London: Routledge, 2005).

30. On the "track" as a Russian understanding of path dependency, see Aleksandr Auzan, "Lovushka 'kolei,'" *Colta.ru*, September 4, 2015, http://www.colta.ru/articles/society/8428, accessed September 7, 2021.

31. For a detailed account of the "Cotton Affair," the most notorious case of high-level corruption in Soviet Uzbekistan, see Riccardo Mario Cucciolla, *The Crisis of Soviet Power in Central Asia: The 'Uzbek Cotton Affair, 1975–1991* (PhD dissertation, Lucca: IMT School of Advanced Studies, 2017), http://e-theses.imtlucca.it/213/1/Cucciolla_phdthesis.pdf, accessed September 7, 2021.

32. See Bruce Bueno de Mesquita, Alastair Smith, *The Dictator's Handbook: Why Bad Behavior Is Almost Always Good Politics* (New York: Public Affairs, 2011), especially chapter 3.

33. See Konstantin Sonin, "Why the Rich May Favor Poor Protection of Property Rights," *Journal of Comparative Economics* 31, no. 4 (2003): 715–731; Anders Åslund, *Russia's Capitalist Revolution: Why Market Reforms Succeeded and Democracy Failed* (Washington, DC: Peterson Institute for International Economics, 2007); Oleksandr Fisun, "Rethinking Post-Soviet Politics from a Neopatrimonial Perspective,"

Demokratizatsiya: The Journal of Post-Soviet Democratization 20, no. 2 (2012): 87–96; Hale, *Patronal Politics*, especially chapter 6.

34. See North, *Institutions*, 3.

35. Stephen Kotkin, Mark R. Beissinger, "The Historical Legacies of Communism: An Empirical Agenda," in *Historical Legacies of Communism in Russia and Eastern Europe*, eds. Mark R. Beissinger, Stephen Kotkin (Cambridge: Cambridge University Press, 2014), 7.

36. Ibid., 16.

37. See Clifford G. Gaddy, "Room for Error: The Economic Legacy of Soviet Spatial Misallocation," in *Historical Legacies of Communism in Russia and Eastern Europe*, eds. Mark R. Beissinger, Stephen Kotkin (Cambridge: Cambridge University Press, 2014), 52–67.

38. See Vladimir Gel'man, Otar Marganiya, Dmitry Travin, *Reexamining Economic and Political Reforms in Russia, 1985–2000: Generations, Ideas, and Changes* (Lanham, MD: Lexington Books, 2014), especially chapter 6.

39. See Arthur Denzau, Douglass C. North, "Sharing Mental Models: Ideologies and Institutions," *Kyklos* 47, no. 1 (1994): 3–31.

40. See Eugene Huskey, "Legacies and Departures in the Russian State Executive," in *Historical Legacies of Communism in Russia and Eastern Europe*, eds. Mark R. Beissinger, Stephen Kotkin (Cambridge: Cambridge University Press, 2014), 111–127.

41. See Brian Taylor, "From Police State to Police State? Legacies and Law Enforcement in Russia," in *Historical Legacies of Communism in Russia and Eastern Europe*, eds. Mark R. Beissinger, Stephen Kotkin (Cambridge: Cambridge University Press, 2014), 128–151.

42. See Vadim Volkov, Ivan Griroriev, Arina Dmitrieva, Ekaterina Moiseeva, Ella Paneyakh, Mikhail Pozdnyakov, Kirill Titaev, Irina Chetverikova, Maria Shklyaruk, *Kontseptsiya kompleksnoi organizatsionno-upravlencheskoi reformy pravookhranitel'nykh organov RF* (Saint Petersburg, European University at Saint Petersburg, Institute for the Rule of Law, 2013), http://www.enforce.spb.ru/images/Issledovanya/IRL_KGI_Reform_final_11.13.pdf, accessed September 7, 2021; Ella Paneyakh, "Faking Performances Together: Systems of Performance Evaluation in Russian Enforcement Agencies and Production of Bias and Privilege," *Post-Soviet Affairs* 30, no. 2–3 (2014): 115–136; Brian D. Taylor, "The Transformation of the Russian State," in *The Oxford Handbook of Transformations of the State*, eds. Stephan Leibfried, Evelyne Huber, Matthew Lange, Johan D. Levy, John D. Stephens (Oxford: Oxford University Press, 2015), 637–653.

43. On the "power vertical," see Vladimir Gel'man, Sergei Ryzhenkov, "Local Regimes, Sub-National Governance, and the Power Vertical" in Contemporary Russia," *Europe-Asia Studies* 63, no. 3 (2011): 449–465.

44. For example, workplace mobilization during the 2011–2012 national elections in Russia was less typical for private enterprises in comparison with state-owned companies and the public sector. See Timothy Frye, Ora John Reuter, David Szakonyi, "Political Machines at Work: Voter Mobilization and Electoral Subversion in the Workplace," *World Politics* 66, no. 2 (2014): 195–228.

45. See Vadim Volkov, *Violent Entrepreneurs: The Role of Force in the Making of Russian Capitalism* (Ithaca, NY: Cornell University Press, 2002), chapters 5 and 6.

46. See Gulnaz Sharafutdinova, "Subnational Governance in Russia: How Putin Changed the Contract with His Agents and the Problems It Created for Medvedev," *Publius* 40, no. 4 (2010): 672–696; Gel'man, Ryzhenkov, "Local Regimes."

47. For comparisons of subnational governance in China and Russia, see Michael Rochlitz, Vera Kulpina, Thomas Remington, Andrei Yakovlev, "Performance Incentives and Economic Growth: Regional Officials in Russia and China," *Eurasian Geography and Economics* 56, no. 4 (2015): 421–445; Alexander Libman, Michael Rochlitz, *Federalism in China and Russia: Story of Success and Story of Failure?* (Cheltenham: Edward Elgar, 2019).

48. See Eugene Huskey, *Presidential Power in Russia* (Armonk, NY: M. E. Sharpe, 1999).

49. For an in-depth analysis of the complex web of relationships between Russia's law enforcement agencies and its effects on their performance, see Ella Paneyakh, Kirill Titaev, Maria Shklyaruk, *Traektoriya ugolovnogo dela: institutsional'nyi analiz* (Saint Petersburg: European University at Saint Petersburg Press, 2018).

50. For example, more than 10 percent of Russian city mayors faced with criminal charges during the period between 2002 and 2018. See Noah Buckley, Ora John Reuter, Michael Rochlitz, Anton Aisin, "Staying Out of Trouble: Criminal Cases Against Russian Mayors," *Comparative Political Studies*, online first, https://journals.sagepub.com/doi/full/10.1177/00104140211047399, accessed February 18, 2022.

51. See Kirill Rogov, "The Art of Coercion: Repressions and Repressiveness in Putin's Russia," *Russian Politics* 3, no. 2 (2018): 151–174.

52. For empirical evidence and analyses, see Keith Darden, "The Integrity of Corrupt State: Graft as an Informal Political Institution," *Politics and Society* 36, no. 1 (2008): 35–59; Ledeneva, *Can Russia Modernise?*

53. On the role of schools in vote delivery during elections in Russia, see Natalia Forrat, "Shock-Resistant Authoritarianism: Schoolteachers and Infrastructural State Capacity in Putin's Russia," *Comparative Politics* 50, no. 3 (2018): 417–449.

54. See Ivan Petrov, Viktor Yadukha, "Molodezh' mechtaet o trube," *rbc.ru*, May 27, 2009, https://www.udbiz.ru/novosti/38/5792/, accessed September 7, 2021.

55. See *Kontseptsiya kompleksnoi organizatsionno-upravlencheskoi reformy*; Paneyakh, Titaev, Shklayruk, *Traektoriya ugolovnogo dela*, chapter 2.

56. For a detailed account, see Thane Gustafson, *Wheel of Fortune: The Battle for Oil and Power in Russia* (Cambridge, MA: Belknap Press of Harvard University Press, 2012).

57. For various interpretations of intraelite relationships in Russia, see Petrov, "Nomenklatura and the Elite"; Evgeny Minchenko, Kirill Petrov, *Politburo 2.0: Renovation Instead of Dismantling*, October 12, 2017, https://minchenko.ru/netcat_files/userfiles/2/Dokumenty/Politburo_2.0_October_2017_ENG.pdf, accessed September 7, 2021. See also "The Foreign Policy Attitudes of Russian Elites, 1993–2016," *Post-Soviet Affairs* 35, no. 5–6 (2019), special issue.

58. See Erdmann, Engel, *Neopatrimonialism Revisited.*

59. See Bratton, van de Walle, "Neopatrimonial Regimes and Political Transitions."

60. For a detailed overview, see *Russia after the Global Economic Crisis*, eds. Anders Åslund, Sergei Guriev, Andrew C. Kuchins (Washington, DC: Peterson Institute for International Economics, 2010).

61. See Michael Bratton, Nicolas van de Walle, *Democratic Experiments in Africa: Regime Transitions in Comparative Perspective* (Cambridge: Cambridge University Press, 1997); Erdmann, Engel, *Neopatrimonialism Revisited.*

62. See *Zastoi-2: Posledstviya, riski i al'ternativy dlya rossiiskoi ekonomiki*, ed. Kirill Rogov (Moscow: Liberal'naya missiya, 2021).

63. For this argument, see Kirill Rogov, "Forty Years in the Desert: The Political Cycles of Post-Soviet Transition," in *Russia 2025: Scenarios for the Russian Future*, eds. Maria Lipman, Nikolay Petrov (London: Palgrave Macmillan, 2013), 18–45.

64. For an in-depth analysis, see Brian Taylor, "The Police Reform in Russia: Policy Process in a Hybrid Regime," *Post-Soviet Affairs* 30, no. 2–3 (2014): 226–255.

65. See William R. Easterly, *The Elusive Quest for Growth: Economists' Adventures and Misadventures in the Tropics* (Cambridge, MA: MIT Press, 2001), part II.

66. See Geddes, *Politician's Dilemma.*

67. See Mancur Olson, *The Rise and Decline of Nations: Economic Growth, Stagflation, and Social Rigidities* (New Haven, CT: Yale University Press, 1982).

68. For the essence of these risk perceptions among Russia's liberal reformers, see "Zhestkim kursom . . . Analiticheskaya zapiska Leningradskoi assotsiatsii sotsial'no-ekonomicheskikh nauk," *Vek XX i mir*, no. 6 (1990): 15–19.

69. For an account of the effects of distributional coalitions in Russia's regions, see Anton Shirikov, *Anatomiya bezdeistviya: politicheskie instituty i byudzhetnye konflikty v regionakh Rossii* (Saint Petersburg: European University at Saint Petersburg Press, 2010).

70. For a classic account, see Jeffrey L. Pressman, Aaron B. Wildavsky, *Implementation* (Berkeley: University of California Press, 1973).

71. For a critique of "high modernism," see James C. Scott, *Seeing Like a State: How Certain Schemes to Improve the Human Condition Have Failed* (New Haven, CT: Yale University Press, 1998).

72. See Paneyakh, "Faking Performances Together"; Paneyakh, Titaev, Shklyaruk, *Traektoriya ugolovnogo dela*, chapter 3.

73. For an analysis of the "loyalty versus efficiency" dilemma among Russia's regional chief executives, see Ora John Reuter, Graeme B. Robertson, "Subnational Appointments in Authoritarian Regimes: Evidence from Russian Gubernatorial Appointments," *Journal of Politics* 74, no. 4 (2012): 1023–1037.

74. See Lev Lyubimov, "Ne nuzhno vsem vydavat' attestaty. Pochemu v Rossii pora menyat' podkhod k obucheniyu v shkolakh," *Lenta.ru*, February 19, 2015, http://lenta.ru/articles/2015/02/19/school/, accessed September 7, 2021.

75. On these changes, see *Doing Business 2015: Going beyond Efficiency* (Washington, DC: World Bank, 2015), http://www.doingbusiness.org/reports/global-reports/

doing-business-2015, accessed September 7, 2021. For a critical overview of the use of global rankings in various countries, see *Ranking the World: Grading States as a Tool of Global Governance*, ed. Alexander Cooley, Jack Snyder (Cambridge: Cambridge University Press, 2015).

76. For a detailed yet controversial account, see Grigory Rodchenkov, *The Rodchenkov Affair: How I Brought Down Russia's Secret Doping Empire* (London: Penguin Random House, 2020).

77. See "Doing Business—Data Irregularities Statement," *The World Bank*, August 27, 2020, https://www.worldbank.org/en/news/statement/2020/08/27/doing-business -data-irregularities-statement, accessed September 7, 2021.

78. For a critical account, see Andrei Yakovlev, Denis Ivanov, "Tekhnicheskii uspekh: pochemu vzlet Rossii v Doing Business ne pomog biznesu," *Rbc.ru*, November 14, 2018, https://www.rbc.ru/opinions/economics/14/11/2018/5bebd6db9a7947c705e43594, accessed September 7, 2021.

79. For a detailed overview, see *The Oxford Handbook of the Russian Economy*.

80. See Easterly, *The Elusive Quest for Growth*, part I.

81. See Daron Acemoglu, James A. Robinson, *Why Nations Fail: The Origins of Power, Prosperity, and Poverty* (New York: Crown Business, 2012), especially chapter 3.

82. On these strategies, see Yaroslav Kuzminov, Vadim Radaev, Andrei Yakovlev, Yevgeny Yasin, "Instituty: ot zaimstvovaniya k vyrashchivaniyu (opyt rossiiskikh reform i vozmozhnosti kul'tivirovaniya institutsional'nykh izmenenii)," *Voprosy ekonomiki*, no. 5 (2005): 5–27.

83. On the role of experts in policy-making under authoritarianism, see, in particular, William R. Easterly, *The Tyranny of Experts: Economists, Dictators, and the Forgotten Rights of the Poor* (New York: Basic Books, 2014), especially chapter 13; Calvert W. Jones, "Adviser to the King: Experts, Rationality, and Legitimacy," *World Politics* 71, no. 1 (2019): 1–43.

84. See Andrey Zaostrovtsev, "Zakon vseobshchei shitizatsii," *fontanka.ru*, August 11, 2009, http://www.fontanka.ru/2009/08/11/116/, accessed September 7, 2021.

85. For a detailed account of implementation of the EGE in the 2000s, see Andrey Starodubtsev, "How Does the Government Implement Unpopular Reforms? Evidence from Education Policy in Russia," in *Authoritarian Modernization in Russia: Ideas, Institutions, and Policies*, ed. Vladimir Gel'man (Abingdon: Routledge, 2017), 148–165.

86. North, *Institutions*, 16.

87. See Vladimir Gel'man, *Authoritarian Russia: Analyzing Post-Soviet Regime Changes* (Pittsburgh, PA: University of Pittsburgh Press, 2015), chapter 5.

88. The minister, Mikhail Abyzov, a close ally of Dmitry Medvedev, left this post in 2018 because the ministerial office as such was abolished. In 2019, he was jailed due to accusations of embezzling state funds.

89. See Nikolay Petrov, Maria Lipman, Henry E. Hale, "Three Dilemmas of Hybrid Regime Governance: Russia from Putin to Putin," *Post-Soviet Affairs* 30, no. 1 (2014): 1–26.

90. See chapter 4 of this book.

91. For a vivid account, see Alexei Navalny. "Dlya bor'by s korruptsiei v pravitel'stve net kvoruma," *navalny.com*, February 9, 2015, https://navalny.com/p/4117/, accessed September 7, 2021.

92. See Geddes, *Politician's Dilemma*, 63–69; *The Politics of Public Sector Performance: Pockets of Effectiveness in Developing Countries*, ed. Michael Roll (London: Routledge, 2014).

93. See Easterly, *The Tyranny of Experts*, especially part II.

94. For polemics, see Steven Levitsky, Lucan A. Way, *Competitive Authoritarianism: Hybrid Regimes after the Cold War* (Cambridge: Cambridge University Press, 2010); Valerie J. Bunce, Sharon Wolchik, *Defeating Authoritarian Leaders in Postcommunist Countries* (Cambridge: Cambridge University Press, 2011); Lucan A. Way, *Pluralism by Default: Weak Autocrats and the Rise of Competitive Politics* (Baltimore: Johns Hopkins University Press, 2015).

95. See Levitsky, Way, *Competitive Authoritarianism*, especially chapter 2.

96. For a critical insider's account of Russia's relations with the IMF in the 1990s, see Martin Gilman, *No Precedent, No Plan: Inside Russia's 1998 Default* (Cambridge, MA: MIT Press, 2010).

97. See Easterly, *The Elusive Quest for Growth*, part III.

98. For a critique about Eastern Europe see Neil Abrams, M. Steven Fish, "Policies First, Institutions Second: Lessons from Estonia's Economic Reforms," *Post-Soviet Affairs* 31, no. 6 (2015): 491–513.

99. For a perceptive account of the behavior of Central Asian leaders and elites, see Alexander Cooley, John Heathershaw, *Dictators without Borders: Power and Money in Central Asia* (New Haven, CT: Yale University Press, 2017). For analysis of the legalization of status and wealth of Russian elites in the West, see Gulnaz Sharafutdinova, Karen Dawisha, "The Escape from Institution-Building in a Globalized World: Lessons from Russia," *Perspectives on Politics* 15, no. 2 (2017): 361–378.

100. For an in-depth analysis, see Juliet Johnson, *Priests of Prosperity: How Central Bankers Transformed the Postcommunist World* (Ithaca, NY: Cornell University Press, 2016).

101. See Yoshiko M. Herrera, *Mirrors of the Economy: National Accounts and International Norms in Russia and Beyond* (Ithaca, NY: Cornell University Press, 2010).

102. See Hilary Appel, *Tax Politics in Eastern Europe: Globalization, Regional Integration, and the Democratic Compromise* (Ann Arbor: University of Michigan Press, 2011).

103. For a similar argument, see Hale, *Patronal Politics*, 458–466.

104. See Balint Magyar, *Post-Communist Mafia State: The Case of Hungary* (Budapest: Central European University Press, 2016); see also chapter 7 of this book.

Chapter 3

1. For the most vigorous arguments in favor of authoritarian modernization during the Cold War, see Samuel P. Huntington, *Political Order in Changing Societies* (New

Haven, CT: Yale University Press, 1968). For a detailed critical account of practical uses of this approach in developing countries, see William R. Easterly, *The Tyranny of Experts: Economists, Dictators, and the Forgotten Rights of the Poor* (New York: Basic Books, 2014).

2. For twenty-first-century discussions, see, for example, Parag Hanna, *The Second World: Empires and Influence in the New Global Order* (New York: Random House, 2008); Roberto Stefan Foa, "Modernization and Authoritarianism," *Journal of Democracy* 29, no. 3 (2018): 129–140. Scholars of the political economy of populism concentrate on the controversial impact of populist politicians on government performance. See Sergei Guriev and Elias Papaioannou, "The Political Economy of Populism," *Journal of Economic Literature*, forthcoming https://www.aeaweb.org/articles?id=10.1257/jel.20201595&from=f, accessed February 15, 2022.

3. For a comprehensive account of various aspects of Russia's modernization, see *Russian Modernization: A New Paradigm*, eds. Markku Kivinen, Brendan Humphreys (Abingdon: Routledge, 2021).

4. On the concept of "triple transition," see Claus Offe, "Capitalism by Democratic Design? Democratic Theory Facing the Triple Transition in East Central Europe," *Social Research* 58, no. 4 (1991): 865–892.

5. See Vladimir Gel'man, *Authoritarian Russia: Analyzing Post-Soviet Regime Changes* (Pittsburgh, PA: University of Pittsburgh Press, 2015), especially chapter 3.

6. For various accounts, see Anders Åslund, *Russia's Capitalist Revolution: Why Market Reforms Succeeded and Democracy Failed* (Washington, DC: Peterson Institute for International Economics, 2007); Clifford G. Gaddy, Barry W. Ickes, *Bear Traps on Russia's Road to Modernization* (London: Routledge, 2013); Alena V. Ledeneva, *Can Russia Modernise? Sistema, Power Networks, and Informal Governance* (Cambridge: Cambridge University Press, 2013).

7. See Brian Taylor, *The Code of Putinism* (Oxford: Oxford University Press, 2018); *The New Autocracy: Information, Politics, and Policy in Putin's Russia*, ed. Daniel Treisman (Washington, DC: Brookings Institution Press, 2018); Timothy Frye, *Weak Strongman: The Limits of Power in Putin's Russia* (Princeton, NJ: Princeton University Press, 2021).

8. See Åslund, *Russia's Capitalist Revolution*; Gaddy, Ickes, *Bear Traps*; *The Oxford Handbook of the Russian Economy*, eds. Michael Alexeev, Shlomo Weber (Oxford: Oxford University Press, 2013).

9. See Vadim Volkov, *Violent Entrepreneurs: The Role of Force in the Making of Russian Capitalism* (Ithaca, NY: Cornell University Press, 2002); Brian Taylor, *State Building in Putin's Russia: Policing and Coercion after Communism* (Cambridge: Cambridge University Press, 2011); Gerald Easter, *Coercion, Capital, and Postcommunist States* (Ithaca, NY: Cornell University Press, 2012).

10. See Marie Mendras, *Russian Politics: The Paradox of a Weak State* (New York: Columbia University Press, 2011); Ledeneva, *Can Russia Modernise?*; Taylor, *The Code of Putinism*, especially chapter 5.

11. See *Historical Legacies of Communism in Russia and Eastern Europe*, eds. Mark R. Beissinger, Stephen Kotkin (Cambridge: Cambridge University Press, 2014).

12. See Steven Levitsky, Lucan A. Way, *Competitive Authoritarianism: Hybrid Regimes after the Cold War* (Cambridge: Cambridge University Press, 2010), especially chapter 2.

13. See Henry E. Hale, *Patronal Politics: Eurasian Regime Dynamics in Comparative Perspective* (Cambridge: Cambridge University Press, 2014), especially chapter 12; Daniel Treisman, "Income, Democracy, and Leader Turnover," *American Journal of Political Science* 59, no. 4 (2007): 927–942.

14. For various accounts, see Sergey Aleksashenko, *Putin's Counterrevolution: How Putin's Autocracy Undercut Russia's Economy and Chances for Democracy* (Washington, DC: Brookings Institution Press, 2018); Anders Åslund, *Russia's Crony Capitalism: The Path from Market Economy to Kleptocracy* (New Haven, CT: Yale University Press, 2019).

15. For classical accounts of the 1960s, see Walt Whitman Rostow, *The Stages of Economic Growth: A Non-Communist Manifesto* (Cambridge: Cambridge University Press, 1960); Cyril Black, *The Dynamics of Modernization: A Study in Comparative History* (New York: Harper & Row, 1966); Huntington, *Political Order in Changing Societies*.

16. See Adam Przeworski, Michael Alvarez, Jose Cheibub, Fernando Limongi, *Democracy and Development: Political Institutions and Well-Being in the World, 1950–1990* (Cambridge: Cambridge University Press, 2000); Ronald Inglehart, Christian Welzel, *Modernization, Cultural Changes, and Democracy: A Human Development Sequence* (Cambridge: Cambridge University Press, 2005).

17. "Neoliberalism" is widely used in present-day social science as a pejorative term. See David Harvey, *A Brief History of Neoliberalism* (Oxford: Oxford University Press, 2005). For a more balanced perspective in analysis of post-Communist neoliberal policies, see Hilary Appel, Mitchell Orenstein, *From Triumph to Crisis: Neoliberal Economic Reform in Postcommunist Countries* (Cambridge: Cambridge University Press, 2018).

18. See Douglass C. North, John J. Wallis, Barry R. Weingast, *Violence and Social Orders: A Conceptual Framework for Interpreting Recorded Human History* (Cambridge: Cambridge University Press, 2009).

19. See Daron Acemoglu, James A. Robinson, *Why Nations Fail: The Origins of Power, Prosperity, and Poverty* (New York: Crown Business, 2012).

20. See Charles Tilly, *Coercion, Capital, and European States, AD 990–1992* (Oxford: Basil Blackwell, 1992); Francis Fukuyama, *The Origins of Political Order: From Prehuman Times to the French Revolution* (New York: Farrar, Straus, and Giroux, 2011); Francis Fukuyama, *Political Order and Political Decay: From the Industrial Revolution to the Globalization of Democracy* (New York: Farrar, Straus, and Giroux, 2014).

21. For a critical account, see Easterly, *The Tyranny of Experts*.

22. For an overview, see *The Macroeconomics of Populism in Latin America*, eds. Rudiger Dornbusch, Sebastian Edwards (Chicago: University of Chicago Press, 1991).

23. See Huntington, *Political Order in Changing Societies*; Mancur Olson, *The Rise and Decline of Nations: Economic Growth, Stagflation, and Social Rigidities* (New Haven, CT: Yale University Press, 1982).

24. See Francis Fukuyama, *The End of History and the Last Man* (New York: Free Press, 1992).

25. See Offe, "Capitalism by Democratic Design?"

26. For the essence of these arguments, see Victor Polterovich, Vladimir Popov, "Democratization, Quality of Institutions and Economic Growth," *TIGER Working Papers*, no. 102, 2007, http://www.tiger.edu.pl/publikacje/TWP102.pdf, accessed September 7, 2021; Vladimir Popov, *Mixed Fortunes: An Economic History of China, Russia, and the West* (Oxford: Oxford University Press, 2014).

27. See "Zhestkim kursom . . . Analiticheskaya zapiska Leningradskoi assotsiatsii sotsial'no-ekonomicheskikh nauk"; *Vek XX i mir* no. 6 (1990): 15–19.

28. For the full text of this manifesto, see Dmitry Medvedev, "Rossiya, Vpered!," *Gazeta.ru*, September 25, 2009, http://www.gazeta.ru/comments/2009/09/10_a_3258568.shtml, accessed September 7, 2021.

29. See Huntington, *Political Order in Changing Societies*, 32–58.

30. See William Nordhaus, "The Political Business Cycle," *Review of Economic Studies* 42, no. 2 (1975): 169–190. On political business cycles in Russia in the 1990s, see Daniel Treisman, Vladimir Gimpelson, "Political Business Cycles and Russian Elections, or The Manipulations of 'Chudar,'" *British Journal of Political Science* 31, no. 2 (2001): 225–246.

31. See George Tsebelis, *Veto Players: How Political Institutions Work* (Princeton, NJ: Princeton University Press, 2002).

32. See Fritz W. Sharpf, "The Joint-Decision Trap: Lessons from German Federalism and European Integration," *Public Administration* 66, no. 3 (1988): 239–278.

33. See Hanna Bäck, Wolfgang C. Muller, Benjamin Nyblade, "Multiparty Government and Economic Policy-Making," *Public Choice* 170 (2017): 33–62.

34. See Olson, *The Rise and Decline of Nations*, especially chapter 3.

35. See Barbara Geddes, *Politician's Dilemma: Building State Capacity in Latin America* (Berkeley: University of California Press, 1994); Stephan Haggard, Robert Kaufman, *The Political Economy of Democratic Transitions* (Princeton, NJ: Princeton University Press, 1995).

36. See Venelin I. Ganev, "The Dorian Gray Effect: Winners as State Breakers in Postcommunism," *Communist and Post-Communist Studies* 34, no. 1 (2001): 1–25; Anna Grzymala-Busse, "Political Competition and the Politicization of the State in East Central Europe," *Comparative Political Studies* 36, no. 10 (2003): 1123–1147.

37. See Offe, "Capitalism by Democratic Design?"

38. See Przeworski, Alvarez, Cheibub, Limongi, *Democracy and Development*, especially chapter 3.

39. See Popov, *Mixed Fortunes*, especially chapters 4 and 5.

40. For critical accounts, see Thomas Carothers, "The 'Sequencing' Fallacy," *Journal of Democracy* 18, no. 1 (2007): 12–27; Dani Rodrik, "The Myth of Authoritarian

Growth," *Project Syndicate*, August 9, 2010, http://www.project-syndicate.org/commentary/the-myth-of-authoritarian-growth, accessed September 7, 2021.

41. See Alexander Gerschenkron, *Economic Backwardness in Historical Perspective* (Cambridge, MA: Harvard University Press); Black, *The Dynamics of Modernization*.

42. See Peter Evans, *Embedded Autonomy: States and Industrial Transformation* (Princeton, NJ: Princeton University Press, 1995).

43. See Peter Evans, James E. Rauch, "Bureaucracy and Growth: A Cross-National Analysis of Effects of the 'Weberian' State Structures on Economic Growth," *American Sociological Review* 64, no. 5 (1999): 748–765.

44. See Barbara Geddes, Joseph Wright, Erica Frantz, *How Dictatorships Work: Power, Personalization, and Collapse* (Cambridge: Cambridge University Press, 2018), especially chapters 8 and 9. See also Nicolas Charron, Victor Lapuente, "Which Dictators Produce Quality of Government?," *Studies in Comparative International Development* 46, no. 4 (2011): 397–423.

45. See Beatriz Magaloni, *Voting for Autocracy: Hegemonic Party Survival and Its Demise in Mexico* (Cambridge: Cambridge University Press, 2006); Kenneth Greene, "The Political Economy of Authoritarian Single-Party Dominance," *Comparative Political Studies* 43, no. 7 (2010): 803–834.

46. See Hale, *Patronal Politics*, especially chapter 4.

47. See also chapter 4 of this book.

48. See Geddes, Wright, Frantz, *How Dictatorships Work*.

49. See Evans, *Embedded Autonomy*.

50. See Bruce Bueno de Mesquita, Alastair Smith, *The Dictator's Handbook: Why Bad Behavior Is Almost Always Good Politics* (New York: Public Affairs, 2011); Milan Svolik, *The Politics of Authoritarian Rule* (Cambridge: Cambridge University Press, 2012).

51. See Richard Pipes, *Russia under the Old Regime* (New York: Scribner, 1974).

52. For a comprehensive account by a Russian historian, see Boris Mironov, *Rossiiskaya imperiya: ot traditisii k modernu*, 3 vols. (Saint Petersburg: Dmitry Bulanin, 2018).

53. See Beissinger, Kotkin, eds., *Historical Legacies of Communism in Russia and Eastern Europe*.

54. See Gaddy, Ickes, *Bear Traps*, especially chapters 2 and 3.

55. See Levitsky, Way, *Competitive Authoritarianism*, chapter 2.

56. See, in particular, Paul R. Gregory, *The Political Economy of Stalinism: Evidence from the Soviet Secret Archives* (Cambridge: Cambridge University Press, 2004); Anton Cheremukhin, Mikhail Golosov, Sergei Guriev, Aleh Tsyvinski, "Was Stalin Necessary for Russia's Economic Development?," *NBER Working Papers*, no. 19425 (2013), https://www.nber.org/papers/w19425.pdf, accessed September 7, 2021.

57. See Yegor Gaidar, *Collapse of an Empire: Lessons for Modern Russia* (Washington, DC: Brookings Institution Press, 2007), chapter 4; Popov, *Mixed Fortunes*, chapter 3.

58. See Vladimir Gel'man, Otar Marganiya, Dmitry Travin, *Reexamining Economic and Political Reforms in Russia, 1985–2000: Generations, Ideas, and Changes* (Lanham, MD: Lexington Books, 2014), especially chapter 3.

82 *Notes*

59. See Andrei Shleifer, Daniel Treisman, *Without a Map: Political Tactics and Economic Reform in Russia* (Cambridge MA: MIT Press, 2000); Åslund, *Russia's Capitalist Revolution*.

60. See Volkov, *Violent Entrepreneurship*, chapter 6; Kathryn Stoner-Weiss, *Resisting the State: Reform and Retrenchment in Post-Soviet Russia* (Cambridge: Cambridge University Press, 2006).

61. See Joel S. Hellman, "Winners Take All: The Politics of Partial Reforms in Post-Communist Transitions," *World Politics* 50, no. 2 (1998): 203–234; Shleifer, Treisman, *Without a Map*.

62. See Vadim Volkov, "Standard Oil and Yukos in the Context of Early Capitalism in the United States and Russia," *Demokratizatsiya: The Journal of Post-Soviet Democratization* 16, no. 3 (2008): 240–264; Vladimir Gel'man, "Leviathan's Return? The Policy of Recentralization in Contemporary Russia," in *Federalism and Local Politics in Russia*, eds. Cameron Ross, Adrian Campbell (London: Routledge, 2009), 1–24.

63. See Robert J. Brym, Vladimir Gimpelson, "The Size, Composition, and Dynamics of the Russian State Bureaucracy in the 1990s," *Slavic Review* 63, no. 1 (2004): 90–112; *The State after Communism: Governance in the New Russia*, eds. Timothy J. Colton, Stephen Holmes (Lanham, MD: Rowman and Littlefield, 2006); Taylor, *State Building in Putin's Russia*.

64. For an empirical analysis, see Ora John Reuter, Graeme B. Robertson, "Subnational Appointments in Authoritarian Regimes: Evidence from Russian Gubernatorial Appointments," *Journal of Politics* 74, no. 4 (2012): 1023–1037.

65. For a theoretical account, see Georgy Egorov, Konstantin Sonin, "Dictators and Their Viziers: Endogenizing the Loyalty-Competence Trade-off," *Journal of European Economic Association* 9, no. 5 (2011): 903–930.

66. See Treisman, Gimpelson, "Political Business Cycles and Russian Elections."

67. See Andrey Scherbak, "Ekonomicheskii rost i itogi dumskikh vyborov 2003 goda," in *Tretii elektoral'nyi tsikl v Rossii, 2003–2004 gody*, ed. Vladimir Gel'man (Saint Petersburg: European University at Saint Petersburg Press, 2007), 196–216; Andrey Starodubtsev, *Federalism and Regional Policy in Contemporary Russia* (Abingdon: Routledge, 2018).

68. See Stephen E. Hanson, *Post-Imperial Democracies: Ideology and Party Formation in Third Republic France, Weimar Germany, and Post-Soviet Russia* (Cambridge: Cambridge University Press, 2010).

69. For some implications of the "good Soviet Union" for bad governance in Russia, see chapter 2 of this book.

70. See Greene, "The Political Economy of Authoritarian Single-Party Dominance."

71. For this argument, see Sergei Guriev, Daniel Treisman, "Informational Autocrats," *Journal of Economic Perspectives* 33, no. 4 (2019): 100–127; Sergei Guriev, Daniel Treisman, "A Theory of Informational Autocracy," *Journal of Public Economics* 186 (2020), https://www.sciencedirect.com/science/article/pii/S0047272720300220, accessed February 18, 2022.

72. See Gel'man, *Authoritarian Russia*, especially chapter 5.

73. See Rodrik, "The Myth of Authoritarian Growth."

74. For an in-depth account of the reception of Western economic ideas among Russia's experts and policymakers, see Joachim Zweynert, *When Ideas Fail: Economic Thought, the Failure of Transition, and the Rise of Institutional Instability in Post-Soviet Russia* (Abingdon: Routledge, 2018); for an analysis of surveys of Russian elites, see "The Foreign Policy Attitudes of Russian Elites, 1993–2016," *Post-Soviet Affairs* 35, no. 5–6 (2019), special issue: 359–476.

75. See Shleifer, Treisman, *Without a Map*, especially chapters 1 and 9.

76. See Ivan Grigoriev, Anna Dekalchuk, "Collective Learning and Regime Dynamics under Uncertainty: Labour Reform and the Way to Autocracy in Russia," *Democratization* 24, no. 3 (2017): 481–497.

77. See Hilary Appel, *Tax Politics in Eastern Europe: Globalization, Regional Integration, and the Democratic Compromise* (Ann Arbor: University of Michigan Press, 2011), especially chapter 6.

78. See Medvedev, "Rossiya, Vpered!"

79. On Skolkovo, a beloved pet project of Dmitry Medvedev that served as a symbol of "modernization" during the period of his presidency, see Svetlana Reiter, Ivan Golunov, "Rassledovanie RBK: chto sluchilos' so Skolkovo," *rbc.ru*, March 23, 2015, http://daily.rbc.ru/special/business/23/03/2015/5509710a9a7947327e5f3a18, accessed September 7, 2021.

80. For a detailed critical account, see Dmitry Travin, *Osobyi put' Rossii: ot Dostoevskogo do Konchalovskogo* (Saint Petersburg: European University at Saint Petersburg Press, 2018); see also Zweynert, *When Ideas Fail*.

81. See the interview Gleb Pavlovsky, "Real'nost' otomstit Kremlyu i bez oppozitsii," *BBC Russian Service*, December 31, 2014, http://www.bbc.com/russian/russia/2014/12/141231_pavlovsky_putin_interview, accessed September 7, 2021.

82. See Gerschenkron, *Economic Backwardness in Historical Perspective*, chapter 3.

83. See Vladimir Gel'man, "The Politics of Fear: How Russia's Rulers Counter Their Rivals," *Russian Politics* 1, no. 1 (2016): 27–45; Kirill Rogov, "The Art of Coercion: Repressions and Repressiveness in Putin's Russia," *Russian Politics* 3, no. 2 (2018): 151–174.

84. See Andrei Shleifer, Daniel Treisman, "A Normal Country," *Foreign Affairs* 83, no. 2 (2004): 20–38.

85. See Huntington, *Political Order in Changing Societies*, 177–191.

86. On the wave of protests in Russia in 2011–2012 and their preconditions, see Graeme B. Robertson, "Protesting Putinism: The Election Protests of 2011–2012 in Broader Perspective," *Problems of Post-Communism* 60, no. 2 (2013): 11–23; Samuel A. Greene, *Moscow in Movement: Power and Opposition in Putin's Russia* (Stanford, CA: Stanford University Press, 2014). On controversies of the role of the Russian middle class in these protests, see Evgeny Gontmakher, Cameron Ross, "The Middle Class and Democratisation in Russia," *Europe-Asia Studies* 67, no. 2 (2015): 269–284; Bryn Rosenfeld, "Reevaluating the Middle-Class Protest Paradigm: A Case Control Study of Democratic Protest Coalition in Russia," *American Political Science Review* 111, no. 4 (2017): 637–652.

87. See Geddes, Wright, Frantz, *How Dictatorships Work*, especially chapters 4 and 5.

88. See Jennifer Gandhi, *Political Institutions under Dictatorship* (Cambridge: Cambridge University Press, 2008); Svolik, *The Politics of Authoritarian Rule*, especially chapter 4.

89. See Nikolay Petrov, Maria Lipman, Henry E. Hale, "Three Dilemmas of Hybrid Regime Governance: Russia from Putin to Putin," *Post-Soviet Affairs* 30, no. 1 (2014): 1–26; Carolina Vendil Pallin, "Internet Control through Ownership: The Case of Russia," *Post-Soviet Affairs* 33, no. 1 (2017): 16–33.

90. See Hilary Appel, Vladimir Gel'man, "Revising Russia's Economic Model: The Shift from Development to Geopolitics," *PONARS Policy Memos*, no. 397 (2015), http://www.ponarseurasia.org/memo/revising-russias-economic-model-shift-development-geopolitics, accessed September 7, 2021.

91. See Geddes, *Politician's Dilemma*, especially chapter 2.

92. Ibid., 61–73.

93. See Susanne Wengle, Michael Rasell, "The Monetisation of L'goty: Changing Patterns of Welfare Politics and Provision in Russia," *Europe-Asia Studies* 60, no. 5 (2008): 739–756; Brian Taylor, "The Police Reform in Russia: Policy Process in a Hybrid Regime," *Post-Soviet Affairs* 30, no. 2–3 (2014): 226–255. See also chapter 4 of this book.

94. See Anna Dekalchuk, "Choosing between Bureaucracy and the Reformers: The Russian Pension Reform of 2001 as a Compromise Squared," in *Authoritarian Modernization in Russia: Ideas, Institutions, and Policies*, ed. Vladimir Gel'man (Abingdon, NY: Routledge, 2017), 166–182. For an analysis from an alternative perspective, see Sarah Wilson Sokhey, "Market-Oriented Reform as a Tool of State-Building: Russian Pension Reform of 2001," *Europe-Asia Studies* 67, no. 5 (2015): 695–717.

95. See Linda Cook, Aadne Aasland, Daria Prisyazhnyuk, "Russian Pension Reform under Quadruple Influence," *Problems of Post-Communism* 66, no. 2 (2019): 96–108; Elena Maltseva, "The Politics of Retirement Age Increase in Russia: Proposals, Protests, and Concessions," *Russian Politics* 4, no. 3 (2019): 375–399.

96. See Grigoriev, Dekalchuk, "Collective Learning and Regime Dynamics."

97. See Gaidar, *Collapse of an Empire*, chapter 4.

98. For some critical interpretations, see Stefan Hedlund, *Russian Path Dependency: A People with Troubled History* (London: Routledge, 2005); Andrey Zaostrovtsev, *Polemika o modernizatsii: obshchie dorogi ili osobye puti?* (Saint Petersburg: European University at Saint Petersburg Press, 2020).

99. See Bruce Bueno de Mesquita, Alastair Smith, Randolph M. Siverson, James D. Morrow, *The Logic of Political Survival* (Cambridge, MA: MIT Press, 2003).

100. For a critical overview, see *Zastoi-2: Posledstviya, riski i al'ternativy dlya rossiiskoi ekonomiki*, ed. Kirill Rogov (Moscow: Liberal'naya missiya, 2021).

101. See Kirill Rogov, "Forty Years in the Desert: The Political Cycles of Post-Soviet Transition," in *Russia 2025: Scenarios for the Russian Future*, eds. Maria Lipman, Nikolay Petrov (London: Palgrave Macmillan, 2013), 18–45.

102. For a content analysis, see Jukka Pietiläinen, "Framing of Modernization in Russian Newspapers: Words, Not Deeds," in *Authoritarian Modernization in*

Russia: Ideas, Institutions, and Policies, ed. Vladimir Gel'man (Abingdon: Routledge, 2017), 71–89.

103. See Rogov, ed., *Zastoi-2: Posledstviya, riski i al'ternativy dlya rossiiskoi ekonomiki*.

Chapter 4

1. For a detailed account of policy reforms in Russia during the 1990s, see Andrei Shleifer, Daniel Treisman, *Without a Map: Political Tactics and Economic Reform in Russia* (Cambridge, MA: MIT Press, 2000).

2. For an initial assessment, see Kirill Rogov, "O sovetnikakh i begemote,"*Novaya Gazeta*, June 7, 2010, http://www.novayagazeta.ru/politics/3214.html, accessed September 7, 2021. For a more detailed analysis, see *Analiz faktorov realizatsii dokumentov strategicheskogo planirovaniya verkhnego urovnya*, eds. Mikhail Dmitriev (Moscow: Center for Strategic Research, 2016), https://polit.ru/media/files/2016/12/27/Report-on-strategy.pdf, accessed September 7, 2021.

3. See Shleifer, Treisman, *Without a Map*.

4. For a critical account, see Anders Åslund, *Russia's Crony Capitalism: The Path from Market Economy to Kleptocracy* (New Haven, CT: Yale University Press, 2019).

5. See Stephan Haggard, Matthew D. McCubbins, eds., *Presidents, Parliaments, and Policy* (Cambridge: Cambridge University Press, 2001).

6. For some exceptions, see Joseph Wright, "Do Authoritarian Institutions Constrain? How Legislatures Affect Economic Growth and Investment," *American Journal of Political Science* 52, no. 2 (2008): 322–343; Alexander Libman, Michael Rochlitz, *Federalism in China and Russia: Story of Success and Story of Failure?* (Cheltenham: Edward Elgar, 2019).

7. For a comparative analysis, see Jennifer Gandhi, *Political Institutions under Dictatorship* (Cambridge: Cambridge University Press, 2008).

8. For a theoretical account, see Matthew S. Shugart, John M. Carey, *Presidents and Assemblies: Constitutional Design and Electoral Dynamics* (Cambridge: Cambridge University Press, 1992); for a detailed analysis of intraexecutive relations in Russia, see Edward Morgan-Jones, Petra Shleiter, "Governmental Change in a Presidential-Parliamentary Regime: The Case of Russia, 1994–2003," *Post-Soviet Affairs* 20, no. 2 (2004): 123–163.

9. See Eugene Huskey, *Presidential Power in Russia* (Armonk, NY: M. E. Sharpe, 1999); Iulia Shevchenko, *The Central Government of Russia: From Gorbachev to Putin* (Aldershot: Ashgate, 2004); Fabian Burkhardt, "The Institutionalization of Relative Advantage: Formal Institutions, Subconstitutional Presidential Powers, and the Rise of Authoritarian Politics in Russia, 1994–2012," *Post-Soviet Affairs* 33, no. 6 (2017): 472–495.

10. On the impact of policy performance on presidential support in Russia, see Richard Rose, William Mishler, Neil Munro, *Popular Support for an Undemocratic Regime: The Changing Views of Russians* (Cambridge: Cambridge University Press, 2011);

Daniel Treisman, "Presidential Popularity in a Hybrid Regime: Russia under Yeltsin and Putin," *American Journal of Political Science* 55, no. 3 (2011): 590–609.

11. For this analytical perspective, see Henry E. Hale, "Democracy or Autocracy on the March? The Colored Revolutions as Normal Dynamics of Patronal Presidentialism," *Communist and Post-Communist Studies* 39, no. 3 (2006): 305–329.

12. See Shevchenko, *The Central Government of Russia*; Eugene Huskey, "Elite Recruitment and State-Society Relationships in Technocratic Authoritarian Regimes: The Russian Case," *Communist and Post-Communist Studies* 43, no. 4 (2010): 363–372. See also chapter 5 of this book.

13. For a firsthand account, see Mikhail Kasyanov, *Bez Putina: politicheskie dialogi s Evgeniem Kiselevym* (Moscow: Novaya gazeta, 2009).

14. See Martin Gilman, *No Precedent, No Plan: Inside Russia's 1998 Default* (Cambridge, MA: MIT Press, 2010).

15. For an account of the period of the 1990s, see Huskey, *Presidential Power in Russia*, chapter 5.

16. See Gilman, *No Precedent, No Plan.*

17. See Evgeniya Pismennaya, *Sistema Kudrina: istoriya klyuchevogo ekonomista putinskoi epokhi* (Moscow: Mann, Ivanov, and Ferber, 2013), especially chapter 5.

18. For some accounts, see Gulnaz Sharafutdinova, "Subnational Governance in Russia: How Putin Changed the Contract with His Agents and the Problems It Created for Medvedev," *Publius* 40 no. 4 (2010): 672–696; Vladimir Gel'man, Sergey Ryzhenkov, "Local Regimes, Sub-National Governance, and the 'Power Vertical' in Contemporary Russia," *Europe-Asia Studies* 63, no. 3 (2011): 449–465.

19. See Murray J. Horn, *The Political Economy of Public Administration: Institutional Choice in the Public Sector* (Cambridge: Cambridge University Press, 1995).

20. For an assessment, see Robert J. Brym, Vladimir Gimpelson, "The Size, Composition, and Dynamics of the Russian State Bureaucracy in the 1990s," *Slavic Review* 63, no. 1 (2004): 90–112. See also Fabian Burkhardt, "Institutionalising Authoritarian Presidencies: Polymorphous Power and Russia's Presidential Administration," *Europe-Asia Studies* 73, no. 3 (2021): 472–504.

21. See Treisman, "Presidential Popularity in a Hybrid Regime."

22. For a detailed analysis, see Thomas F. Remington, "Presidential Support in the Russian State Duma," *Legislative Studies Quarterly* 31, no. 1 (2006): 5–32.

23. See Gerald M. Easter, "The Russian State in the Time of Putin," *Post-Soviet Affairs* 24, no. 3 (2008): 199–230.

24. See Vladimir Gel'man, "Leviathan's Return? The Policy of Recentralization in Contemporary Russia," in *Federalism and Local Politics in Russia*, eds. Cameron Ross, Adrian Campbell (London: Routledge, 2009), 1–24.

25. See John W. Kingdon, *Agendas, Alternatives, and Public Policies* (New York: Longman, 2003).

26. See Shleifer, Treisman, *Without a Map*; Anders Åslund, *Russia's Capitalist Revolution: Why Market Reforms Succeeded and Democracy Failed* (Washington, DC: Peterson Institute for International Economics, 2007).

27. For a programmatic statement, see Vladimir Putin, "Rossiya na rubezhe tysyache-letii," *Nezavisimaya Gazeta*, December 30, 1999, www.ng.ru/politics/1999-12-30/4 _millenium.html, accessed September 7, 2021.

28. See Gerald M. Easter, "Building Fiscal Capacity," in *The State after Communism: Governance in the New Russia*, eds. Timothy J. Colton, Stephen Holmes (Lanham, MD: Rowman and Littlefield, 2006), 21–51.

29. See Beatriz Magaloni, *Voting for Autocracy: Hegemonic Party Survival and Its Demise in Mexico* (Cambridge: Cambridge University Press, 2006); Kenneth F. Greene, "The Political Economy of Authoritarian Single-Party Dominance," *Comparative Political Studies* 43, no. 7 (2010): 803–834.

30. See Daniel Treisman, Vladimir Gimpelson, "Political Business Cycles and Russian Elections, or the Manipulations of 'Chudar,'" *British Journal of Political Science* 31, no. 2 (2001): 225–246.

31. See Kas'yanov, *Bez Putina*; Pismennaya, *Sistema Kudrina*, chapter 5.

32. For a classic account, see Jeffrey L. Pressman, Aaron Wildavsky, *Implementation* (Berkeley: University of California Press, 1973).

33. For critical assessments, see Vadim Volkov, *Violent Entrepreneurs: The Role of Force in the Making of Russian Capitalism* (Ithaca, NY: Cornell University Press, 2002), especially chapter 6; Gerald M. Easter, *Capital, Coercion, and Postcommunist States* (Ithaca, NY: Cornell University Press, 2012).

34. For a detailed overview, see Vladimir Nazarov, "Nalogovaya sistema Rossii v 1991–2008 godakh," in *Istoriya novoi Rossii: ocherki, interv'yu*, vol. 1, ed. Petr Filippov (Saint Petersburg: Norma, 2011), 449–516.

35. For an analysis of Russian tax reform from a comparative perspective, see Hilary Appel, *Tax Politics in Eastern Europe: Globalization, Regional Integration, and the Democratic Compromise* (Ann Arbor: University of Michigan Press, 2011), especially chapter 6.

36. See Nazarov, "Nalogovaya sistema Rossii,"495.

37. See Andrey Zaostrovtsev, "Oil Boom and Government Finance in Russia: Stabilization Fund and Its Fate," in *Resource Curse and Post-Soviet Eurasia: Oil, Gas, and Modernization*, eds. Vladimir Gel'man, Otar Marganiya (Lanham, MD: Lexington Books, 2010), 123–147; Eva Dabrowska, Joachim Zweynert, "Economic Ideas and Institutional Change: The Case of the Russian Stabilization Fund," *New Political Economy* 20, no. 4 (2015): 518–544.

38. See Appel, *Tax Politics in Eastern Europe*, chapter 6.

39. For accounts, see Pauline Jones Luong, Erika Weinthal, *Oil Is Not a Curse: Ownership Structure and Institutions in Soviet Successor States* (Cambridge: Cambridge University Press, 2010); Thane Gustafson, *Wheel of Fortune: The Battle for Oil and Power in Russia* (Cambridge, MA: Belknap Press of Harvard University Press), especially chapter 5; Pismennaya, *Sistema Kudrina*, chapter 5.

40. See Remington, "Presidential Support in the Russian State Duma."

41. See Gustafson, *Wheel of Fortune*, chapter 5.

42. See Pismennaya, *Sistema Kudrina*, chapter 5.

43. See Nazarov, "Nalogovaya sistema Rossii."

44. See Zaostrovtsev, "Oil Boom and Government Finance in Russia."

45. See Ilya Sokolov, "Byudzhetnaya Sistema Novoi Rossii," in *Istoriya novoi Rossii: ocherki, interv'yu*, vol. 1, ed. Petr Filippov (Saint Petersburg: Norma, 2011), 517–551; Pismennaya, *Sistema Kudrina*.

46. For an overview, see Mark Agranovich, Olga Kozhevnikova, *Sostoyanie i razvitie sistemy obshchego srednego obrazovaniya v Rossiiskoi Federatsii: natsional'nyi doklad* (Moscow: Aspekt-Press, 2006).

47. See Boris Startsev, *Khroniki obrazovatel'noi politiki: 1991–2011* (Moscow: National Research University—Higher School of Economics, 2012).

48. See Tatiana Kliachko, "Gosudarstvennye imennye finansovye obyazatel'stva (GIFO)," *Universitetskoe Upravlenie*, no. 4 (2002): 70–73.

49. See Sergey Podosenov, "Rossiyane stali dumat' o EGE eshche khuzhe chem ran'she," *Izvestiya*, June 6, 2013, http://izvestia.ru/news/551551, accessed September 7, 2021.

50. See Startsev, *Khroniki obrazovatel'noi politiki*, 107.

51. See Alexander Chernykh, "Andrey Fursenko popal v nestandartnoe polozhenie," *Kommersant*, April 20, 2011, https://www.kommersant.ru/doc/1625019, accessed September 7, 2021.

52. For a detailed account, see Andrey Starodubtsev, "How Does the Government Implement Unpopular Reforms? Evidence from Education Policy in Russia," in *Authoritarian Modernization in Russia: Ideas, Institutions, and Policies*, ed. Vladimir Gel'man (Abingdon: Routledge, 2017), 148–165.

53. See Ivan Sterligov, "Experiment po vvedeniyu GIFO nuzhdaetsya v novoi otsenke," *RIA Novosti*, July 17, 2009, http://ria.ru/education/20090709/176794627.html, accessed September 7, 2021.

54. See Michael Lipsky, *Street-Level Bureaucracy: Dilemmas of the Individual in Public Services* (New York: Russell Sage Foundation, 1980).

55. See Vladimir Popov, "The State in the New Russia (1992–2004): From Collapse to Gradual Revival?" *PONARS Policy Memos*, no. 324 (2004), https://www.ponarseurasia.org/the-state-in-the-new-russia-1992-2004-from-collapse-to-gradual-revival/, accessed September 7, 2021.

56. See Joel S. Hellman, "Winners Take All: The Politics of Partial Reforms in Post-Communist Transitions," *World Politics* 50, no. 2 (1998): 203–234.

57. See William Thompson, "From 'Clientelism' to a 'Client-Centered Orientation'? The Challenge of Public Administration Reform in Russia," *OECD Economics Department Working Papers*, no. 536 (2007), http://dx.doi.org/10.1787/332450142780, accessed September 7, 2021.

58. See Daniel Treisman, *After the Deluge: Regional Crises and Political Consolidation in Russia* (Ann Arbor: University of Michigan Press, 1999); Mikhail Filippov, Olga Shvetsova, "Asymmetric Bilateral Bargaining in the New Russian Federation: A Path-Dependent Explanation," *Communist and Post-Communist Studies* 32, no. 1

(1999): 61–76; Kathryn Stoner-Weiss, *Resisting the State: Reform and Retrenchment in Post-Soviet Russia* (Cambridge: Cambridge University Press, 2006).

59. That year saw the initial implementation of the federal program "Reforming Public Service in the Russian Federation (2003–2005)."

60. For an overview, see Alexei Barabashev, Jeffrey D. Strausmann, "Public Service Reform in Russia, 1991–2006," *Public Administration Review* 67, no. 3 (2007): 373–382.

61 According to World Bank data; https://info.worldbank.org/governance/wgi/, accessed September 7, 2021, in 2012 the percentile rank of Governance Effectiveness in Russia approached 41, and the rank of Regulatory Quality approached 39, while the reformers had set a target of 70 for both indicators by 2010. See "Rasporyazhenie Pravitel'stva Rossiiskoi Federatsii ot 25 oktyabrya 2005 goda no. 1889-r (v redaktsii rasporyazheniya Pravitel'stva RF ot 09.02.2008 no. 157-r, postanovlenii Pravitel'stva RF ot 28.03.2008 no. 221, ot 10.03.2009 no. 219)," *Konsul'tant*, http://www.consultant.ru/document/cons_doc_LAW_86001/, accessed September 7, 2021. Russia's position in the rankings of the Transparency International Corruption Perceptions Index has declined: in 2012, Russia took 133th place out of 174. See http://www.transparency.org/cpi2012/results, accessed September 7, 2021.

62. For a detailed analysis, see Andrey Starodubtsev, *Federalism and Regional Policy in Contemporary Russia* (Abingdon: Routledge, 2018).

63. See Mikhail Dmitriev, "Administrativnaya reforma," *Istoriya novoi Rossii: ocherki, interv'yu*, vol. 1, ed. Petr Filippov (Saint Petersburg: Norma, 2011), 198–216.

64. See Brym, Gimpelson, "The Size, Composition, and Dynamics of the Russian State Bureaucracy."

65. See Andrei Logunov, "Administrativnaya reforma v Rossiiskoi Federatsii: osnovnye etapy realizatsii,"*Analiticheskii Vestnik*, no. 22 (2006): 23.

66. For the text of the 2003 annual address, see Vladimir Putin, *Poslanie Federal'nomu Sobraniyu Rossiiskoi Federatsii*, May 16, 2003, www.kremlin.ru/events/president/transcripts/21998, accessed September 7, 2021.

67. Dmitriev, "Administrativnaya reforma," 202–203.

68. See *Chislennost' rabotnikov gosudarstvennykh organov i organov mestnogo samoupravleniya po vetvyam vlasti i urovnyam upravleniya*, www.gks.ru/free_doc/new_site/gosudar/chisl_vetv.htm, accessed September 7, 2021.

69. For some critical assessments, see Peter Solomon, "Law in Public Administration: How Russia Differs," *Journal of Communist Studies and Transition Politics* 24, no. 1 (2008): 115–135; Dmitry Goncharov, Anton Shirikov, "Public Administration in Russia," in *Public Administration in Post-Communist Countries: Former Soviet Union, Eastern Europe, and Mongolia*, eds. Saltanat Liebert, Stephen E. Condrey, Dmitry Goncharov (Abingdon: Routledge, 2013), 23–43.

70. See Gustafson, *Wheel of Fortune*, chapters 6 and 8.

71. For accounts of state-business relations in Russia in the 2000s, see Andrey Yakovlev, "The Evolution of Business-State Interactions in Russia: From State Capture to Business Capture?" *Europe-Asia Studies* 58, no. 7 (2006): 1033–1056; Vladimir Gel'man,

"The Logic of Crony Capitalism: Big Oil, Big Politics, and Big Business in Russia," in *Resource Curse and Post-Soviet Eurasia: Oil, Gas, and Modernization*, eds. Vladimir Gel'man, Otar Marganiya (Lanham, MD: Lexington Books, 2010), 97–122.

72. See Pismennaya, *Sistema Kudrina*, chapter 6.

73. For analyses of "monetization," see Anastassia Alexandrova, Raymond J. Stryuk, "Reform of In-Kind Benefits in Russia: High Cost for a Small Gain," *Journal of European Social Policy* 17, no. 2 (2007): 153–166; Susanne Wengle, Michael Rasell, "The Monetisation of L'goty: Changing Patterns of Welfare Politics and Provision in Russia," *Europe-Asia Studies* 60, no. 5 (2008): 739–756.

74. For an overview of regional elections in Russia in the 2000s, see Grigorii V. Golosov, "Regional Roots of Electoral Authoritarianism in Russia," *Europe-Asia Studies* 63, no. 4 (2011): 623–639.

75. See Pismennaya, *Sistema Kudrina*, chapter 6.

76. For a detailed account of police reform, see Brian Taylor, "The Police Reform in Russia: Policy Process in a Hybrid Regime," *Post-Soviet Affairs* 30, no. 2–3 (2014): 226–255.

77. See Ella Paneyakh, "Faking Performances Together: Systems of Performance Evaluation in Russian Enforcement Agencies and Production of Bias and Privilege," *Post-Soviet Affairs* 30, no. 2–3 (2014): 115–136; Ella Paneyakh, Kirill Titaev, Maria Shklyaruk, *Traektoriya ugolovnogo dela: institutsional'nyi analiz* (Saint Petersburg: European University at Saint Petersburg Press, 2018).

78. See Ekaterina Alyab'eva, "VShE o reforme meditsiny: imitatsiya i pokazukha," *Slon.ru*, February 9, 2014, https://republic.ru/posts/l/1081189, accessed September 7, 2021.

79. For a comprehensive account of military reforms in post-Soviet Russia, see Alexander Golts, *Military Reform and Militarism in Russia* (Washington, DC: Jamestown Foundation, 2018).

80. For different accounts, see "Crisis in the Caucasus, Russia, Georgia, and the West," *Small Wars and Insurgencies* 20, no. 2 (2009): special issue; *The Great Power (Mis)management: The Russian-Georgian War and Its Implications for Global Political Order*, ed. Alexander Astrov (Aldershot: Ashgate, 2011).

81. For a detailed account, see Kirill Shamiev, "Against a Bitter Pill: The Role of Interest Groups in Armed Forces Reform in Russia," *Armed Forces and Society* 47, no. 2 (2021): 319–342. Some observers noted that in 2011 Serdyukov endorsed the idea of a second term in office for then-President Dmitry Medvedev, and that this could have been perceived as a sign of his political disloyalty to Putin. See Golts, *Military Reform and Militarism in Russia*, chapter 2.

82. For different accounts of the effects of the military reforms initiated by Serdyukov, see Dmitry Gorenburg, "The Russian Military under Sergei Shoigu: Will the Reform Continue?," *PONARS Eurasia Policy Memos*, no. 253 (2013), www.ponarseurasia.org/memo/russian-military-under-sergei-shoigu-will-reform-continue, accessed September

7, 2021; Pavel Baev, *Ukraine: A Test for Russian Military Reforms* (Paris, IFRI, 2015), https://www.ifri.org/sites/default/files/atoms/files/ifri_rnr_19_pavel_baev_russian_military_reform_eng_may_2015_0.pdf, accessed September 7, 2021.

83. See Golts, *Military Reform and Militarism in Russia*, chapter 2.

84. See Pismennaya, *Sistema Kudrina*, chapter 6.

85. See Bruce Bueno de Mesquita, Alastair Smith, *The Dictator's Handbook: Why Bad Behavior Is Almost Always Good Politics* (New York: Public Affairs, 2011).

Chapter 5

1. Alexey Ulyukaev, "Liberalizm i politika perekhodnogo perioda v sovremennoi Rossii," *Mir Rossii* 4, no. 2 (Summer 1995): 8.

2. See Milan Svolik, *The Politics of Authoritarian Rule* (Cambridge: Cambridge University Press, 2012), especially chapters 5 and 6.

3. For theoretically driven arguments, see Mancur Olson, "Dictatorship, Democracy, and Development," *American Political Science Review* 87, no. 3 (1993): 567–576; Ronald Wintrobe, *The Political Economy of Dictatorship* (Cambridge: Cambridge University Press, 1998).

4. See Bruce Bueno de Mesquita, Alastair Smith, *The Dictator's Handbook: Why Bad Behavior Is Almost Always Good Politics* (New York: Public Affairs, 2011), especially chapter 5.

5. See Barbara Geddes, *Politician's Dilemma: Building State Capacity in Latin America* (Berkeley: University of California Press, 1994), chapter 2.

6. See William Easterly, *The Tyranny of Experts: Economists, Dictators, and the Forgotten Rights of the Poor* (New York: Basic Books, 2014), especially chapter 1.

7. On awkward combinations of politics and policy-making during market transitions in Russia and other post-Communist countries, see Andrei Shleifer, Daniel Treisman, *Without a Map: Political Tactics and Economic Reform in Russia* (Cambridge, MA: MIT Press, 2000); Timothy M. Frye, *Building States and Markets after Communism: The Perils of Polarized Democracy* (Cambridge: Cambridge University Press, 2010).

8. For a strong critique, see Anders Åslund, *Russia's Capitalist Revolution: Why Market Reforms Succeeded and Democracy Failed* (Washington, DC: Peterson Institute for International Economics, 2007).

9. See chapter 4 of this book.

10. See Ivan S. Grigoriev, Anna A. Dekalchuk, "Collective Learning and Regime Dynamics under Uncertainty: Labour Reform and the Way to Autocracy in Russia," *Democratization* 24, no. 3 (2017): 481–497.

11. See Svolik, *The Politics of Authoritarian Rule*, chapter 1.

12. There are numerous intermediate forms of interaction between politics and policy-making, but their analysis lies beyond the scope of this discussion.

13. See Bueno de Mesquita, Smith, *The Dictator's Handbook*, especially chapter 3.

14. For a systematic account, see Georgii Egorov, Konstantin Sonin, "Dictators and Their Viziers: Endogenizing the Loyalty-Competence Trade-off," *Journal of the European Economic Association* 9, no. 5 (2011): 903–930.

15. See Mancur Olson, *The Rise and Decline of Nations: Economic Growth, Stagflation, and Social Rigidities* (New Haven, CT: Yale University Press, 1982), especially chapter 3.

16. See Shleifer, Treisman, *Without a Map*, chapter 1; Åslund, *Russia's Capitalist Revolution*, especially chapters 3–5.

17. For this argument, see Adam Przeworski, *Democracy and the Market: Political and Economic Reforms in Eastern Europe and Latin America* (Cambridge: Cambridge University Press, 1991), chapter 4.

18. See Joel Hellman, "Winners Take All: The Politics of Partial Reform in Postcommunist Transitions," *World Politics* 50, no. 2 (1998): 203–234.

19. For an empirical analysis, see Stephen Fortescue, "Russia's Civil Service: Professional or Patrimonial? Executive-Level Officials in Five Federal Ministries," *Post-Soviet Affairs* 36, no. 4 (2020): 365–388.

20. See Fabian Burkhardt, "Foolproofing Putinism," *ridl.io*, March 29, 2021, https://www.ridl.io/en/foolproofing-putinism/, accessed September 7, 2021.

21. See chapter 2 of this book.

22. See Henry E. Hale, *Patronal Politics: Eurasian Regime Dynamics in Comparative Perspective* (Cambridge: Cambridge University Press, 2014), especially chapter 4.

23. See Anna A. Dekalchuk, "Choosing between Bureaucracy and the Reformers: The Russian Pension Reform of 2001 as a Compromise Squared," in *Authoritarian Modernization in Russia: Ideas, Institutions, and Policies*, ed. Vladimir Gel'man (Abingdon: Routledge, 2017), 166–182.

24. Yegor Gaidar, *Days of Defeat and Victory* (Seattle: University of Washington Press, 1999), 259.

25. See Evgeniya Pismennaya, *Sistema Kudrina. Istoriya klyuchevogo ekonomista putinskoi epokhi* (Moscow: Mann, Ivanov & Ferber, 2013), especially chapter 5.

26. See *Analiz faktorov realizatsii dokumentov strategicheskogo planirovaniya verkhnego urovnya*, ed. Mikhail Dmitriev (Moscow: Center for Strategic Research, 2016), https://polit.ru/media/files/2016/12/27/Report-on-strategy.pdf, accessed September 7, 2021.

27. For a detailed comparative analysis, see Hilary Appel, *A New Capitalist Order: Privatization and Ideology in Russia and Eastern Europe* (Pittsburgh, PA: University of Pittsburgh Press, 2004).

28. See Shleifer, Treisman, *Without a Map*; Martin Gilman, *No Precedent, No Plan: Inside Russia's 1998 Default* (Cambridge, MA: MIT Press, 2010).

29. See Frye, *Building States and Markets*, chapter 8.

30. See Vladimir Gel'man, Dmitry Travin, "Fathers versus Sons: Generational Changes and the Ideational Agenda of Reforms in Late Twentieth-Century Russia,"

in *Authoritarian Modernization in Russia: Ideas, Institutions, and Policies*, ed. Vladimir Gel'man (Abingdon: Routledge, 2017), 22–38; Vladimir Gel'man, "'Liberals' versus 'Democrats': Ideational Trajectories of Russia's Post-Communist Transformation," *Social Sciences* 51, no. 2 (2020): 4–24.

31. For a detailed analysis, see Yegor Gaidar, *Collapse of an Empire: Lessons for Modern Russia* (Washington, DC: Brookings Institution Press, 2007), chapter 4.

32. For firsthand accounts by former members of the Russian government, see Petr Aven, Alfred Kokh, *Gaidar's Revolution: The Inside Account of the Economic Transformation in Russia* (London: I. B. Tauris, 2015).

33. See Vladimir Gel'man, *Authoritarian Russia: Analyzing Post-Soviet Regime Changes* (Pittsburgh, PA: University of Pittsburgh Press, 2015), chapter 3.

34. See Richard Rose, William Mishler, Neil Munro, *Popular Support for an Undemocratic Regime: The Changing Views of Russians* (Cambridge: Cambridge University Press, 2011); Daniel Treisman, "Presidential Popularity in a Hybrid Regime: Russia under Yeltsin and Putin," *American Journal of Political Science* 55, no. 3 (2011): 590–609.

35. See chapter 4 of this book.

36. See Pismennaya, *Sistema Kudrina*, chapter 6.

37. See Hale, *Patronal Politics*, chapter 4.

38. For a detailed account of politics of expertise in Russia, see Marina Khmelnitskaya, "Socio-Economic Development and the Politics of Expertise in Putin's Russia: The 'Hollow Paradigm' Perspective," *Europe-Asia Studies* 73, no. 4 (2021): 625–646.

39. See chapter 4 of this book.

40. See *Analiz faktorov*.

41. See Yuliya Starostina, Egor Gubernatorov, Elizaveta Efimovich, Lyudmila Podobedova, Svetlana Burmistrova, "Shchetnaya palata ukazala nedostatki i riski natsproektov," *rbc.ru*, January 13, 2020, https://www.rbc.ru/economics/13/01/2020/5e184e-2a9a79470bf49655c3, accessed September 7, 2021.

42. See Polina Khimshiashvili, Artem Filippenok, "Kreml' ob'yasnil ischeznovenie tseli voiti v top-5 krupneishikh ekonomik," *rbc.ru*, July 21, 2020, https://www.rbc.ru/economics/21/07/2020/5f16b4479a7947289fd7c751, accessed September 7, 2021.

43. See Vladislav Inozemtsev, "Priglasite psikhiatra: Pravitel'stvo RF predstavilo proekt edinogo plana po dostizheniyu natsional'nykh tselei razvitiya do 2030 goda," *Novaya gazeta*, September 10, 2020, https://novayagazeta.ru/articles/2020/09/10/87037-priglasite-psihiatra, accessed September 7, 2021.

44. For an in-depth analysis of post-Communist neoliberalism, see Hilary Appel, Mitchell Orenstein, *From Triumph to Crisis: Neoliberal Economic Reform in Postcommunist Countries* (Cambridge: Cambridge University Press, 2018).

45. See Vladimir Gel'man, "Political Opposition in Russia: A Dying Species?," *Post-Soviet Affairs* 21, no. 3 (2005): 226–246.

46. For a critical overview of "systemic liberals" (regime loyalists), see Lilia Shevtsova, "Russia: Did Liberals Bury Liberalism?," *IWM Post*, no. 119 (June, 23, 2017), https://

www.eurozine.com/russia-did-liberals-bury-liberalism/?pdf, accessed September 7, 2021; for a more positive account, see Philip Hanson, Elizabeth Teague, *Liberal Insiders and Economic Reform in Russia* (London: Chatham House, 2013), https://www.chathamhouse.org/sites/default/files/public/Research/Russia%20and%20Eurasia/0113pr_hansonteague.pdf, accessed September 7, 2021. The trend of Russia's liberals becoming an open opposition to the regime was exemplified by Boris Nemtsov, a former deputy prime minister of Russia under Yeltsin who was assassinated in February 2015. See *Boris Nemtsov and Russian Politics: Power and Resistance*, eds. Andrey Makarychev, Alexandra Yatsyk (Stuttgart: Ibidem Verlag, 2018).

47. For a detailed account of reforms of the electricity sector in Russia in the 2000s, see Susanne A. Wengle, *Post-Soviet Power: State-Led Development and Russia's Marketization* (Cambridge: Cambridge University Press, 2015).

48. For critical accounts, see Anders Åslund, "Sergey Glazyev and the Revival of Soviet Economics," *Post-Soviet Affairs* 29, no. 5 (2013): 375–386; Andrey Movchan, "Glazyev's Economic Policy of the Absurd," *Carnegie Moscow Center*, September 15, 2015, https://carnegie.ru/commentary/61271, accessed September 7, 2021.

49. For a detailed overview of the impact of economic ideas on policy-making in post-Soviet Russia, see Joachim Zweynert, *When Ideas Fail: Economic Thought, the Failure of Transition, and the Rise of Institutional Instability in Post-Soviet Russia* (Abingdon: Routledge, 2018).

50. For a critical overview, see *Zastoi-2: Posledstviya, riski i al'ternativy dlya rossiiskoi ekonomiki*, ed. Kirill Rogov (Moscow: Liberal'naya missiya, 2021). See also Andrei Yakovlev, "Composition of Ruling Elite, Incentives for Productive Usage of Rents, and the Prospects of Russia's Limited Access Order," *Post-Soviet Affairs* 37, no. 5 (2021): 417–434.

51. See Hilary Appel, *Tax Politics in Eastern Europe: Globalization, Regional Integration, and the Democratic Compromise* (Ann Arbor: University of Michigan Press, 2011), especially chapter 6.

52. See Juliet Johnson, *Priests of Prosperity: How Central Bankers Transformed the Postcommunist World* (Ithaca, NY: Cornell University Press, 2016).

53. See Bueno de Mesquita, Smith, *The Dictator's Handbook*, chapter 3.

54. See chapter 1 of this book.

55. For a detailed analysis of the introduction of EGE in Russia in the 2000s, see Andrei Starodubtsev, "How Does the Government Implement Unpopular Reforms? Evidence from Education Policy in Russia," in *Authoritarian Modernization in Russia: Ideas, Institutions, and Policies*, ed. Vladimir Gel'man (Abingdon: Routledge, 2017), 148–165.

56. See chapter 4 of this book.

57. For a systematic overview of the evolution of EGE, see Aleksandr Chernykh, "Sdachnyi roman. Vo chto prevratilsya Edinyi gosudarstvennyi ekzamen," *Kommersant-Vlast'*, February 15, 2016, http://www.kommersant.ru/doc/2911647, accessed September 7, 2021.

58. See Starodubtsev, "How Does the Government Implement Unpopular Reforms?"

59. See Shleifer, Treisman, *Without a Map*, chapter 2; David Hoffman, *The Oligarchs: Wealth and Power in the New Russia* (New York: Public Affairs Books, 2002), part II; Andrew Barnes, *Owning Russia: The Struggle over Factories, Farms and Power* (Ithaca, NY: Cornell University Press, 2006). For analysis of the impact of privatization on property rights in Russia, see Konstantin Sonin, "Why the Rich May Favor Poor Protection of Property Rights," *Journal of Comparative Economics* 31, no. 4 (2003): 715–731.

60. For these accounts, see Sergei Guriev, Andrei Rachinsky, "The Role of Oligarchs in Russian Capitalism," *Journal of Economic Perspectives* 19, no. 1 (2005): 131–150; Daniel Treisman, "'Loans for Shares' Revisited," *Post-Soviet Affairs* 26, no. 3 (2010): 207–227.

61. For a comparative analysis, see Irina Denisova, Markus Eller, Timothy Frye, Ekaterina Zhurvaskaya, "Who Wants to Revise Privatization? The Complementarity of Market Skills and Institutions," *American Political Science Review* 103, no. 2 (2009): 284–304.

62. See Andrei Yakovlev, "The Evolution of Business-State Interactions in Russia: From State Capture to Business Capture?" *Europe-Asia Studies* 58, no. 7 (2006): 1033–1056.

63. See Maria Leiva, "FAS zayavila o kontrole gosudarstva nad 70% rossiskoi ekonomiki," *rbc.ru*, September 29, 2016, http://www.rbc.ru/economics/29/09/2016/57ec-d5429a794730e1479fac, accessed September 7, 2021.

64. See Vladimir Gel'man, "Leviathan's Return? The Policy of Recentralization in Contemporary Russia," in *Federalism and Local Politics in Russia*, eds. Cameron Ross, Adrian Campbell (London: Routledge, 2009), 1–24.

65. See Appel, *Tax Politics in Eastern Europe*, chapter 6.

66. For a comprehensive account, see Brian Taylor, "The Police Reform in Russia: Policy Process in a Hybrid Regime," *Post-Soviet Affairs* 30, no. 2–3 (2014): 226–255.

67. See chapter 4 of this book.

68. See Johnson, *Priests of Prosperity*, especially chapter 6.

69. See Wengle, Rasell, "The Monetisation of L'goty"; Meri Kulmala, Markus Kainu, Jouko Nikula, Markku Kivinen, "Paradoxes of Agency: Democracy and Welfare in Russia," *Demokratizatsiya: The Journal of Post-Soviet Democractization* 22, no. 4 (2014): 523–552. For an original version of the concept, see Charles E. Lindbom, "The Science of 'Muddling Through,'" *Public Administration Review* 19, no. 1 (1959): 79–88.

70. For a detailed and positive account, see Maxim Boycko, Andrei Shleifer, Robert W. Vishny, *Privatizing Russia* (Cambridge, MA: MIT Press, 1995). For a similar view by an insider, see Alfred Kokh, *The Selling of the Soviet Empire: Politics and Economics of Russia's Privatization* (New York: S. P. I. Books, 1998).

71. For critical accounts, see Chrystia Freeland, *Sale of the Century: Russia's Wild Ride from Communism to Capitalism* (New York: Crown Business, 2000); Hoffman, *The Oligarchs*, especially chapters 12–14.

72. See chapter 6 of this book.

73. See Appel, *Tax Politics*, chapter 6.

74. See Dekalchuk, "Choosing Between Bureaucracy and the Reformers."

75. See Olson, "Dictatorship, Democracy, and Development."

76. For a critique, see Easterly, *The Tyranny of Experts*, especially chapter 13.

77. For a critical analysis, see Ella Paneyakh, "Zaregulirovannoe gosudarstvo," *Pro et Contra* 13, no. 1–2 (2013): 58–92; Ella Paneyakh, "The Overregulated State," *Social Sciences* 45, no. 1 (2014): 20–33.

78. See Stanislav Markus, *Property, Predation, and Protection: Piranha Capitalism in Russia and Ukraine* (Cambridge: Cambridge University Press, 2015).

79. For a typology of corruption, see Andrei Shleifer, Robert W. Vishny, "Corruption," *Quarterly Journal of Economics* 108, no. 3 (1993): 599–617.

80. On this possible trajectory of Russia's further development, see, in particular, *Zastoi-2.*

81. For journalist accounts Ilya Zhegulev, Ivan Golunov, Evgenii Berg, Alexandr Gorbachev, "Chelovek Gaidara, sporivshii s Putinym," *Meduza*, November 15, 2016, https://meduza.io/feature/2016/11/15/chelovek-gaydara-sporivshiy-s-putinym, accessed September 7, 2021; "Spetsoperatsiya 'privatizatsiya.' Kogo perekhitril Igor Sechin," *Finanz.ru*, December 15, 2016, http://www.finanz.ru/novosti/aktsii/specoperaciya-privatizaciya-kogo-perekhitril-igor-sechin-1001608380, accessed September 7, 2021.

Chapter 6

1. See Andrey Starodubtsev, "Usloviya uspeshnogo upravleniya v sovremennoi Rossii (subnatsional'nyi uroven')," *Politeia*, no. 4 (2018): 70–89; Andrei Yakovlev, Lev Freinkman, Sergey Makarov, Victor Pogodaev, "How Do Russia's Regions Adjust to External Shocks? Evidence from the Republic of Tatarstan," *Problems of Post-Communism* 66, no. 4–5 (2020): 417–431.

2. See Susanne Wengle, "The New Plenty: Why Are Some Post-Soviet Farms Thriving?," *Governance* 33, no. 4 (2020): 915–933; Susanne Wengle, *Black Earth, White Bread: A Technopolitical History of Russian Agriculture and Food* (Madison: University of Wisconsin Press, 2022).

3. See Juliet Johnson, *Priests of Prosperity: How Central Bankers Transformed the Postcommunist World* (Ithaca, NY: Cornell University Press, 2016), especially chapter 6.

4. See Barbara Geddes, *Politician's Dilemma: Building State Capacity in Latin America* (Berkeley: University of California Press, 1994).

5. See *The Politics of Public Sector Performance: Pockets of Effectiveness in Developing Countries*, ed. Michael Roll (London: Routledge, 2014).

6. See Michael Roll, "Pockets of Effectiveness: Review and Analytical Framework," in *The Politics of Public Sector Performance: Pockets of Effectiveness in Developing Countries*, ed. Michael Roll (London: Routledge, 2014), 22–42.

7. See Loren Graham, *Lonely Ideas: Can Russia Compete?* (Cambridge, MA: MIT Press, 2013).

8. See Geddes, *Politician's Dilemma*, 61–73.

9. See Roll, "Pockets of Effectiveness."

10. See Graham, *Lonely Ideas.*

11. On the role of policy entrepreneurs as key drivers of policy changes, see John W. Kingdon, *Agendas, Alternatives, and Public Policies* (New York: Longman, 2003).

12. See Michael Roll, "Comparative Analysis: Deciphering Pockets of Effectiveness," in *The Politics of Public Sector Performance: Pockets of Effectiveness in Developing Countries*, ed. Michael Roll (London: Routledge, 2014), 194–241.

13. For a classical analysis of mechanisms of governance in the last decades of the Soviet Union, see Jeffrey F. Hough, Merle Fainsod, *How the Soviet Union Is Governed* (Cambridge, MA: Harvard University Press, 1979); on subnational governance, see Jerry F. Hough, *The Soviet Prefects: The Local Party Organs in Industrial Decision-Making* (Cambridge, MA: Harvard University Press, 1969); Peter Rutland, *The Politics of Economic Stagnation in the Soviet Union: The Role of Local Party Organs in Economic Management* (Cambridge: Cambridge University Press, 1993).

14. Although the case of the Soviet space program was the most visible technological advancement of that time, it is not unique for this period. Without claiming to make an exhaustive list, certain outstanding achievements and technological and educational developments of the Soviet period after World War II are worthy of mention, such as the production of lasers, specialized high-level math training, the nuclear industry before the Chernobyl disaster, and some other cases. See: Graham, *Lonely Ideas*, chapter 10; Sonja Schmid, *Producing Power: The Pre-Chernobyl History of the Soviet Nuclear Industry* (Cambridge, MA: MIT Press, 2015); Slava Gerovitch, "'We Teach Them to be Free': Specialized Math Schools and the Cultivation of the Soviet Technical Intelligentsia," *Kritika: Explorations in Russian and Eurasian History* 20, no. 4 (2019): 717–754.

15. For 2008 survey results, see "Naibolee znachimye sobytiya rossiiskoi istorii," *Levada Center*, June 9, 2008, https://www.levada.ru/2008/06/09/naibolee-zna-chimye-sobytiya-rossijskoj-istorii/, accessed September 7, 2021.

16. This section makes extensive use of an overview of works of several Western authors: James E. Oberg, *Red Star in Orbit* (Houston: NASA Johnson Space Center, 1981); Walter A. McDougall, *Heavens and the Earth: A Political History of the Space Age* (New York: Basic Books, 1985); Asif A. Siddiqui, *Challenge to Apollo: The Soviet Union and the Space Race* (Washington, DC: NASA, 2000); Bart Hendrickx, Bert Vis, *Energiya-Buran: The Soviet Space Shuttle* (Chichester: Springer/Praxis Publishing, 2007); Grujica S. Ivanovich, *Salyut—The First Space Station: Triumph and Tragedy* (Chichester: Springer/Praxis Publishing, 2008); *Cold War Space Sleuths: The Untold Secrets of the Soviet Space Program*, ed. Dominic Phelan (Chichester: Springer/Praxis Publishing, 2012); for Russian-language sources, see Nikolai Kamanin, *Skrytyi kosmos: kosmicheskie dnevniki generala Kamanina*, 4 vols. (Moscow: Infotekst-M, 1997); Yaroslav Golovanov, *Korolev: mify i fakty* (Moscow: Nauka, 1994).

17. For some details, see Golovanov, *Korolev*, 583, 595, 731; Boris Chertok, *Rockets and People, Vol. 3: Hot Days of the Cold War* (Washington, DC: NASA History Division, 2009), 207.

18. These issues are reflected in Khrushchev's biographies. See William Taubman, *Khrushchev: The Man and His Era* (New York: W. W. Norton, 2003), especially 480–506.

19. For critical assessments, see Taubman, *Khrushchev: The Man and His Era*, 129–132, 616–619; David Jouravsky, *The Lysenko Affair* (Chicago: University of Chicago Press, 1986).

20. See Golovanov, *Korolev*, 569, 718; Chertok, *Rockets and People*, 340; for an insider's account, see Kamanin, *Skrytyi kosmos*, vol. 1, 154–155.

21. See Slava Gerovitch, "Why Are We Telling Lies? The Creation of Soviet Space History Myths," *Russian Review* 70, no. 3 (2011): 460–484.

22. For a critical account, see Yegor Gaidar, *Collapse of an Empire: Lessons for Modern Russia* (Washington, DC: Brookings Institution Press, 2007), chapter 4.

23. See Siddiqui, *Challenge to Apollo*.

24. See Ivanovich, *Salyut—The First Space Station*.

25. See Hendrickx, Vis, *Energiya—Buran*.

26. See Geddes, *Politician's Dilemma*; Roll, "Pockets of Effectiveness."

27. See Roll, "Comparative Analysis."

28. See Gaidar, *Collapse of an Empire*, chapter 4.

29. For a detailed analysis, see Benjamin Peters, *How Not to Network a Nation: The Uneasy Story of the Soviet Internet* (Cambridge, MA: MIT Press, 2016).

30. For a skeptical account, see Katri Pynnöniemi, "Science Fiction: President Medvedev's Campaign for Russia's 'Technological Modernization,'" *Demokratizatsiya: The Journal of Post-Soviet Democratization* 22, no. 4 (2014): 605–626.

31. See Graham, *Lonely Ideas*, chapter 19.

32. For some details, see Svetlana Reiter, Ivan Golunov, "Rassledovanie RBK: chto sluchilos' so Skolkovo," *rbc.ru*, March 24, 2015, https://www.rbc.ru/special/business/2 3/03/2015/5509710a9a7947327e5f3a18, accessed September 7, 2021.

33. See Alexei Navalny, "Byt' dochkoi Putina," *navalny.com*, April 7, 2015, https:// navalny.com/p/4185/, accessed September 7, 2021.

34. See Geddes, *Politician's Dilemma*; *Institutions Count: Their Role and Significance in Latin American Development*, eds. Alejandro Portes, Lori D. Smith (Berkeley: University of California Press, 2012); Roll, ed., *The Politics of Public Sector Performance*.

35. See chapter 2 of this book.

36. See Bruce Bueno de Mesquita, Alastair Smith, *The Dictator's Handbook: Why Bad Behavior Is Almost Always Good Politics* (New York: Public Affairs, 2011), especially chapter 3.

37. See Matrin Muller, "Higher, Larger, Costlier: Sochi and the 2014 Winter Olympics," *Russian Analytical Digest*, no. 143 (2014); Robert W. Orttung, Sufian Zhemukhov, "The 2014 Sochi Olympic Mega-Project and Russia's Political Economy," *East European Politics* 30, no. 2 (2014): 175–191.

38. For a comparative analysis, see Jason Brownlee, "Hereditary Succession in Modern Autocracies," *World Politics* 59, no. 4 (2007): 595–628.

39. See Mancur Olson, "Dictatorship, Democracy, and Development," *American Political Science Review* 87, no. 3 (1993): 567–576.

40. See *Analiz faktorov realizatsii dokumentov strategicheskogo planirovaniya verkhnego urovnya*, ed. Mikhail Dmitriev (Moscow: Center for Strategic Research, 2016), https://polit.ru/media/files/2016/12/27/Report-on-strategy.pdf, accessed September 7, 2021.

41. For comparisons of incentives for Russian and Chinese officials, see Michael Rochlitz, Vera Kulpina, Thomas F. Remington, Andrei Yakovlev, "Performance Incentives and Economic Growth: Regional Officials in Russia and China," *Eurasian Geography and Economics* 56, no. 4 (2015): 421–445; Alexander Libman, Michael Rochlitz, *Federalism in China and Russia: Story of Success and Story of Failure?* (Cheltenham: Edward Elgar, 2019).

42. See Ora John Reuter, Graeme B. Robertson, "Subnational Appointments in Authoritarian Regimes: Evidence from Russian Gubernatorial Appointments," *Journal of Politics* 74, no. 4 (2012): 1023–1037.

43. See Ella Paneyakh, "Zaregulirovannoe gosudarstvo," *Pro et Contra* 13, no. 1–2 (2013): 58–92: Ella Paneyakh, "The Overregulated State," *Social Sciences* 45, no. 1 (2014): 20–33.

44. On these regulatory models, see Matthew D. McCubbins, Thomas Schwartz, "Congressional Oversight Overlooked: Police Patrols versus Fire Alarms," *American Journal of Political Science* 28, no. 1 (1984): 165–179.

45. See Vadim Volkov, Ivan Griroriev, Arina Dmitrieva, Ekaterina Moiseeva, Ella Paneyakh, Mikhail Pozdnyakov, Kirill Titaev, Irina Chetverikova, Maria Shklyaruk, *Kontseptsiya kompleksnoi organizatsionno-upravlencheskoi reformy pravookhranitel'nykh organov RF* (Saint Petersburg: European University at Saint Petersburg, Institute for the Rule of Law, 2013), http://www.enforce.spb.ru/images/Issledovanya/IRL_KGI_Reform_final_11.13.pdf, accessed September 7, 2021; Ella Paneyakh, "Faking Performances Together: Systems of Performance Evaluation in Russian Enforcement Agencies and Production of Bias and Privilege," *Post-Soviet Affairs* 30, no. 2–3 (2014): 115–136.

46. On Gref, see Evgenyi Karasyuk, *Slon na tantspole: kak German Gref i ego komanda uchat Sberbank tantsevat'* (Moscow: Mann, Ivanov and Ferber, 2013). For a critical account of Sberbank, see Jardar Østbø, "Hybrid surveillance capitalism: Sber's model for Russia's modernization," *Post-Soviet Affairs* 37, no. 5 (2021): 435–452.

47. See Graham, *Lonely Ideas*, especially chapters 1 and 2.

48. See Johnson, *Priests of Prosperity*, chapter 6.

49. See Geddes, *Politician's Dilemma*; Michael Roll, "Comparative Analysis."

50. Hereafter, I use materials from the HSE official website, www.hse.ru, accessed September 7, 2021.

51. See *Istoriya Vyshki*, https://www.hse.ru/info/hist/, accessed September 7, 2021.

52. See Andrei Kolesnikov, Yevgeny Yasin, *Dialogi s Yevgeniem Yasinym* (Moscow: Novoe literaturnoe obozrenie, 2014).

53. See Marina Khmelnitskaya, "Socio-Economic Development and the Politics of Expertise in Putin's Russia: The 'Hollow Paradigm' Perspective," *Europe-Asia Studies* 73, no. 4 (2021): 625–646.

54. For such an account, see Kirill Benediktov, "GU VSHE: istoriya uspeshnogo eksperimenta," *Russkii zhurnal*, March 10, 2010, http://www.russ.ru/pole/GU-VSHE -istoriya-uspeshnogo-eksperimenta, accessed September 7, 2021.

55. For a journalistic investigation, see Polina Nikol'skaya, "Rassledovanie RBK: kak zarabatyvaet Vysshaya shkola ekonomiki," *rbc.ru*, September 28, 2015, https://www. rbc.ru/investigation/society/28/09/2015/56087c389a794702546d5127, accessed September 7, 2021.

56. See Andrey Starodubtsev, "How Does the Government Implement Unpopular Reforms? Evidence from Education Policy in Russia," in *Authoritarian Modernization in Russia: Ideas, Institutions, and Policies*, ed. Vladimir Gel'man (Abingdon: Routledge, 2017), 148–165.

57See *Strategiya–2020: novaya model' rosta—novaya sotsial'naya politika, Itogovyi doklad ekspertnoi gruppy po aktual'nym problemam sotsial'no-ekonomicheskoi strategii Rossii na period do 2020 g* (Moscow: Delo, 2012), http://2020strategy.ru/ data/2012/03/13/1214585985/itog.pdf, accessed September 7, 2021.

58. See *Istoriya Vyshki*.

59. See the information on the HSE official website at https://strategyunits.hse.ru/ news/keywords/81259457/, accessed September 7, 2021.

60. For an overall highly critical assessment of the HSE, see Anton Oleinik, "Underperformance v teorii i universitetskoi praktike," *Sotsiologiya nauki i tekhnologii* 2, no. 3 (2011): 68–78, http://institutional.narod.ru/papers/oleinik.pdf, accessed September 7, 2021.

61. See Svetlana Pavlova, "Sam sebya uvolil? VShE proshchaetsya s 'nepravil'nymi' prepodavatelyami," *svoboda.org*, June 14, 2019, https://www.svoboda.org/a/29999440. html, accessed September 7, 2021; Evgeny Sen'shin, "V takikh usloviyakh ni odna nauka normal'no sushchestvovat' ne mozhet," *znak.com*, June 25, 2019, https://www.znak. com/2019-06-25/izvestnyy_politolog_rasskazal_chto_segodnya_ugrozhaet_gumanitarnymi_naukami_v_rossii, accessed September 7, 2021.

62. For a critical account, see Margarita Zavadskaya, "Academic Unfreedom," *ridl.io*, July 11, 2019, https://www.ridl.io/en/academic-unfreedom/, accessed September 7, 2021.

63. See Sasha Shvedchenko, "Kto takoi Egor Zhukov i pochemu vse o nem govoryat," *mel.fm*, December 7, 2019, https://mel.fm/povestka_dnya/3680759-egor_zhukov, accessed September 7, 2021.

64. See Nikol'skaya, "Rassledovanie RBK."

65. The official title is "The Project of Increasing Competitiveness of Leading Russian Universities among Leading Global Scientific-Educational Centers." Hereafter, I use materials from the official website of the project, www.5top100.ru, accessed September 7, 2021.

66. See Sergei Guriev, Dmitry Livanov, Konstantin Severinov, "Shest' mifov Akademii nauk," *polit.ru*, December 14, 2009, http://polit.ru/article/2009/12/14/6mifov/, accessed September 7, 2021.

67. See *Strategiya–2020*.

68. Experts differ in their assessments of the motives, mechanisms, and outcomes of these actions. For a polemic, see Natalia Forrat, "The Political Economy of Russian Higher Education: Why Does Putin Support Research Universities?" *Post-Soviet Affairs* 32, no. 4 (2016): 299–337; Igor Chirikov, "Do Russian Universities Have a Secret Mission: A Response to Forrat," *Post-Soviet Affairs* 32, no. 4 (2016): 338–344; Natalia Forrat, "A Response to Igor Chirikov," *Post-Soviet Affairs* 32, no. 4 (2016): 345–349.

69. For some critical analyses, see Mikhail Sokolov, Vladimir Volokhonskii, "Politicheskaya ekonomiya rossiiskogo vuza," *Otechestvennye zapiski*, no. 4 (2013), http://www.strana-oz.ru/2013/4/politicheskaya-ekonomiya-rossiyskogo-vuza, accessed September 7, 2021; Mikhail Sokolov, Kirill Titaev, "Provintsial'naya i tuzemnaya nauka," *Antropologicheskii forum*, no. 19 (2013): 239–275; Serghei Golunov, *The Elephant in the Room: Corruption and Cheating in Russian Universities* (Stuttgart: Ibidem-Verlag, 2014). For a detailed treatment of the involvement of Russian universities in production of fake dissertations and other instances of academic dishonesty collected by the Dissernet community of scholars and experts, see "Disseropediya rossiiskikh vuzov: rossiiskie vuzy pod lupoi Disserneta," *dissernet.org*, http://rosvuz.dissernet.org/, accessed September 7, 2021.

70. On the Chinese experience, see Guanzi Shen, "Building World-Class Universities in China: From the View of National Strategies," *Global University Network for Innovation*, May 30, 2018, www.guninetwork.org/articles/building-world-class-universities-china-view-national-strategies, accessed September 7, 2021.

71. For a highly critical account of the School of Advanced Studies, see Natalia Savelyeva, "How 'Love What You Do' Went Wrong in an 'Academic Sweatshop' in Siberia," *Opendemocracy.net*, March 13, 2020, https://www.opendemocracy.net/en/odr/how-love-what-you-do-went-wrong-in-an-academic-sweatshop-in-siberia/, accessed September 7, 2021. For self-presentation by the school, see its official website, https://sas.utmn.ru/ru/, accessed September 7, 2021.

72. In 2019, the number of Russian universities listed in the *Times Higher Education* ranking tables was thirty-nine, compared to two in 2012. In the QS World University Rankings, there were thirty-six (compared to fourteen in 2012), and in the ARWU (Academic Ranking of World Universities, also known as the Shanghai ranking) there were sixteen universities (compared to two in 2012). See https://www.5top100.ru/rankings/, accessed September 7, 2021.

73. See Igor Chirikov, *Does Conflict of Interest Distort Global University Rankings?* Research & Occasional Paper Series CSHE 5:2021 (Berkeley: Berkeley Center for Studies in Higher Education, 2021), https://escholarship.org/uc/item/8hk672nh, accessed September 7, 2021.

74. *Programma Prioritet 2030*, https://minobrnauki.gov.ru/action/priority2030/, accessed February 18, 2022.

75. See Paul J. DiMaggio, Walter W. Powell, "The 'Iron Cage' Revisited: Institutional Isomorphism and Collective Rationality in Organizational Analysis," *American Sociological Review* 48, no. 2 (1983): 149.

76. Ibid.

77. See Andrei Shleifer, Daniel Treisman, "A Normal Country," *Foreign Affairs* 83, no. 2 (2004): 20–38.

78. See chapter 3 of this book.

79. For a critical account, see Sergei Medvedev, *The Return of the Russian Leviathan* (Cambridge: Polity Press, 2019).

Chapter 7

1. According to Levada-Center mass surveys, the Soviet-style political and economic system is perceived by many Russians as the only relevant and desirable alternative to the status quo. In January 2016, 37 percent of all respondents in a nationwide survey (N = 1600) opted for the Soviet system as the best model, 23 percent supported the status quo, and 13 percent choose Western-style democracy. At the same time, 52 percent of the respondents in this survey preferred a planned economy over the market and private property. See "Predpochtitel'nye modeli politicheskoi i ekonomicheskoi sistem," *Levada-Center*, February 17, 2016, https://www.levada.ru/2016/02/17/predpochtitelnye-modeli-ekonomicheskoj-i-politicheskoj-sistem/, accessed September 7, 2021.

2. See Dmitry Travin, *Prosushchestvuet li putinskaya sistema do 2042 goda?* (Saint Petersburg: Norma, 2016).

3. See Henry E. Hale, *Patronal Politics: Eurasian Regime Dynamics in Comparative Perspective* (Cambridge: Cambridge University Press, 2014); Daniel Treisman, "Income, Democracy, and Leader Turnover," *American Journal of Political Science* 59, no. 4 (2015): 927–942.

4. For these assessments, see Keith Grane, Shanthi Natharaj, Patrick B. Johnston, Gursel Rafig oglu Aliyev, *Russia's Mid-Term Economic Prospects* (Santa Monica, CA: Rand Corporation, 2016); Marek Dabrowski, Antoine Mathieu Collin, "Russia's Growth Problem," *Bruegel Policy Contribution*, no. 4 (February 2019). Some critically minded observers have discussed the total lack of prospects for economic growth and development in Russia under its current political regime. See *Zastoi-2: Posledstviya, riski i al'ternativy dlya rossiiskoi ekonomiki*, ed. Kirill Rogov (Moscow: Liberal'naya missiya, 2021).

5. For this translation of Nekrasov, see "Russian Poetry in Translation," *allthelyrics.com*, January 23, 2013, https://www.allthelyrics.com/forum/showthread.php?t=141341&page=2, accessed September 7, 2021.

6. See Steven Levitsky, Daniel Ziblatt, *How Democracies Die* (New York: Crown, 2018); Sergei Guriev, Elias Papaioannou, "The Political Economy of Populism," *Journal*

of Economic Literature, forthcoming, https://www.aeaweb.org/articles?id=10.1257/ jel.20201595&from=f, accessed February 16, 2022; Stephen E. Hanson, Jeffrey S. Kopstein, "Understanding the Global Neopatrimonial Wave," *Perspectives on Politics,* "20, no. 1 (2022): 237-249."

7. For the essence of these discussions of the 1970s, see Michel Crozier, Samuel P. Huntington, Joji Watanuki, *The Crisis of Democracy: Report on the Governability of Democracies to the Trilateral Commission* (New York: New York University Press, 1975).

8. For these assessments, see Timothy Frye, "Russian Studies Are Thriving, Not Dying," *The National Interest*, October 3, 2017, https://nationalinterest.org/feature/ russian-studies-thriving-not-dying-22547, accessed September 7, 2021. Judging from this perspective, the slogan "Know Your Enemy!" which served as a major driver of Soviet studies during the Cold War, has not lost its relevance. See David C. Engerman, *Know Your Enemy: The Rise and Fall of America's Soviet Experts* (Oxford: Oxford University Press, 2009).

9. See Samuel P. Huntington, "Political Development and Political Decay," *World Politics* 17, no. 3 (1965): 386–430.

10. See Francis Fukuyama, *Political Order and Political Decay: From the Industrial Revolution to the Globalization of Democracy* (New York: Farrar, Straus, and Giroux, 2014), especially chapter 31.

11. See Huntington, "Political Development and Political Decay," 493; Fukuyama, *Political Order and Political Decay*, 27–28.

12. For an analysis of interconnections between formal and informal institutions, see Gretchen Helmke, Steven Levitsky, "Informal Institutions and Comparative Politics: A Research Agenda," *Perspectives on Politics* 2, no. 4 (2004): 725–740. For a more comprehensive overview, see *International Handbook on Informal Governance*, eds. Thomas Christiansen, Christine Newhold (Cheltenham: Edward Elgar, 2012).

13. See Hanson, Kopstein, "Understanding the Global Neopatrimonial Wave."

14. For divergent perspectives of analysis, see Pippa Norris, Ronald Inglehart, *Cultural Backlash: Trump, Brexit, and Authoritarian Populism* (Cambridge: Cambridge University Press, 2019); Guriev, Papaioannou, "The Political Economy of Populism."

15. See Javier Coralles, "Authoritarian Legalism in Venezuela," *Journal of Democracy* 26, no. 2 (2015): 37–51; Kirk A. Hawkins, "Responding to Radical Populism: Chavismo in Venezuela," *Democratization* 23, no. 2 (2016): 242–262.

16. See "Exit from Democracy: Illiberal Governance in Turkey and Beyond," *Southeast European and Black Sea Studies* 16, no. 4 (2008): special issue; "Critical Crossroads: Erdogan and the Transformation of Turkey," *Mediterranean Quarterly* 29, no. 3 (2018): special issue.

17. See Roger E. Hamilton, "Russia's Attempts to Undermine Democracy in the West: Effects and Causes," *Orbis* 63, no. 3 (2019): 334–348; Anders Åslund, *Russia's Crony Capitalism: The Path from Market Economy to Kleptocracy* (New Haven, CT: Yale University Press, 2019), especially chapter 6.

18. See, for example, Levitsky, Ziblatt, *How Democracies Die*; David Cay Johnson, *It's Even Worse Than You Think: What the Trump Administration Is Doing to America*

(New York: Simon and Schuster, 2018); *American Political Development and the Trump Presidency*, eds. Zachary Callen, Philip Rocco (Philadelphia: University of Pennsylvania Press, 2020).

19. On the practices of *kompromat*, see Alena Ledeneva, *How Russia Really Works: The Informal Practices That Shaped Post-Soviet Politics and Business* (Ithaca, NY: Cornell University Press, 2006), especially chapter 3.

20. On the impact of the global economic crisis on Hungary, see, for example, Laszlo Andor, "Hungary in the Financial Crisis: A (Basket) Case Study," *Debatte: Journal of Contemporary Central and Eastern Europe* 17, no. 3 (2009): 285–296. For broader overviews of economic and political changes in post-Communist Hungary, see Umut Korkut, *Liberalization Challenges in Hungary: Elitism, Progressivism, and Populism* (New York: Palgrave Macmillan, 2012); Adam Fabry, *The Political Economy of Hungary: From State Capitalism to Authoritarian Neoliberalism* (Cham: Palgrave Macmillan, 2019).

21. See Hilary Appel, Mitchell Orenstein, *From Triumph to Crisis: Neoliberal Economic Reform in Postcommunist Countries* (Cambridge: Cambridge University Press, 2018).

22. See Juliet Johnson, Andrew Barnes, "Financial Nationalism and Its International Enablers: The Hungarian Experience," *Review of International Political Economy* 22, no. 3 (2015): 535–569.

23. See Dorottya Szikra, "Democracy and Welfare in Hard Times: Social Policy of the Orban Government in Hungary between 2010 and 2014," *Journal of European Social Policy* 24, no. 5 (2014): 486–500; Fabry, *The Political Economy of Hungary*.

24. For example, Hungary was ranked as 50th among the countries in the annual Corruption Perception Index in 2010, while in 2019 its rank declined to 70th. See https://www.transparency.org, accessed September 7, 2021. According to the Rule of Law Index of the World Justice Project, Hungary was ranked as 36th in 2014, but was downgraded to 60th out of 128 countries by 2020. See https://worldjusticeproject.org/, accessed September 7, 2021.

25. For some accounts, see Anne Appelbaum, "Creeping Authoritarianism Has Finally Prevailed," *The Atlantic*, April 3, 2020, https://www.theatlantic.com/ideas/archive/2020/04/hungary-coronavirus-just-excuse/609331/, accessed September 7, 2021; Will Collins, "Soft Authoritarianism Comes to Hungary," *The National Review*, April 3, 2020, https://www.nationalreview.com/2020/04/soft-authoritarianism-comes-to-hungary, accessed September 7, 2021; John Stuttack, "Victor Orban's Viral Authoritarianism," *The American Prospect*, April 6, 2020, https://prospect.org/coronavirus/viktor-orban-viral-authoritarianism-hungary/, accessed September 7, 2021.

26. See Balint Magyar, *Post-Communist Mafia State: The Case of Hungary* (Budapest: Central European University Press, 2016).

27. For a systematic analysis of mafia as a phenomenon, see Diego Gambetta, *The Sicilian Mafia: The Business of Private Protection* (Cambridge, MA: Harvard University Press, 1993).

28. See *Stubborn Structures: Reconceptualizing Post-Communist Regimes*, ed. Balint Magyar (Budapest: Central European University Press, 2019), 97–176.

29. For this argument, see Jussi Lassila, "Putin as a Non-Populist Autocrat," *Russian Politics* 3, no. 2 (2018): 175–195.

30. See Fukuyama, *Political Order and Political Decay*, especially part IV.

31. See William R. Easterly, *The Elusive Quest for Growth: Adventures and Misadventures in the Tropics* (Cambridge, MA: MIT Press, 2001), especially part II.

32. On these developments, see Vladimir Gel'man, "The Politics of Fear: How Russia's Rulers Counter Their Rivals," *Russian Politics* 1, no. 1 (2016): 27–45; Kirill Rogov, "The Art of Coercion: Repressions and Repressiveness in Putin's Russia," *Russian Politics* 3, no. 2 (2018): 151–174.

33. See Barbara Geddes, Joseph Wright, Erica Frantz, *How Dictatorships Work: Power, Personalization, and Collapse* (Cambridge: Cambridge University Press, 2018), 187–190.

34. See Linda Cook, Aadne Aasland, Daria Prisyazhnyuk, "Russian Pension Reform under Quadruple Influence," *Problems of Post-Communism* 66, no. 2 (2019): 96–108; Elena Maltseva, "The Politics of Retirement Age Increase in Russia: Proposals, Protests, and Concessions," *Russian Politics* 4, no. 3 (2019): 375–399.

35. For an account of the 2020 constitutional changes in Russia, see Henry Hale, "Putin's End Game," *PONARS Policy Memos*, no. 638 (2020), www.ponarseurasia.org/memo/putins-end-game, accessed September 7, 2021.

36. See Milan Svolik, *The Politics of Authoritarian Rule* (Cambridge: Cambridge University Press, 2012), especially chapter 4; Alexander Baturo, *Democracy, Dictatorship, and Term Limits* (Ann Arbor: University of Michigan Press, 2014); Geddes, Wright, Frantz, *How Dictatorships Work*, especially chapter 6.

37. See *The Politics of Presidential Term Limits*, eds. Alexander Baturo, Robert Elgie (Oxford: Oxford University Press, 2019); Farid Guliyev, "Is Putin Emulating Azerbaijan in 2008–09? Modifying Term Limits under Economic Uncertainty," *PONARS Policy Memos*, no. 647 (2020), www.ponarseurasia.org/memo/putin-emulating-azerbaijan-2008-09-modifying-term-limits, accessed September 7, 2021.

38. See *Russia after the Global Economic Crisis*, eds. Anders Åslund, Sergei Guriev, Andrew C. Kuchins (Washington, DC: Peterson Institute for International Economics, 2010).

39. See Anton Feinberg, "Gil'otina ot pravitel'stva: kak vlasti khotyat snizit' trebovaniya k biznesu," *rbc.ru*, January 15, 2019, https://www.rbc.ru/economics/15/01/2019/5c3df76f9a7947214d11adcf, accessed September 7, 2021; "Tsel' regulyatornoi gil'otiny—ne ubit' kontrol' i nazdor, a sozdat' novuyu sistemu," *hse.ru*, April 11, 2019, https://www.hse.ru/news/science/261723973.html, accessed September 7, 2021.

40. See Ivan Grigoriev, Anna Dekalchuk, "Collective Learning and Regime Dynamics under Uncertainty: Labour Reform and the Way to Autocracy in Russia," *Democratization* 24, no. 3 (2017): 481–497; see also chapter 4 of this book.

41. For analysis of the case of police reform in Russia, which was loudly announced by Dmitry Medvedev but had a negligible effect, see Brian Taylor, "The Police Reform in Russia: Policy Process in a Hybrid Regime," *Post-Soviet Affairs* 30, no. 2–3 (2014): 226–255.

42. See Mikhail Sokolov, "Can Russian Research Policy Be Called Neoliberal? A Study in the Comparative Sociology of Quantification," *Europe-Asia Studies* 73, no. 6 (2021): 989–1009; Katerina Guba, Angelika Tsivinskaya, "Evaluating the Evaluators in Russia: When Academic Citizenship Fails," *Europe-Asia Studies* 73, no. 6 (2021): 1010–1036.

43. On "regulatory capture," see George J. Stigler, "The Theory of Economic Regulation," *The Bell Journal of Economics and Management Science* 2, no. 1 (1971): 3–21.

44. See "Obshchestvennyi sovet pri Ministerstve prirodnykh resursov i ekologii Rossiiskoi Federatsii," *Doklad No.2, Rabochaya gruppa po realizatsii mekhanizma "regulyatornoi gil'otiny,"* July 17, 2020 (document, author's archive). I would like to thank Angelina Davydova for this valuable information.

45. For a critical account of Gref's approach to digitalization, see Jardar Østbø, "Hybrid Surveillance Capitalism: Sber's Model for Russia's Modernization," *Post-Soviet Affairs* 37, no. 5 (2021): 435–452. The criticism became much stronger in the wake of the COVID-19 pandemic when digital technologies were arbitrarily and rather ineffectively used by the Russian subnational authorities for control over the movement of people in big cities.

46. For an overview, see Carolina Vendil Pallin, "Internet Control through Ownership: The Case of Russia," *Post-Soviet Affairs* 33, no. 1 (2017): 16–33.

47. See "Rostelekom zakryl natsional'nyi poiskovik 'Sputnik,'" *Kommersant*, September 8, 2020, https://www.kommersant.ru/doc/4483248, accessed September 7, 2021.

48. See Lada Shamardina, "'Pomenyaite vash algoritm': Duma otlozhila vopros o 'Yandex. Novostyakh,'" *The Bell*, August 19, 2019, https://thebell.io/pomenyajte-vash-algoritm-gosduma-otlozhila-vopros-o-yandeks-novostyah/, accessed September 7, 2021.

49. For various assessments, see Larry Diamond, "The Road to Digital Unfreedom: The Threat of Postmodern Totalitarianism," *Journal of Democracy* 30, no. 1 (2019): 20–24; *Towards Digital Enlightenment: The Essays on the Dark and Light Sides of the Digital Revolution*, ed. Dirk Helbing (Cham: Springer Nature, 2019).

50. See Leonid Volkov, "Kto zarabotaet na 'pakete Yarovoi,'" *leonidvolkov.ru*, August 3, 2016, https://www.leonidvolkov.ru/p/160/, accessed September 7, 2021; Mariya Plyusnina, "Blokirovka Youtube mozhet sozdat' okolorevoluyutsionnuyu situatsiyu," *znak.com*, December 25, 2019, https://www.znak.com/2019-12-25/pochemu_rossiyskim_vlastyam_vazhno_nauchitsya_tochechno_otklyuchat_internet_k_2021_godu, accessed September 7, 2021.

51. See Matt Burgess, "This Is Why Russia's Attempts to Block Telegram Have Failed," *Wired*, April 28, 2018, https://www.wired.co.uk/article/telegram-in-russia-blocked-web-app-ban-facebook-twitter-google, accessed September 7, 2021; Ksenia Ermoshina, Francesca Musiani, "The Telegram Ban: How Censorship 'Made in Russia' Faced Global Internet," *First Monday* 26, no. 5 (2021), https://hal.archives-ouvertes.fr/hal-03215281/ document, accessed September 9, 2021.

52. See Mark Krutov, Robert Coalson, "The Insulted and the Injured: 'Streisand Effect' Dulls Impact of Law on Dissing Russian Authorities," *Radio Free Europe/Radio*

Liberty, October 6, 2019, https://www.rferl.org/a/streisand-effect-dulls-impact-of-insult-law-putin/30202144.html, accessed September 7, 2021.

53. See Tatyana Vasil'chuk, "'Mishki' na servere. Kak onlain-golosovanie privelo v Mosgordumu kandidatov, podderzhannykh 'Edinoi Rossiei,'" *Novaya gazeta*, September 12, 2019, https://www.novayagazeta.ru/articles/2019/09/12/81950-mishki-na-servere, accessed September 7, 2021.

54. For a description, see Dmitry Kuznets, Alexander Ershov, "Tak vse-taki byli fal'sifikatsii na elektronnom golosovanii—ili vlasti prosto mobilizovali na nego bol'she svoikh storonnikov?," *meduza.io*, September 24, 2021, https://meduza.io/feature/2021/09/24/tak-vse-taki-byli-falsifikatsii-na-elektronnom-golosovanii-ili-vlasti-prosto-mobilizovali-na-nego-bolshe-svoih-storonnikov, accessed February 16, 2022. For a discussion, see Andrei Yu. Buzin, Alexander A. Isavnin, Dmitry A. Kuznetsov, Dmitry V. Nesterov, Boris V. Ovchinnikov, Oleg Ch. Reut, Aleksei V. Rybin, Viktor L. Tolstoguzov, Yevgeny V. Fedin, "Experience and Prospects of Remote Electronic Voting," *Electoral Politics* 2, no. 6 (2021): 9, https://electoralpolitics.org/en/articles/distantsionnoe-elektronnoe-golosovanie-opyt-i-perspektivy/, accessed February 16, 2022.

55. For in-depth analyses, see Carolina Schlaufer, "Why Do Non-Democratic Regimes Promote E-Participation? The Case of Moscow Active Citizen Online Voting Platform," *Governance* 34, no. 3 (2021): 821–836; Daria Gritsenko, Andrey Indukaev, "Digitalising City Governance in Russia: The Case of the 'Active Citizen' Platform," *Europe-Asia Studies* 73, no. 6 (2021): 1102–1124.

56. On the use of digitalization by Moscow city government in other policy areas, see Gulnaz Sharafutdinova, Nisan Gorgulu, "Digital Technologies and Authoritarian Regimes: A Case of Pothole Management in Moscow," *PONARS Policy Memos*, no. 661 (2020), https://www.ponarseurasia.org/digital-technologies-and-authoritarian-regimes-a-case-of-pothole-management-in-moscow/, accessed September 9, 2020.

57. For an overview, see Andrey Starodubtsev, *Federalism and Regional Policy in Contemporary Russia* (Abingdon: Routledge, 2018).

58. See Alexander Libman, Andrei Yakovlev, "A Centralist Approach to Regional Development: The Case of the Russian Ministry for the Development of the Far East," *Europe-Asia Studies* 73, no. 6 (2021): 1125–1148.

59. See Andrei Yakovlev, Lev Freinkman, Sergey Makarov, Victor Pogodaev, "How Do Russia's Regions Adjust to External Shocks? Evidence from the Republic of Tatarstan," *Problems of Post-Communism* 67, no. 4–5 (2020): 417–431.

60. On the large-scale program of housing renovation in Moscow, see Regina Smyth, "How the Kremlin Is Using the Moscow Renovation Project to Reward and Punish Voters," *PONARS Policy Memos*, no. 513 (2017), http://www.ponarseurasia.org/memo/kremlin-using-moscow-renovation-project-reward-punish-voters, accessed September 7, 2021. See also Marina Khmelnitskaya, Emmirosa Ihalainen, "Urban Governance in Russia: The Case of Moscow Territorial Development and Housing Renovation," *Europe-Asia Studies* 73, no. 6 (2021): 1149–1175.

61. For these accounts, see Daria Dimke, Aleksey Gilev, "'No Time for Quality': Mechanisms of Local Governance in Russia," *Europe-Asia Studies* 73, no. 6 (2021): 1060–1079; Margarita Zavadskaya, Lev Shilov, "Providing Goods and Votes? Federal Elections and the Quality of Local Governance in Russia" *Europe-Asia Studies* 73, no. 6 (2021): 1037–1059.

62. On "participatory authoritarianism" in China and Russia, see Catherine Owen, "Participatory Authoritarianism: From Bureaucratic Transformation to Civic Participation in China and Russia," *Review of International Studies* 246, no. 4 (2020): 415–434.

63. For a detailed account of the effects of participatory budgeting projects in Russia, see Ivan Shulga, Lev Shilov, Anna Sukhova, Peter Pojarski, "Can Local Participatory Programs Enhance Public Confidence: Insights from the Local Initiatives Support Program in Russia," *World Bank Discussion Papers*, no. 1931 (2019), https://elibrary.worldbank.org/doi/abs/10.1596/31810, accessed September 7, 2021.

64. For an empirical evidence, see Leonid Polishchuk, Alexander Rubin, Igor Shagalov, "Managing Collective Action: Government-Sponsored Community Initiatives in Russia," *Europe-Asia Studies* 73, no. 6 (2021): 1176–1209.

65. On the "triple transition," see Claus Offe, "Capitalism by Democratic Design? Democratic Theory Facing the Triple Transition in East Central Europe," *Social Research* 58, no. 4 (1991): 865–892.

66. On state capture in post-Communist countries, see Joel S. Hellman, "Winners Take All: The Politics of Partial Reform in Postcommunist Transitions," *World Politics* 50, no. 2 (1998): 203–234.

67. See M. Steven Fish, "The Determinants of Economic Reforms in the Postcommunist World," *East European Politics and Societies* 12, no. 1 (1998): 31–78; Michael McFaul, "The Fourth Wave of Democracy and Dictatorship: Non-Cooperative Transitions in the Postcommunist World," *World Politics* 54, no. 2 (2002): 212–244; Timothy M. Frye, *Building States and Markets after Communism: The Perils of Polarized Democracy* (Cambridge: Cambridge University Press, 2010). See also Kirill Rogov, "Krizis perekhoda: Oktyabr' 1993 i uroki makroistorii," *Inliberty.ru*, October 6, 2018, https://www.inliberty.ru/magazine/issue8/, accessed September 7, 2021.

68. For some evidence, see Eric Hanley, Natasha Yershova, Richard Anderson, "Russia—Old Wine in a New Bottle? The Circulation and Reproduction of Russian Elites, 1983–1993," *Theory and Society* 24, no. 5 (1995): 639–668; Olga Kryshtanovskaya, Stephen White, "From Soviet Nomenklatura to Russian Elite," *Europe-Asia Studies* 48, no. 5 (1996): 711–733.

69. For firsthand accounts, see Petr Aven, Alfred Kokh, *Gaidar's Revolution: The Inside Account of the Economic Transformation in Russia* (London: I. B. Tauris, 2015).

70. For various assessments, see Andrei Shleifer, Daniel Treisman, *Without a Map: Political Tactics and Economic Reform in Russia* (Cambridge, MA: MIT Press, 2000);

Chrystia Freeland, *Sale of the Century: Russia's Wild Ride from Communism to Capitalism* (New York: Crown Business, 2000).

71. See Neil Abrams, M. Steven Fish, "Policies First, Institutions Second: Lessons from Estonia's Economic Reforms," *Post-Soviet Affairs* 31, no. 6 (2015): 491–513.

72. See Anton Steen, *Between Past and Future: Elites, Democracy, and the State in Post-Communist Countries. A Comparison of Estonia, Latvia, and Lithuania* (Aldershot: Ashgate, 1997).

73. For some survey data, see Joakim Ekman, Kjetil Duvold, "Ethnic Divides in the Baltic States: Political Orientations after the Russian-Ukrainian Crisis," in *Crises in the Post-Soviet Space: From the Dissolution of the Soviet Union to the Conflict in Ukraine*, eds. Fexit Jaitner, Tina Olteanu, Tobias Spöri (Abingdon: Routledge, 2018), 121–135.

74. For these accounts, see Juan J. Linz, Alfred Stepan, *Problems of Democratic Transitions and Consolidation: Southern Europe, South America, and Post-Communist Europe* (Baltimore: Johns Hopkins University Press, 1996), chapter 20; David D. Laitin, *Identity in Formation: The Russian-Speaking Populations in the Near Abroad* (Ithaca, NY: Cornell University Press, 1998). For a critical assessment, see James Hughes, "'Exit' in Deeply Divided Societies: Regimes of Discrimination in Estonia and Latvia," *Journal of Common Market Studies* 43, no. 4 (2005): 739–762.

75. On the advantages of relative backwardness, see Alexander Gerschenkron, *Economic Backwardness in Historical Perspective* (Cambridge, MA: Harvard University Press, 1962).

76. See Alina Mungiu-Pippidi, "The Quest for Good Governance: Learning from Virtuous Circles," *Journal of Democracy* 27, no. 1 (2016): 95–109; Fredrika Björklund, "E-Government and Moral Citizenship: The Case of Estonia," *Citizenship Studies* 20, no. 6–7 (2016): 914–931; Valts Kalnins, "The World's Smallest Virtuous Circle: Estonia," in *Transitions to Good Governance: Creating Virtuous Circles of Anti-Corruption*, eds. Alina Mingui-Pippidi, Michael Johnston (Cheltenham: Edward Elgar, 2017), 102–127.

77. For similar observations, see Lucan Ahmad Way, Adam Casey, "The Structural Sources of Postcommunist Regime Trajectories," *Post-Soviet Affairs* 34, no. 5 (2018): 317–332.

78. For some accounts, see Stephen Jones, *Georgia: A Political History since Independence* (London: I. B. Tauris, 2013); Jonathan Wheatley, *Georgia from the National Awakening to the Rose Revolution: Delayed Transition in the Former Soviet Union* (Abingdon: Routledge, 2017).

79. For a detailed account, see Larisa Burakova, *Pochemu u Gruzii poluchilos'* (Moscow: United Press, 2011). See also Alexander Kupatadze, "The Quest for Good Governance: Georgia's Break with the Past," *Journal of Democracy* 27, no.1 (2016): 110–123.

80. See Vladimir Fedorin, *Doroga k svobode: besedy s Kakhoi Bendukidze* (Moscow: Novoe izdatel'stvo, 2015).

81. For the self-presentation of Georgian reformers, see Nika Gilauri, *Practical Economics: Economic Transformation and Government Reform in Georgia, 2004–2012* (Cham: Palgrave Macmillan, 2012). For a more critical account, see Lincoln Mitchell, "Compromising Democracy: State Building in Saakashvili's Georgia," *Central Asian Survey* 28, no. 2 (2009): 171–183.

82. For an in-depth analysis, see Ketevan Bolkvadze, "Hitting the Saturation Point: Unpacking the Politics of Bureaucratic Reforms in Hybrid Regimes," *Democratization* 24, no. 4 (2017): 751–769.

83. For a critical account, see Kornely Kakachia, Bidzina Lebanidze, "Georgia's Dangerous Slide Away from Democracy," *Carnegie Europe*, December 10, 2019, https://carnegieeurope.eu/strategiceurope/80542, accessed September 7, 2021.

84. For some accounts, see Andrew Wilson, *Ukraine's Orange Revolution* (New Haven, CT: Yale University Press, 2005); Paul D'Anieri, *Understanding Ukrainian Politics: Power, Politics, and Institutional Design* (Armonk, NY: M. E. Sharpe, 2007); Lucan A. Way, *Pluralism by Default: Weak Autocrats and the Rise of Competitive Politics* (Baltimore: Johns Hopkins University Press, 2015), chapter 3.

85. For a critical assessment, see Serhiy Kudelia, "The Maidan and Beyond: The House That Yanukovych Built," *Journal of Democracy* 25, no. 3 (2014): 19–34.

86. For some accounts, see Oleksandr Fisun, "The Future of Ukraine's Neopatrimonial Democracy," *PONARS Policy Memos*, no. 394 (2015), http://www.ponarseurasia.org/memo/future-ukraine-neopatrimonial-democracy, accessed September 7, 2021; *Beyond Euromaidan: Comparative Perspective of Advancing Reforms in Ukraine*, eds. Henry E. Hale, Robert W. Orttung (Stanford, CA: Stanford University Press, 2016).

87. On the impact of oligarchs, see Judy Dempsey, "The Long Road to Dismantling Ukraine's Oligarchic Democracy," *Carnegie Europe*, April 16, 2015, https://carnegieeurope.eu/strategiceurope/59798, accessed September 7, 2021; Heiko Pleines, "Oligarchs and Politics in Ukraine," *Demokratizatsiya: The Journal of Post-Soviet Democratization* 24, no. 1 (2016): 105–127; Satu Kahkonen, "What Is the Cost of Crony Capitalism for Ukraine?," *The World Bank*, March 15, 2018, https://www.worldbank.org/en/news/opinion/2018/03/15/what-is-the-cost-of-crony-capitalism-for-ukraine, accessed September 7, 2021.

88. For a detailed account, see Maria Popova, Daniel Beers, "No Revolution of Dignity for Ukraine's Judges: Judicial Reform after Euromaidan," *Demokratizatsiya: The Journal of Post-Soviet Democratization* 28, no. 1 (2020): 113–142.

89. See Scott Radnitz, *Weapons of the Wealthy: Predatory Regimes and Elite-Led Protests in Central Asia* (Ithaca, NY: Cornell University Press, 2012).

90. On these issues, see Maria Popova, *Politicized Justice in Emerging Democracies: A Study of Courts in Russia and Ukraine* (Cambridge: Cambridge University Press, 2014).

91. For a more detailed account of challenges to the quality of governance in the post-Soviet region, see *The Struggle for Good Governance in Ukraine, Georgia, and*

Moldova, eds. Michael Emerson, Denis Genusa, Tamara Kovziridze, Veronica Movchan (Lanham, MD: Rowman and Littlefield, 2018).

92. See William R. Easterly, *The Elusive Quest for Growth: Adventures and Misadventures in the Tropics* (Cambridge, MA: MIT Press, 2001); Gero Erdmann, Ulf Engel, *Neopatrimonialism Revisited: Beyond a Catch-All Concept* (Hamburg: German Institute for Global and Area Studies, 2006), GIGA Working Paper no. 16, https://core.ac.uk/download/pdf/71729549.pdf, accessed September 7, 2021.

93. On the coercive and infrastructural capacity of the state, see Michael Mann, "The Autonomous Power of the State: Its Origins, Mechanisms, and Results," *European Journal of Sociology/Archives Européennes de Sociologie* 25, no. 2 (1984): 185–213.

94. See Francis Fukuyama, "The Pandemic and Political Order," *Foreign Affairs* 99, no. 4 (2020), https://www.foreignaffairs.com/articles/world/2020-06-09/pandemic-and-political-order, accessed September 7, 2021.

95. See Anton Troianovski, "'You Can't Trust Anyone': Russia's Hidden Covid Toll Is an Open Secret," *The New York Times*, April 10, 2021, https://www.nytimes.com/2021/04/10/world/europe/covid-russia-death.html, accessed September 7, 2021. See also calculations by Alexey Zakharov, Higher School of Economics, https://www.facebook.com/alexei.zakharov.1/posts/3663318147058819, accessed September 7, 2021.

96. See Charlie Giattino, Hannah Ritchie, Max Roser, Esteban Ortiz-Ospina, Joe Hassel, "Excess Mortality during the Coronavirus Pandemic (COVID-19)," *Our World in Data*, February 14, 2022, https://ourworldindata.org/excess-mortality-covid, accessed February 16, 2022.

97. See Grigorii Yudin, "Edinstvennyi ili nikakoi: chego khochet ot plebiscite Putin i chto mogut sdelat' opponenty," *republic.ru*, June 11, 2020, https://republic.ru/posts/96942, accessed September 7, 2021.

98. See "Doktor Myasnikov: Komu polozheno pomeret', pomrut," *Soloviev. Live*, May 20, 2020, https://www.youtube.com/watch?v=wztfLJLUSWc, accessed September 7, 2021.

99. For an account, see Kristina Safonova, "My vse boimsya—i rukovodstvo, i vrachi," *meduza.io*, April 21, 2020, https://meduza.io/feature/2020/04/21/my-vse-boimsya-i-rukovodstvo-i-vrachi, accessed September 7, 2021.

100. See Sergei Guriev, Daniel Treisman, "Informational Autocrats," *Journal of Economic Perspectives* 33, no. 4 (2019): 100–127.

101. "The authoritarian equilibrium rests mainly on lies, fear, and economic prosperity." Adam Przeworski, *Democracy and the Market: Political and Economic Reforms in Eastern Europe and Latin America* (Cambridge: Cambridge University Press, 1991), 58.

102. On the Russian state officials' manipulations of COVID-19 statistics, see, for example, Sergey Kalashnikov, "Lipetskii gubernator poprosil podchinennykh popravit' statistiku po koronavirusu," *Kommersant*, May 25, 2020, https://www.kommersant.ru/doc/4356084, accessed September 7, 2021.

103. See John Burn-Murdoch, Henry Foy, "Russia's COVID Death Toll Could be 70 Per Cent Higher than Official Figure," *Financial Times*, May 11, 2020; Henry Meyer, "Experts Question Russian Data on COVID-19 Death Toll," *Bloomberg.com*, May 13, 2020, https://www.bloomberg.com/news/articles/2020-05-13/experts-question-russian-data-on-covid-19-death-toll, accessed September 7, 2021.

104. See Maksim Litavrin, David Frenkel, Egor Skovoroda, "Vesnoi kak minimum v 7 regionakh sil'no vyrosla smertnost', i ofitsial'nye dannye po koronavirusu eto ne ob'yasnyayut," *Mediazona*, June 30, 2020, https://zona.media/article/2020/06/30/mortality, accessed September 7, 2021.

105. This practice had a devastating effect during the Chernobyl nuclear disaster in 1986 when Soviet leaders attempted to conceal information. They publicly acknowledged the nuclear accident after a major delay after spread the alarming news in the West. For a detailed account, see Serhii Plokhy, *Chernobyl: History of a Tragedy* (London: Penguin, 2019).

106. On the poor quality of Soviet statistics and its post-Soviet legacies, see Mark Tolz, "Population Trends in the Russian Federation: Reflection on the Legacy of Soviet Censorship and Distortion of Demographic Statistics," *Eurasian Geography and Economics* 49, no. 1 (2008): 87–98.

107. See Farida Rustamova, Andrei Pertsev, "Dazhe slovo 'karantin' starayutsya ne upotreblyat.' Kak president i pravitel'stvo perekladyvayut drug na druga otvetstvennost' v bor'be s koronavirusom," *meduza.io*, April 1, 2020, https://meduza.io/feature/2020/04/01/dazhe-slovo-karantin-starayutsya-ne-upotreblyat, accessed September 7, 2021.

108. On the "optimization" of medical organizations in Russia, see Linda Cook, "Constraints of Universal Health Care in the Russian Federation: Inequality, Informality, and the Failure of Mandatory Health Insurance Reforms," in *Towards Universal Health Care in Emerging Economies*, ed. Ilcheong Yi (Cham: Palgrave Macmillan, 2017), 269–296; Anastasia Novkunskaya, *Professionalism, Agency, and Institutional Change: Case of Maternity Services in Small-Town Russia* (PhD dissertation, University of Helsinki, 2020), especially chapter 2.

109. See Ilya Barabanov, Andrei Soshnikov, Svetlana Reiter, "Ona byla tikhaya-tikhaya: Kto takaya Anna Popova, vozglavivshaya bor'bu s koronavirusom v Rossii," *BBC Russian Service*, May 29, 2020, https://www.bbc.com/russian/features-52775158, accessed September 7, 2021.

110. See Sergei Guriev, "Kak Vladimir Putin proigral koronavirusu," *Internetproekt.com*, June 29, 2020, https://internetproekt.com/novosti/item/688326-sergey-guriev-o-tom-kak-putin-proigral-koronavirusu, accessed September 7, 2021.

111. For an in-depth analysis, see Ella Paneyakh, Kirill Titaev, Mariya Shklyaruk, *Traektoriya ugolovnogo dela: institutstional'nyi analiz* (Saint Petersburg: European University at Saint Petersburg Press, 2018).

112. See Elena Kuznetsova, "Teorema smertnosti: chto proiskhodit so statistikoi po koronavirusu v Rossii," *fontanka.ru*, June 15, 2020, https://www.fontanka.ru/2020/06/15/69316156/, accessed September 7, 2021.

113. See Mary Ilyushina, Frederik Pleitgen, "Reality Bites for Putin's Much hyped COVID-19 Vaccine, as Concerns over Efficacy and Safety Linger," *CNN*, October 27, 2020, https://edition.cnn.com/2020/10/27/health/russia-coronavirus-vaccine-sputnik-v-reality-check/index.html, accessed August 29, 2021; Brendan Cole, "Putin's World-Beating COVID Vaccine Faces Doubts from Doctors and Russians," *Newsweek*, December 8, 2020, https://www.newsweek.com/russia-putin-sputnik-v-coronavirus-vaccine-kremlin-1553136, accessed August 29, 2021.

114. Denis Y. Logunov, Inna V. Dolzhikova, Dmitry V. Shcheblyakov, Amir I. Tukhvatulin, Olga V. Zubkova, Alina S. Dzharullaeva, Anna V. Kovyrshina, Nadezhda L. Lubenets, Daria M. Grousova, Alina S. Erokhova, Andrei G. Botikov, Fatima M. Izhaeva, Olga Popova, Tatiana A. Ozharovskaya, Ilias B. Esmagambetov, Irina A. Favorskaya, Denis I. Zrelkin, Daria V. Voronina, Dmitry N. Shcherbinin, Alexander S. Semikhin, Yana V. Simakova, Elizaveta A. Tokarskaya, Daria A. Egorova, Maksim M. Shmarov, Natalia A. Nikitenko, Vladimir A. Gushchin, Elena A. Smolyarchuk, Sergey K. Zyryanov, Sergei V. Borisevich, Boris S. Naroditsky, Alexander L. Gintsburg, "Safety and Efficacy of an rAd26 and rAd5 Vector-Based Heterologous Prime-Boost COVID-19 Vaccine: An Interim Analysis of a Randomised Controlled Phase 3 Trial in Russia," *The Lancet* 397, no. 10275 (2021): 671–681.

115. See Andrew Higgins, "Slovakia Claims a Bait-and-Switch with the Russian Vaccines it Ordered." *The New York Times*, April 8, 2021, https://www.nytimes.com/2021/04/08/world/europe/slovakia-coronavirus-russia-vaccine-sputnik.html, accessed September 7, 2021; Ladislav Charouz, "Can the Czech Health Minister Have His Cake and Eat It Too?," *The New Federalist*, April 14, 2021, https://www.thenewfederalist.eu/can-the-czech-health-minister-have-his-cake-and-eat-it-too-a-game-of?lang=fr, accessed September 7, 2021.

116. For global data on vaccination, see *Our World in Data*, COVID Vaccination Data, https://ourworldindata.org/covid-vaccinations?country=OWID_WRL, accessed December 28, 2021.

117. On workplace mobilization in Russia, see Timothy Frye, Ora John Reuter, David Szakonyi, "Political Machines at Work: Voter Mobilization and Electoral Subversion in the Workplace," *World Politics* 66, no. 2 (2014): 195–228.

118. For survey results, see Levada-Center, *Obshcherossiiskoe golosovanie po popravkam v konstitutsiyu*, July 2, 2020, https://www.levada.ru/2020/07/02/obshherossijskoe-golosovanie-po-popravkam-v-konstitutsiyu-4/, accessed September 7, 2021.

119. For a data-driven analysis, see Aleksandr Kireev, "Referendum Shredingera," *Novaya gazeta*, July 6, 2020, https://novayagazeta.ru/articles/2020/07/06/86170-referendum-shredingera, accessed September 7, 2021.

120. See Vladislav Gordeev, "Volodin opisal budushchee Rossii slovami 'posle Putina budet Putin'," *rbc.ru*, June 18, 2020, https://www.rbc.ru/society/18/06/2020/5eeb-6d129a794743608c8c2a, accessed September 7, 2021.

121. For a preliminary analysis of effects of political regime continuity on governance in Russia, see Vladimir Gel'man, "Constitution, Authoritarianism, and Bad Governance: The Case of Russia," *Russian Politics* 6, no. 1 (2021): 70–89.

Page numbers in *italics* refer to figures and tables.

Printed and bound by CPI Group (UK) Ltd, Croydon, CR0 4YY

09/06/2025

14686129-0001